BOYS TO MEN

THE STORY OF A
JUNIOR SOLDIER

by
Steven John Burt

Published by Chapel Rank Publications

Frist edition printed by Createspace August 2016

ISBN Book 978-09570538-4-7
ISBN Ebook 978-09570538-5-4

Other titles by the same author.

Growing up in Lederhosen

I would like to say a big thank you to all the ex-Freds who provided information to me for this book; especially Alan Tadd and Las Stewart, who refreshed my memory when it failed and reminded me of events I'd forgotten. We all had a story to tell. This is mine; parts of it are personal to me, but I sincerely hope that the majority of my story will resonate with those who went through Junior Service as boy soldiers; regardless of Regiment or Corps.

Forward

The mid nineteen fifties saw the introduction of Junior Regiments within the British Army.

Boys as young as fifteen could make a life changing decision, and with their parents' consent, undertake theoretical and practical tests to leave home and become a Junior Soldier.

During the three terms of the year, Secondary Schools, and probably Grammar Schools as well would host a careers day.

Exhibiting at these events, along with local business and industry would be teams from the local Army, Navy, and Air Force information offices.

On some occasions, on the stand with the Army Information Officers or NCOs would be a Junior Soldier smartly turned out in his Number Two dress (No2) spending a week working in his local office; there to sing the praises of leaving home for a life of adventure.

In the winter of 1970 I was approaching school leaving age with no idea what to do with my future, until I stopped briefly to talk to a boy in a uniform on an army recruiting stand, and I went home hooked.

Almost every Regiment in the army had a Junior Regiment attached to them, the Marines at Deal in Kent; the Junior Infantry at Shorncliffe, also in Kent, the Para's, the Royal Signals, the Gunners and so on and so on...

It seems unbelievable now that every year, rather than staying on at school and doing 'O' levels thousands of youngsters from all over the country, some only just fifteen years old, would, with an army issue train warrant in hand, say goodbye to mum, dad, and siblings, head for their local railway station, and voluntarily board the train heading off for the army life.

It sounds more like something that happened during the Wellington era rather than post World War Two Britain.

But in truth it worked and it worked well.

There were a multitude of reasons that a youth choose to take this path; broken home, under achieving at school, poor employment prospects, or simply the lure of adventure. The army would give them adventure but also stability, direction and in the right Regiment or Corps, a trade.

Of all the thousands of kids that took this monumentous step only a very small percentage dropped out. The rest went on to make the best soldiers, NCOs, Warrant Officers and in some cases Commissioned Officers in the army.

The reason this was so successful of course was because these kids on leaving school never took the step into civilian life, therefore they never missed the freedom they would have known having gone into civilian employment prior to joining up.

Discipline at home, at school, then with the entry into Junior Soldiering it was just a natural progression of discipline.

Regardless of some serious barracking and bullshit this new life brought with it a whole new incredibly diverse experience to boys so young - outward bound courses, sport, military skills, in some cases far better food then they ever had at home and of course no mum and dad!

You soon learnt that if you done what was asked of you, life was good and a great deal of fun. If you bucked the system or didn't make the effort then you were shat on from a great height and not just you, your room-mates would also bear the brunt of your stupidity and they wouldn't put up with it more than once. You'd be sorted out pretty sharpish.

As I mentioned, I was one of these kids who joined a Junior Regiment.

At the age of fifteen and five months I left home to become a Junior Leader for two years in the Royal Engineers (The Sappers) at Old Park Barracks, Dover, Kent. And I never looked back. I passed out from Dover to adult service in August 1973 to join a Royal Engineers Field Squadron in Germany (BAOR - The British Army of the Rhine) and on that day I felt ten feet tall.

This book is dedicated to the kids of all Junior Regiments who took that gigantic step and won through. It wasn't easy, in fact at times it was damn hard going, I'm sure more than a few kids, at times would have broken down in tears, especially through the first thirteen weeks. But your room mates were in the same boat so you worked together and you got through all the crap.

You returned after your first thirteen week end-of-term leave where you'd walked tall and told your parents, gran, brother and mates how great it was and you were now in your second term; Course 2.

No longer the 'Sprog', no longer the new boys, because a new Intake had arrived who would now bear the brunt of every other Courses jokes.

2

You were on the way to being a real soldier in your chosen Regiment or Corps.

These Junior Regiments no longer exist in the form they did in the fifties, sixties, seventies or eighties. They have been replaced by the AFC (The Army Foundation College) an amalgamation of Regiments and Corps, training together. No doubt the style and method of training has also changed; this may in some case not be such a bad thing; however this book will tell it as it was. There will be bad language because bad language was used, regularly; in fact it was a constant part of the training routine against an individual or a group. It is not my intention to tone down the story to appease the politically correct brigade.

It was what it was....

Well done lads, one and all.

Steve Burt – 'A' Squadron, JLRRE Sept 71 – August 73

Old Park Barracks, Whitfield, Dover, Kent.

About the author

The author grew up in a small West Country village during the sixties.

With a German mum and English dad life was at times confusing but not boring.

Although well-mannered and polite Steven was not the best behaved kid on block and soon began to flash on the radar of the local village policeman. No matter how harsh the punishment misbehaviour persisted and school results plummeted; parents despaired.

John and Elsa's rising concerns were brought to a halt when their now fourteen year old somewhat wayward son came home from school one evening and announced he was leaving home to become a boy soldier in the Royal Engineers.

From that moment life changed; two years as a Junior Leader Royal Engineer stationed at Dover followed by four years in Germany defending the free west from the Soviet hordes posed in readiness behind the iron curtain and two tours on the streets of Northern Ireland changed Steve from boy to man.

The years that followed his time in the army were interesting and exciting with jobs in the oil industry and the world of International marine tourism, the latter taking him all over the world through numerous contracts and adventures.

Steven eventually married in 2010 and settled in Norfolk where he works in a variety of management roles; now approaching retirement he hopes to fulfil a final ambition to live a few years in the country of his mother's birth, which he dearly loves, Germany and eventually settle back in West Wiltshire.

Chapters

The Corps of Royal Engineers - 'The Sappers'.

The Corps of Royal Engineers has a long heritage that not many Corps can rival. They are the direct descent from William the Conqueror's Military Engineers, following his invasion of England in 1066.

By the end of the Peninsular War in 1814 there were five companies serving with Wellington's army.

In 1856, the Corps of Royal Sappers and Miners were amalgamated with the Corps of Royal Engineers. The rank of 'Private' in the newly formed Corps of Royal Engineers was changed to 'Sapper' and still exists today.

Sapper comes from the French word Sappe (Spade) Sapping referred to digging trenches or tunnels leading toward or under the enemy's fortifications.

However the role of the Royal Engineers throughout its history has been far greater than just digging trenches or fortifications.

They provide roads, water-supply, fuel supply, accommodation and camps. They carry out surveys, produce maps, run trains, and manage port infrastructure. They provide Chippy's, Bricky's, Sparky's and Plumbers. They drive and operate cranes, dozers, graders, dig wells and provide fuel and power. They provide mobile amphibious bridging and ferry units.

On the battlefield they build roads, blow roads; build bridges, blow bridges; lay and clear mine fields. They search for IEDs and carry out bomb disposal.

They have their own Para's and Commandos who provide Engineer support for any infiltration by sea or air. The list goes on...

Although the motto of the Royal Engineers is 'Ubique' meaning everywhere it should also be 'Quidvis' which is Latin for 'Everything'. The Engineers are not just everywhere, they do everything. The army in short could not operate without them.

This was the Corps I'd chosen to join and I still wear the Corps pin with pride.

Old Park Barracks – Layout

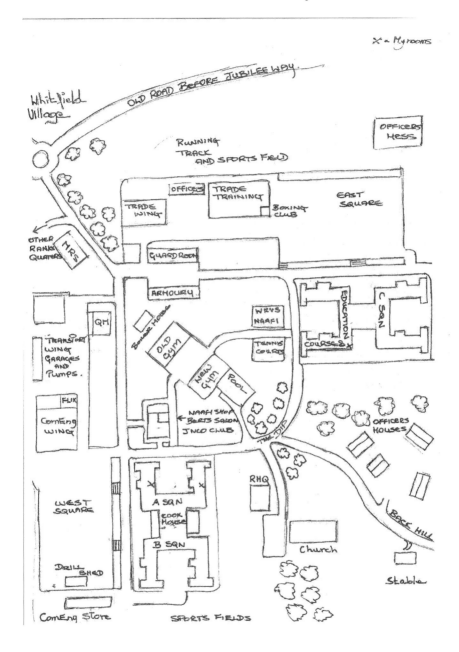

Whitfield and surrounds.

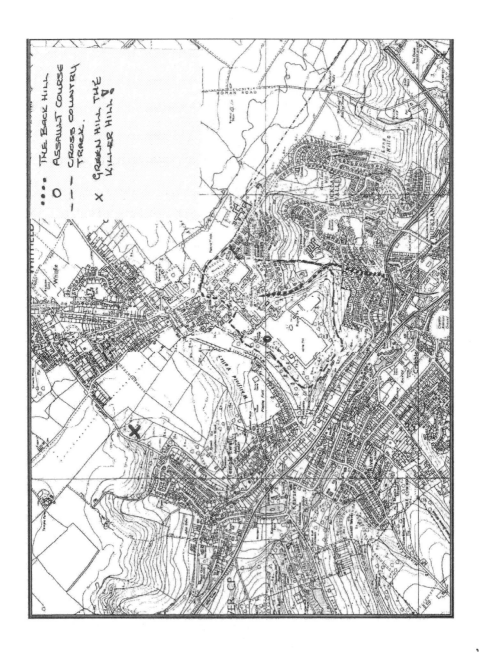

Day 1

Hugs - kisses, take care, be safe, write soon....

'Please Steven let us know you've arrived if you can,' mum shouted as the train pulled away from the platform; a request she had repeated at ever decreasing intervals over the last three weeks.

I watched as my parents and brother became small waving dots in the distance before closing the door window and returning to my compartment and a seat below the ridiculously large suitcase balanced precariously on the luggage rack above my head.

As the Breydon mud flats slipped by outside and the train gathered momentum from Great Yarmouth toward Norwich I leant back into the corner of my seat and reflected back over just how I got here.

The date was September 16th 1971 and I was on the train to London, then on to Dover in Kent to start a career as a Junior Soldier with the Royal Engineers.

Three weeks previously our family had migrated from our farmhouse home in the lovely county of Wiltshire to Norfolk, where my parents had taken joint jobs as broiler farm managers with 'Buxted Poultry.'

This move was due to major job stability concerns at my father's place of work, 'Marcos Sports Cars' in Westbury. At least that's what my brother and I were led to believe; the company was under threat of closure and dad couldn't find work locally. Forty five years on I look back at this move and wonder if this really was the reason.

All this is explained in depth in volume one - 'Growing up in Lederhosen'.

Almost a year earlier failing at school and unsure of any post-school direction, I had returned home from a careers day and announced to my parents I was going to be a Junior Soldier in the army; not only a Junior Soldier but a Paratrooper!

They never sat me down to a lecture about how stupid I was, neither was I dissuaded from my plans. Once they had returned from the ceiling and after the 'not over my dead body, we'll tell you what you will and won't do,' parental type lectures, negotiation took place resulting in my parents' acceptance of my decision.

Although the Parachute Regiment was discarded along with wildly optimistic ideas that my parents had of me joining the Medical Corps, the Army Pay Corps, or the Intelligence Corps; all well above my IQ grade, we settled on the Royal Engineers. A Corps of Gentlemen who would utilize my mechanical aptitude and raw but obvious leadership skills... At least that's what the recruiting Sergeant said.

The pre-selection had taken place; first minor interviews and tests at the Army information office in Bath, then a far more rigorous weekend selection at the Signals Regiment based in Corsham just up the road from where we lived outside Trowbridge.

The final swearing allegiance, presentation of the soldier's 'Prayer Book' and collection of travel documents had taken place in Norwich a few days after our arrival in Norfolk.

This change of recruitment offices may account for a mix-up that would happen later in the day on my arrival at Dover, but which would ultimately be to my benefit in more ways than one.

So, today, all those months later here I am on the train and on my way to an army career.

What had prompted me to make this momentous decision? Well I had always been a free spirit, but that childish free spirit had spilled over into bad behaviour, arguments with my parents and brushes with the law, to the point where it was disrupting family life and giving my parents major concerns.

I hated school, my grades were terrible and I had no idea what to do if I left school. I would have enjoyed working at Marcos with my dad, but that was out of the question, the work situation at Marcos was very unstable, our reason at this point in 1971 for leaving Wiltshire and moving to Norfolk.

Then on a careers day I'd spoken to the lad in the Junior Parachute Regiment and the flash light had gone off in my head; that's the life for me!

Mum and dad saw my departure to the army as a way for me to channel my energies, to get some discipline instilled in me and at the same time get a foundation in a worthwhile future civilian trade. Oh! And of course I would be someone else's responsibility not theirs... harsh but true.

In 1971 the train was still a relatively civilized way to travel; the train from Liverpool Street in London to Gt Yarmouth completed the whole journey without the need of a change at Norwich. Also the carriages had compartments with arm rests between the seats and buffet cars. Although the journey took four hours compared to the present two, you did travel in relative comfort and even in rush hour a seat was generally available, and there weren't endless delays and line closures.

Through Norwich and down through Suffolk and Essex the train arrived in Liverpool Street, London...

Navigation of the capitals underground system didn't faze me, I had the map, I was a well-seasoned traveller and knew how to look after myself and my gear; the ticket collector on the train gave me, with the aid of my map, very concise instructions on how the London underground system worked, which line to take and where to get off.

Little did I realise at that moment how many times over the years I would be sitting on that Circle Line between Liverpool Street, Paddington Waterloo, or Embankment, heading either to my gran in Wiltshire, my parent's new home in Norfolk, or returning to Old Park Barracks in Dover.

The train arrived at Liverpool Street station and down the platform I struggled with my hellishly large suitcase.

When I left for Dover in that September I was only fifteen and-a-bit years old and hadn't yet reached my full potential in the height department. I measured according to my first military ID card only five foot six and a bit which made walking with my giant suitcase pure agony. The now all common holdall was not so common, when you were packed off on holiday to some distant relative, or left home for any reason at all, you did so with a suitcase... what a lovely old fashioned word isn't it. Yes a suitcase, now in 1971 you weren't exactly spoilt for choice when it came to buying a suitcase either; in the main there were two types neither of which were any good for keeping suits in... why you ask? Because when you picked them up by the handle all the contents tumbled to the bottom, unless of course it was full to bursting.

Anyway, as I was saying, two types of case owned by Mr Average, either a mottled tan affair with leather corners unladen weight equal to that of your average car battery or a blue compressed cardboard affair with a spray-on plastic coating. Put engine and wheels on the former and you'd have better value and safer transport then a mid-seventies Fiat 127, the latter was a different kettle of fish entirely, if you attempted carrying anything other than feathers the metal rivets securing the handle would pull straight through the cardboard and God help you if you took it out in the rain without protection, like a Steradent tablet it would dissolve in front of your eyes.

I did own a metal frame German style rucksack but it was not big enough or smart enough to use for my departure to Dover so my mum went out and bought me a suitcase and I had to have a big one, odd considering I had bugger all clothes to put in it.

On reflection it must have been a kind of council estate status symbol, the bigger the suitcase the higher up the social ladder you were.

This particular case mum came home with was massive, I can honestly say I've never seen one bigger, it was a wonder I wasn't charged a second ticket, whole third world families live in smaller spaces. From the floor to the handle measured 30"... yes, I can see you are with me on this? Carrying the thing was a killer, like some medieval torture device I would struggle along the road with my elbow cocked out to the side leaning forty five degrees to 'Port' with veins bulging in my forehead as I attempted to keep the thing off the ground. You see my arms were too low for the handle, my suitcase and I were totally incompatible in the height department; unfortunately at this time there was no such thing as wheeled cases, at least not for our social grouping, if there had been I could have ridden the thing to Dover.

Having successfully negotiated the underground and arrived at Victoria I went to the kiosk to look through the magazines, my eye was drawn to the top shelf where the men's magazines were blatantly on display, devoid at that time of any blacked out packaging.

Playboy, Penthouse, Men Only, and Mayfair to name just a few. Nothing was left to the imagination nor in anyway were the magazines hidden from the view of children, or those that did not wish to view the naked female form.

After much deliberation I bought a copy of Mayfair one of the popular lad's magazines of the day and ten Embassy cigarettes.

Wow! Now I was truly out in the big world on my own.

So fags in pocket, 'Mayfair' under one arm, double garage on the other I wandered down the platforms looking for my train to Dover.

I found it and climbed aboard one of those lovely old carriages which had doors to the platform from every pair of seats and a 'V' shaped net luggage holder suspended above your head. There was no way my case was going to fit up there, it ended up in the guards van, so naturally I sat in the compartment next door.

Over the years that followed I got used to reading the blackboard at the start of platform five, with the hand scribbled information telling you which bit of the train went where; 'this train splits at Canterbury front four carriages to Dover Priory rear four to Ramsgate'?

But this was my first trip into 'Hop' country and I was travelling with a portable eclipse so I missed this sign.

There were no carriage intercoms in those days only the untranslatable voice booming through the station tannoy. CAN*..**B..Y CH**!!*ERE F R**!*!MS!!**TE FR***FO!!**! crackle, crackle, cough, hiss.....TO DOVER, ah to Dover? That's great, then, I'm ok.

I and my double garage went to Ramsgate, good job I had some intellectual reading material with me on Steve Burt's world tour of Kent. Well two hours later and I'm back at Canterbury, no problem you just wait on the train until it returns the way it came.

Off I get and eventually find myself correctly installed on the train going to Dover; another lad is in the compartment I've piled into, a guy called Gerald Dickerson he is also a prospective Royal Engineer and will eventually end up in a room with me, or should I say me with him as he'll be there hours before me. (This name has been changed for reasons that will become obvious later on, other names have also been changed if circumstances warranted).

I was completely mesmerised by Gerald's pustulating face, I had never seen so many spots and weeping sores he was the ultimate advert for teenage zit cream.

I remember thinking that he should wake up on a regular basis throughout the night or he would stick to the pillow. Sadly Gerald was never destined to go the distance. He had a rock solid inability to keep himself, his clothes, or his locker free of gunge and was hounded unmercifully because of this. I'll never forget the evening he was thrown in the shower and sluiced down with a fire hose this was after the stench from his locker was so bad it was deemed he needed to be taught a lesson.

Bullying I suppose you'd could call it today, but the truth is we were being moulded. Being turned into a clean, smart, sharp soldier and either you knuckled down and done what was expected of you in which case life was good, it was interesting, and was also a great deal of fun, or you were shat on from a great height and life was made a misery, not only by the Junior NCOs but by the guys you were letting down in your room. One person didn't suffer, the room did.

But all this was yet to come at this point in time I was beginning to feel tired, nervous and looking at Gerald's face, slightly sick. I leant back in my seat tried to get comfortable and lit a fag...

'Dover Priory'; end of the line - this is it then.

13

Along with Gerald I drag the double garage off the train and look around at the platform, a platform that will become all too familiar over the next two years.

Lots of other blank apprehensive looking youngsters are also dragging a pitiful mixture of suitcases from the other carriages. We shuffle toward the exit while the tannoy tells us again in unrecognisable blurb that Junior Soldiers heading for Old Park Barracks should get their asses into gear and get on the green bus waiting outside the station.

There's the army green bus and a bloke in a khaki uniform with three stripes rounding us up like sheep and trying to be nice and friendly. Of course this is a front for Jo-public during the short time he's been let out of the barracks; I could see it written all over his face 'just wait till you're through those gates, then you're mine.'

Help! Was this a good idea after all?

As the bus groaned its way out of Dover town centre up the hill to Whitfield our guide in green was talking us through the coming procedure, what would happen to us on arrival at Old Park, something about the WRVS rooms (Women Royal Voluntary Service) for processing and allocations to Squadrons.

The bus stopped at the Guardroom, we were unloaded pretty sharpish and told to get into three rows, we then had to walk to a building about 200 yards away while the bus pulled away from us and drove, yes you guessed it, straight past the building we were heading for, odd? So why drop us here?

This was my first experience of walking very quickly out of step while struggling with a portable double garage and the bloke behind continually stepping on my heels. By the time we got to the WRVS, I was all in.

There was tea. It had an odd sort of smell, a smell which I would become accustomed to over the years and even having left the army, when attending an annual kit and documentation check as a reservist in Colchester, army tea would always have that smell. There were also biscuits and sarnies (sandwiches) with turned up edges.

One by one we boys were called forward for processing to our Squadrons; my turn came.

'Name son?'

'Burt sir'... *silence - pause?*

'Is that your Christian name or Surname?'

'Surname sir.'

Uum.... another long pause...

'Are you sure?'

'Yes sir, Steven Burt, since birth.' (I said this with a grin thinking the guy may have a sense of humour… I was wrong).

'Right, less of the cheek smart ass, sit yourself down over there'…

I sat and watched all the other guys getting processed and then another coach load arrives.

Eventually a soldier with a double stripe on his arm comes in and asks me to follow him - we were off.

His name was Corporal Johnny Spriggs.

I follow him across the road to what was 'C' Squadron office he introduces himself and asks if he can check my name against their personnel Intake lists.

No luck, so off we go again, me and the double garage staggering along the road, through the dip, (a point in the circular road that drops towards what I would later find out was the start of the back hill) and up the other side.

'So what seems to be the problem Corporal,' I ask expectantly? I know he's a Corporal because it was made very clear to a group of us during our assessment at Corsham that two strips indicated Corporal, not Corp.

'Well it's like this son; you don't seem to be on anyone's Intake list? So we're going round the Squadrons checking the allocation they hold. Are you sure you were told you'd be a Junior Sapper?'

'Yes Corporal and my train warrant was made out to Dover.'

So…I'm a non-person, it had to be me didn't it, couldn't happen to some other bugger, had to be me.

The next stop was 'B' Squadron; we left the road and walked up across a lovely grassed area to the furthest block in the distance entering through a side door into an office area. Once more we had no luck; my name was not on 'B' Squadron list either.

From here we went out through a side door across a large square open area surrounded on three sides by three-story windows, though another set of doors, through a small corridor which was obviously an accommodation area and out into a roadway.

Johnny Spriggs was explaining to me how things worked.

'We've three Squadrons here Steven,' he said. 'A', 'B' and 'C'.'

Opposite the WRVS we've just left is the education block and beyond that 'C' Squadron. There's two main buildings both in an 'H' design this one has 'B' Squadron forming one end and 'A' Squadron the other. The cookhouse is in the middle joining the two. The other one has

'C' Squadron at one end and the education block on the other. Each Squadron is made up of around two hundred and fifty Junior Leaders and Permanent Staff; the lads are split between eight ongoing Courses.

I doubt you'll do all eight Courses... how old are you?'

'Fifteen and four month's Corporal.' I said.

'Crikey, you are a kid aren't you, in that case I reckon you'll do over two years here, probably six Courses in all.'

'We don't know if I'm wanted yet Corporal, it doesn't seem as if I'm supposed to be here at all.' I said despondently.

'Don't worry', said Spriggsy. 'We'll sort it out.'

At this point he was very decent and took my suitcase off me, he could see I was really knackered.

'Ok, here's what we'll do; I'm a member of 'A' Squadron - 'Shiny A'.

All the Squadrons like to think they are the best, the thing is we in 'A' know we are,' he said laughing.

'If you're supposed to be a Junior Sapper, and we don't know that for sure yet, you'll be in 'A' Squadron, I'll make sure of that; do you like sport?'

'Yeah, all sport.' I replied.

'Good, 'A' is the place for you then,' said Spriggsy.

We had arrived at another side door and again went through an accommodation corridor and out across a quadrangle identical to 'B' Squadron before entering an office area.

'Right let's talk to the Chief Clerk,' said Spriggsy knocking at a door.

'Hi Chief, can you look at 'A' Squadron Intake list for a Steven Burt?'

The chief handed the list to Spriggsy and he ran his finger down the column of names.

'No you're not on here either son,' he said.

'Chief, these couple of names with lines through them... are they no-shows?'

'Yeah that's right, why?'

'This lad has no Squadron allocated, in fact he's not on a list anywhere and until we find out whether he's even in the right

'A' Squadron quad doors ahead to the dining room and to the left into the office area. Another set of doors mirror these out of shot on the right hand side.

16

Regiment he'll need a pit (a bed and bed space) somewhere; can we put him up in Intake lines for the time being?'

'Take him back to the WRVS and I'll make some inquiries with RHQ,' said the Chief Clerk.

With this action plan in place we headed back to the WRVS.

I was dumped once more in the corner and beginning to feel very despondent; I must have been sitting for an hour with no one taking the slightest bit of notice of me when I decided to go home; I had just reached that point I'd had enough. I stood up, picked up my double garage and walked out.

I got as far as the main road before Johnny Spriggs caught up with me.

He explained that the Chief Clerk had been waiting while RHQ (Regimental Headquarters) made phone calls to track down where I should be and it seemed I was not supposed to be at Dover at all but at the Regiment of the Junior Para's.

I was dumfounded.

Whether the Para's new Intake kicked-off on the same day or not wasn't clear. What was clear, the paperwork at their end showed me as an entrant with them for that September and I wasn't down to be a Junior Royal Engineer. (I later found out my parents were not even made aware of this hick-up).

I was taken back to 'A' Squadron where I explained that I had been accepted at Bath information office to be a Royal Engineer; that yes, my second choice was to have been a Junior Para, but I had passed all the necessary tests to be an Engineer.

Obviously the recruiting office in Norwich thought I was going to Dover and had issued travel warrant and instructions to that effect.

'Give him a bed,' said the Chief Clerk. 'We'll sort it out tomorrow.'

I was taken upstairs to the new Intake lines on the top floor and given a bed space in room 96 where once again I met my co-traveller Gerald Dickerson.

Spriggsy left me there after introducing me to the Junior Lance Corporal who was in charge of the room; Lance Corporal (L/Cpl) Smudge Smith.

At all Junior Regiments the training of Junior Soldiers was carried out by a Permanent Staff group of Adult Soldiers.

These guys, picked for their ability, volunteered, applied, or were asked if they would like to serve as training NCOs for a given period of time, roughly two to three years.

At Dover they instructed in all aspects of Royal Engineer soldiering.

Drill, weapons training, field craft, etc. Also advanced trade training, and Combat Engineering.

When a Junior Soldier left Dover he was an extremely well trained addition to any Royal Engineer unit and a prime candidate for quick promotion through the ranks; hence the name Junior Leaders.

However the day to day running of the Squadron, its discipline and management was controlled by Junior NCOs.

These Junior NCOs were promoted following their first couple of terms in their respective Squadron (terms or Courses as they were also called; a term being thirteen to fifteen weeks depending on whether it was summer winter or Easter).

They were promoted on their commitment, leadership skills and abilities. So we had Junior Lance Corporals, Junior Corporals, Junior Sergeants as well as each Squadron having a Junior Squadron Sergeant Major. Ultimately after every term and passing-out (departure) of Course 8 into adult service we would also have one of the three Junior SSMs promoted to Junior Regimental Sergeant Major; a really outstanding honour for the lad concerned and for the Squadron from which he was elected.

The room allocations were in alphabetical order. By rights having a surname beginning with 'B' I should have been in the big-end room, a large room containing around fourteen beds at the end of the corridor.

Because of my homelessness I'd ended up in a room with 'Cs' and 'Ds'. I was replacing a lad called 'Downs' who for whatever reason had failed to turn up and his bed space was free.

The other lads in the room were surrounded with kit, clothing and other stuff; there was a charged atmosphere of utter chaos.

As for me, I only had only what was in my own suitcase. I wasn't going to be issued with anything until my situation had been sorted.

Smudge was doing his best to explain how to arrange clothing in lockers, where to put suitcases and what kit to put to one side that would be needed in the short term.

I was somewhat detached from this chaos which made me feel very much the outsider. I wanted to go home.

Smudge must have sensed this and came over.

'What's your story then mate,' he asked?

I gave him a run down on my day and the history leading up to being in his room.

'I know Winsley and North Bradley,' he said. 'My dad delivers coal there; my family own a coal yard in Westbury.'

I knew I recognised the face...

'I know you,' I said. I thought I recognised you; you've delivered coal to our house loads of times!'

What a coincidence, we both laughed and I felt a whole lot better. These little quirky tricks of fate go a long way to smoothing the road of life, I had something in common with my Room-jack and it would stand me in good stead.

'You need to come over here and listen in to this Steve,' said Smudge. 'Even though you haven't got your own kit yet you'll need to know how things work.'

I went across the room to a lad in the far corner and asked if I could give him a hand with anything.

Ray Dakers a lad from the North East - Sunderland. I helped him to start folding the items from a large kit bag and suitcase he had lying on his bed. I couldn't understand a word he said – he was the first person I'd ever met from the North East and the accent was completely double-dutch to me, 'Geordie'.

It wasn't long after this that we were called out onto the landing for a briefing by all our room NCOs. We were on the third level – the top landing. Off this landing, as you reach the top to the left a door led into the washrooms, three rows of five sinks; from the sink area there was a step up leading into two bathrooms and four showers.

Off the landing to the right a corridor lead to a block of toilet cubicles. To get to these you passed a room for washing clothes with two big farmhouse type sinks and a room with hooks around the walls, the drying room.

These rooms would be where we done all our own clothes washing by hand; everything from socks and under-pants to our woollen jumpers, denim work wear and even our heavy-duty combat gear. It would be a steep learning curve for all of us. I don't believe there was one boy amongst us who had ever experienced anything like this before. Even those who were worldly or street wise had never been in a position where they needed to wash and rinse their own clothes, then, when dry, iron them. It was a real shock to the system.

We mustered on the landing with our JNCOs in front of us; they told us what would happen...

Following our evening meal to which we would head straight after this briefing; we would be shown more kit preparation, we would be shown how to dress ourselves, and how to make bed packs. We would be delegated tasks to carry out in the mornings which would change week by week.

These tasks included just about everything; cleaning all the washrooms, baths, toilets, and showers; the clothes drying room and the clothes washing room.

All floors would be 'bumped'? Bumped - what the hell was that...? A bumper was brought forth and shown to us; a huge heavy lump of metal with a felt pad on the bottom. We would be shown how to use it later on.

Every morning we were told there would be a room inspection by our Course Junior Sergeant, once a week the inspection would be carried out by our Course Permanent Staff NCOs and Troop Officer.

It was now 5pm, 1700 in military time keeping. We were told to pick up our irons, nosh-rods, or rods - slang for a knife, fork, and spoon set (KFS); a set of three held together with a clip also an enamelled metal mug.

We were told we'd be shown by our Room-jacks where to go to queue for the cook house.

Be back on this landing at 1830 we were told. We dispersed back to our rooms.

I never had mug or any Irons - because I'd no kit issue; the irons and mug were part of it. I went to tell Smudge.

'Ok, don't worry about it, stay here till I get back,' he said.

A few moments later he returned with a mug and a set of nosh-rods.

'Borrow these,' he said. 'And for fuck sake don't lose them, I've borrowed them from another Junior NCO and you'll be well fucked if they disappear.'

I hoped against hope he didn't mean literally!

'We need to get you sorted ASAP or it's going to create a fucking heap of problems in more ways than one.'

At that point I heard a heck of a ruckus going on. The guys in my room were all looking out the windows - I joined them.

20

'It's the 'C' Squadron Intake.' Smudge told us. 'They'll get a heap of stick for the next few days; new Intakes always do.'

Every window overlooking the quadrangle had a multitude of heads sticking out, the guys were laughing and shouting at the poor old ramble who'd tried to march over in a squad from 'C' Squadron.

They did look a forlorn bunch, desperately trying to keep in step in their motley, multi-coloured civi-clothes.

Not only was this a daunting first day for them as well as for us, they had to attempt a march to the cookhouse and go through this very public humiliation as well.

An 'A' Squadron Permanent Staff NCO came out into the quad and shouted at the heads to get back inside and quit the noise. Slowly everything returned to normal.

'Ok, grab your irons and follow me,' said Smudge. 'I'll show you what's-what tonight, then you'll know where to go and what to do tomorrow for breakfast.'

We left the room, turned left, left again at the end of the corridor and through a set of double swing fire doors. This brought us to the top of the main stairs, two floors above the main entrance doors leading off the quad into the building where the main doors to the canteen or cookhouse were – this is where the dinner queue began.

'We'll need to wait here, they've probably allowed the 'C' Squadron guys in first,' said Smudge. 'They need to get them fed and back over the other side, they're going through the same crap as you guys; don't expect an early night.'

While we waited and shuffled downward, still more rooms and individuals were joining the queue behind us.

'It's not normally like this,' Smudge told us. 'It's because it's new-Intake first night. It'll sort itself out by this time tomorrow; there'll always be a small queue but nothing like this.'

We were moving slowly toward the ground floor two landings below us.

We were talking among ourselves while we waited.

The other guys in my room were Paul Dodwell who came from Morton-in-the-Marsh in Gloucestershire, Gary Cutting from Cumbria, Ray Dakers who I'd already spoken to and tried to understand, was from Geordie land, Sunderland in Tyne-and-Wear. Gerald Dickerson who I'd travelled on the train and who I now shared a room with came from somewhere in the Midlands. Steve Cottle came from Tilbury and finally a right wise ass called Les Dixon who came from Manchester. Les and I

21

would become firm friends through our Dover days and remain so until we left 3 Training Regiment for our adult units two years up the road.

Eventually we were inside the canteen and queuing at the hotplate. Tables stretched the whole length of a massive hall and I noticed there were in fact two hot plates one for the guys coming in from 'B' Squadron end and one from 'A'. The guys coming over from 'C' had to join whichever queue was the shortest.

I was already - based on what I'd witnessed so far, extremely grateful I hadn't been left in 'C' Squadron.

I seemed to have joined a decent Squadron with a decent Room-jack and a good set of roommates.

I can't remember after all these years just what the menu was that first night; however I remember there was a great deal of choice, the food was well cooked and tasty and we were all bloody hungry.

During my two years at Dover I would have no complaints about the food it was always very good with heaps of choice.

On the opposite side of the cookhouse to the hotplates an archway took you through to a separate eating area, this I believe was an extension build the other side of the full length windows. This was the salad bar area and also the area where Permanent Staff Sappers, NCOs such as Lance Corporals and Corporals and also Junior Sergeant and above ate. Most of course were married and went back to their quarters for lunch time meal, Permanent Sergeants and above had their own mess as did the Officers.

The salad bar was a whole new world to me - well all of us I suppose, it was full of the most wonderful cuts of cold meat. It was also the place where I saw my first cooked whole salmon. Gary and I went down to lunch one day and he suggested a salad, I pooh-hooed it saying I wanted real food.

'No no,' he said. 'Come and look at what they've got its amazing.'

So I tagged along and sure enough it was.

There laying out in all its glory was the biggest fish I'd ever seen - with the head and tail still on! A salmon at least a meter long.

The serving chef stood there in his 'whites' and asked us what we'd like; we both went for the salmon. He peeled back the skin with a narrow spatula and then with a pair of tongs lifted a section of flesh onto our plates. It was absolutely mega. I'd only ever had a small bit of tinned salmon at my grans Christmas time when she bought a tin for my dad and granddad, in truth there was no comparison.

We collected our food and found a table where we could all sit together including Smudge.

'Right,' he said, 'while you're stuffing your faces let me fill you guys in on a few details. There are over ninety of you in this Intake, and that's just in this Squadron alone. There are the same numbers in the other Squadrons as well; it's the biggest Intake ever. The numbers have caused some headaches that's for sure. You guys occupy the whole of the top floor and the upper bridge level, that's one of two corridors that link 'A' and 'B' Squadrons over the top of the cookhouse; we have the top level which is sealed off at the far end, and 'B' Squadron have the second level which is closed off at our end.

What you need to remember is this - you guys are in Course one, the bottom of the pecking order for thirteen weeks and believe me it'll be thirteen weeks of pure shit – not all of you will survive; for one reason or another you'll either leave or be kicked off. If you want to leave you best get kicked out as they won't let you go just because you don't like it. Like it or not you're in the army now.' He was looking at us grinning.

'However,' he continued on... 'You do get to go home for a weekend at mid-term. Enjoy the weekend at home, get through the second half of term and you'll be ok. You'll come back after Christmas in Course two; you'll still be Sprogs, but you'll be Course two Sprogs; one step up the JL pecking order.'

We'd all stopped eating and I think we were all a bit shell shocked, it had been a long day, it was far from over, and we'd just been told in no uncertain terms, the consequences of the decision we'd made while sitting in the comfort of our front rooms at home with our parents.

'So when do we finally stop being Sprogs?' Queried Les.

'Once you've completed the first two terms, you're looked at with a bit more respect in Course three; we've all been through it. Ok we're going back up now and parade on the landing, now the fun starts; you'll be shown how to use a bumper, how to clean the bogs and the washrooms and when I say clean I mean clean, not a speck of dust or crap anywhere. We'll then run through your kit, belt, boots, and beret. How many of you practiced using an iron before you got here?'

'I have,' I answered. 'So did I,' answered both Paul and Les.

The others shook their heads.

I'll show you all how to do this, we have a long evening ahead of us and tomorrow morning we'll be up fucking early; I doubt you'll be parading in uniform tomorrow; that'll probably happen Sunday or Monday, but you'll learning how to clean the 'Lines.'

'What are Lines?' Asked Gary.

'Our floor, your rooms and all the other rooms on the landing, including the stairs as far down as the Course two landing below us.

Ok, all finished? Let's go.' He was in a hurry now, time had slipped rapidly past while we had queued and eaten.

'Scrape your waste food in the bin, stack your plates and bring your rods back upstairs to wash and put back in your locker. Steve, keep hold of those rods and don't fucking loose them. We'll get you a set tomorrow.'

We followed Smudge back upstairs like a flock of sheep, we went in the washrooms and washed our nosh-rods and went to put them back in our lockers.

'Right we have ten minutes,' said Smudge. 'Who smokes?'

Four of said we did.

'Ok light up if you want to and one of you give me a fag.'

Paul, Gary, Les and I pulled out our cigarettes, Les gave one to Smudge.

'Thanks,' said Smudge drawing on his fag.

'Grab the ashtray off the table, we don't want to make any mess in here tonight; ok gather round, who knows what hospital corners are?'

'I do,' said Les.

'Army Cadet eh?' queried Smudge.

'Yes Corporal,' replied Les.

'Yeah and I bet you know a load more shit as well, which is going to help you and your room-mates no end. Know how to bull boots?'

'I've done it once or twice but I'm not that good at it.'

'You will be. Ok I'm quickly going to show you how to make your bed up, this'll take a few minutes before we go onto the landing. Sheets and pillow cases get changed alternately every week on a Monday ok? So you change one of each every week, basically you keep them for two weeks. Personally I put the clean sheet on the bottom and the bottom sheet to the top but it's up to you. Oh, and don't for fuck sake wet the bed you'll never live it down.'

Smudge chucked - unceremoniously, all Gary's bedding onto Paul's bed. He then started going through the process of putting on the bottom sheet, the top sheet and the blankets – two grey coloured horrible looking blankets with a maroon stripe down the middle.

I'd never seen anything like it; I'd spent my whole life sleeping under a big fluffy duvet. To put it bluntly I was horrified. The blankets looked like bedding you'd be issued with in prison.

Smudge tucked in the end of the bed, pulled up the material hanging over the side so that it formed a triangle and then tucked in the hanging corner. When he dropped the piece he was holding a nice neat angled corner appeared.

'That,' said Smudge, 'is a hospital corner.'

'RIGHT, lets ave you out here! Cum-on step on it!' A voice boomed from the corridor.

'Half six I said on the landing, CUM-ON WHERE ARE YOU!'

'Get going,' said Smudge.

We hastily stubbed out our fags in the ash tray and piled out of the door straight into another mass of bodies heading for the landing. Eventually we were all there, around forty five of us, half the Course. The other half were on the same floor on the opposite side of the building.

We gathered in a congested group with our Junior Sergeant, Junior Corporals and Lance Corporals in front of us.

'Right,' said our Sergeant this will be the last time I ever call you out onto this landing, in future if I tell you to be out here at a given time you'll be here waiting for me, not the other way round. Any late comers will find themselves in trouble and by trouble I mean doing something miserable for a long period of time. Who wants to go home?'

There was silence.

'Good then I take it you're all loving it so far. Did I make myself clear?'

'Yes,' we collectively mumbled.

'Right, let's start again. When I ask you a question you reply in a loud voice, YES SERGEANT! I am Kevin Perry, Junior Sergeant in charge of this side of the Intake lines. I am a Junior Sergeant because I have three stripes on my arm, Abe and Martin over there are Corporals because they have two stripes and although Smudge and Mick have one stripe they are also Corporal to you lot. We are not Sarg or Corp... we may be later when you've won some respect from us but until then our rank is not abbreviated, we are also not called by our Christian names is that clear?'

'Yes Sergeant,' we mumbled.

'LOUDER!'

'YES SERGEANT!' We shouted.

'Good, now we're getting somewhere. This is how your evening and tomorrow morning is going to pan-out...'

The three hours we had spent working since our meeting on the landing had consisted of being given tasks for the morning and being shown how to carry them; out not a speck of dirt or dust must remain on anything.

We were shown how to use the bumper to polish our barrack-room floors and the corridors.

Each room had a bumper, a metal block on a long pole weighing roughly 8lbs or 4 kilos. Soft wax polish would be splattered on the floors and the bumper swung from side to side across the space until the polish hardened into a surface so shiny you could almost shave in it.

Woe-betide anyone who then walked on it! His life wouldn't be worth living.

Bumping was a killer of a job; as the days and weeks went past we knew, if we mucked up, we could spend hours as a punishment individually or collectively as a room bumping for hours into the night, up and down the corridors.

Failure to come up to standard with our turn-out would impact on the individual or if the standard was low across the troop we'd be punished with a 'Changing Parade'. We'd parade in the quad, be inspected and then get four minutes to change into another uniform – it could be our best uniform No2s, combats, BDs, or PT kit... well anything really. We'd be dismissed and go hell-for-leather up the stairs – manically get changed and charge back down, form up and be inspected again.

Of course with our gear just being thrown on, we were far from smart. We'd get a bollocking and then the JNCOs would send us to get changed into another uniform. Of course the last to get back and get fell-in would really be shat-on. Finally after doing this for an unspecified time and through numerous changes we'd be told we had fifteen minutes before a locker inspection.

Following the cleaning demonstrations we were briefed on how to prepare and fold our clothing which had to be nine inches wide, every item! How to lay out our lockers; every locker had to be identical with army stuff on some shelves and civi stuff on others.

Civi suitcase went under the bed with your army case on top of your locker; inside the case went your green kit bag and 37 pattern webbing.

We were shown how to thread the laces into our boots Engineer style; which is using one lace knotted at one end. How to polish our boots, including the rubber rim and the underside of the sole. The bullshit was unbelievable, our heads were spinning.

We were told that our first morning we would be parading in our civi clothing. Following parade we would be taken to the barbers for a haircut and to the NAAFI to buy whatever items we had failed to bring with us.

We had been given a list of items to bring – a padlock for our lockers, washing powder, scrubbing brush, boot cleaning brushes and polish, dusters, Brasso or Duraglit; this stuff as well as our personnel kit such as soap, toothbrush and paste...

Also we were told to bring a housewife? Yes a housewife - this is the name given to a sewing kit; assorted size needles and various coloured thread. Mum packed me up a neat box which included not only a thimble but a sock mushroom! I'm sure nobody in 2015 has a sock mushroom in their house or even knows what it is. It's made of wood and looks just like a mushroom, a short wooden handle with a convex top that unscrews. You push it into the toe or heel of a sock where the hole is and then carry out a latticework of wool darning. I bet I was the only kid ever to turn up at Dover having had darning lessons from their mum before I left home but over the years I did use it; especially in Germany where replacement kit was almost impossible to get hold of.

Whatever we had failed to bring with us we were expected to buy. This included a very strange dull green substance in a tin called blanco; this would be used on our No2 dress belt, bayonet scabbard holder and rifle sling on parade days.

Never, during my 2 years at Dover would I get the hang of blancoing and throughout my time at Old Park, Les Dixon my mate would do my belt for me. In return I'd polish his belt brasses. That's how things worked.

We eventually got to bed around 2300, 11pm! At home I was only allowed to stay up to 11pm on a Saturday night to watch Match of the Day. Mum would have a blue-fit!

Lights went out and I was asleep instantly.

At this point I need to break from my story and do a small amount of explaining - how the Regiment operated and how we worked our way through the system.

The first three terms, Courses 1, 2, 3, were basic training Courses where we learnt foot drill, small arms drill, basic field craft and weapons training.

Weapons training covered two personnel weapon the 9mm SMG (Stirling Sub Machine Gun or Carbine as some called it; I'll refer to it from here on as just the SMG) and the 7.62 mm SLR (Self Loading Rifle). I loved this weapon and won many shooting competitions with it during my years at Dover and in Germany; although considered outdated due to its lack of an automatic mode and also heavy (It would be replaced following the Falkland's conflict in 1982). Of all the weapons I fired in the army, British and others the SLR was my weapon of choice.

We were also trained to use the section machine gun the 7.62 mm LMG (Light Machine Gun); this weapon had taken over from the Bren but preceded the belt fed GPMG (General Purpose Machine Gun) which I never used till I arrived in my unit in Germany.

Our academic education also continued while at Dover.

We had to pass tests called modules.

The basic modules we had to pass were based on secondary school 'O' levels and covered subjects - Math, English, and Technical Drawing. I'm sure we studied other subjects as well, such as History and Geography. But my memory has deserted me.

The modules were numbered one-to-seven.

These basic units were the academic levels required for basic trades such as driver, signaller, bricklayer and plumber, for certain high grade trades such as electrician or my plant operator trade there were further modules to take and pass.

Any lad that failed to pass the basics was obliged to complete another term of education, known as 4E.

During our Intake Course - Course one, we had three days education per week, in Course two, two days a week and Course three one day per week.

We all loathed education days for two reasons – the first being the simple fact we'd left school behind us and didn't want to sit in classrooms any longer doing crappy sums. The second reason was due to the hideous uniform we had to wear on education days.

For some bizarre reason we were issued with a set of World War Two Battle Dress (BDs); old fashioned, hairy, and very uncomfortable. We've all seen soldiers wearing these in series like 'Dads Army' and the black and white war films of the thirties, forties and fifties.

How British and Commonwealth soldiers wore this uniform and managed to win a war in it defies belief.

It's the most hideous and uncomfortable stuff I've ever worn. But wear it we did, every time we were attending education classes. The army must have had thousands of sets of this stuff left in storage and no idea how to get rid of them...

They were in fact wool serge... the logic behind the use of this material was that it would keep a soldier warm even when wet. The fact that they doubled in weight when wet and you boiled when the sun shone, itched like mad as the sweet ran down your legs, didn't seem to be issues that bothered the designers who never had to wear it.

Have you ever tried ironing or pressing wool serge?

No, I doubt you have... well it's almost impossible. Yet we were compelled to have razor sharp creases in the trousers and a razor sharp 9" box crease ironed into the back of the jacket.

To obtain these creases we turned the trouser or jacket inside out and shaved the material very carefully down the line of the crease with a safety razor (the razor that had a separate blade). Then with a bar of soap we rubbed over the length of the shaved crease line. When turned back the right way and pressed, the creases would look immaculate.

However... can you imagine how sticky and uncomfortable this made the trousers when we had to sit for five hours in a classroom.

To match this hideous uniform we were issued a military 'Great Coat', another relic of British uniform history.

Fortunately going to education classes was the only time we had to wear the BDs, as they were known; along with a pair of black issue shoes.

Our other work clothing consisted of beret plus RE badge, two shirts KF (khaki flannel), a denim jacket and a couple of pairs of denim trousers. Our matching accessories were - a work belt gleaming with black polish, gaiters also in black polish, also minor items such as pants, vests, socks, etc, all in khaki and a pure wool pullover.

This pullover was another item of clothing that caused a great deal of grief. It was worn almost every day during the winter months which meant of course that it had to be washed pretty regularly as it was pure wool and would very quickly smell sweaty.

For a bunch of lads who'd never, ever, done their own washing in a machine let-alone by hand; washing a pure wool item was always going to end in disaster.

We were never guided in how to carry-out this procedure, so instead of a few pure soap flakes in luke warm water and a gentle manipulation, it was - chuck in the washing powder, water as hot as your hands could stand it, rough wash, rinse, rinse and rinse again, also in almost boiling water, then wring it out and place on red hot radiator to dry. Result – a matted lump of wool that would barely fit an 'Action Man' doll.

The replacement pullover (because there was no possible way to salvage the shrunken garment), had to be paid for. In fact any lost or damaged kit had to be paid for. Holes in socks – darn them!

We had a combat smock and trousers in plain olive green; the DPM (or camouflage as it was more popularly known) combats had not yet been adopted. Gloves - khaki, yes again in wool and a long scarf type item which was called a 'cap comforter'… no I don't know why. This item could be worn as a scarf or turned into a hat.

We were also to be fitted later in the week for a dress uniform known as No2. Surprisingly this uniform was semi-tailored to fit, although 'of-the-peg' minor alterations such as jacket sleeves and trouser length, carried out by the Regimental tailors to improve the cut; the only item in our wardrobe that was.

To go with this uniform we had a second pair of boots, which had to be 'Bulled' to a glass-like finish. A second belt, a peeked-hat with a second badge, two No2 dress shirts which had separate collars held in place with a stud at the back and a further stud at the front. This front stud would push painfully into your Adams-apple and throat. As you stood there on parade with your head held high staring into the distance; you felt like someone had kicked you in the balls every time you swallowed. The collar was pressed using pints of spray starch, (another product we had to buy), until it was as stiff as wood. The collar would also be one size smaller than your neck measurement so it wouldn't sag and leave a gap between material and skin. It was agony just putting it on let-alone wearing it.

Under this collar we wore a narrow, parallel, tightly woven khaki wool tie that had to be tied in the most perfect full Windsor knot, a perfect heart shape with not the trace of a crease where the tail appears from the knot. Some lads would never get the hang of it and had to call for a mate to tie it for them.

Finally along with a pair of super heavy-weight, elastic trouser button-on braces, we had two collar lapel ensigns; the RE exploding grenades.

When we eventually got all this kit into shape and we'd learned how to bull boots, shine brasses, blanco belts, spin hats, and press clothing, we became a bloody smart bunch of Junior Sappers. And we were without doubt very proud of ourselves.

As well as shorts, singlet and pumps for PE (they weren't called trainers in those days) there were three other items that were part of our everyday dress; firstly a 'cravat'. These were in different colours for the three different Squadrons; green for 'C', blue for 'B' and red for 'A'. Worn, with pride I might add, around the neck under your open necked KF shirt.

Secondly we were all issued with, and carried in our top right-hand shirt pocket a stainless steel pocket knife, known as a 'Jack knife'. This was attached to an Royal Engineer blue lanyard.

These knifes have been issued to soldiers for generations, I have my grandfather's and great grandfather's at home to this day. Where the term 'Jack' stems from is hard to track down. It seems to relate to something that bends in the middle and was first used during the American civil war, more than that I don't know.

And finally to the lanyard...

Now, why do the Royal Engineers wear a blue lanyard associated with firing an Artillery field gun on their right shoulder?

Well it's a pretty controversial subject, which I'm sure has caused more than a few Inter-Corps punch-ups over the years.

However I'm going to pass on the story as it was given to me all those years ago as a newly recruited boy soldier at Dover.

The 'Gunners' (Royal Artillery) use or used a lanyard to pull on the firing mechanism of a field gun; this allowed them to stand clear of the recoil. They wore this lanyard under the shoulder epaulette and around the shoulder with the end holding a hoof pick or spike (for the removal of stones from the hoofs of the horses pulling the gun carriages) tucked into the top pocket.

Now here comes the controversial bit... At some point in history the military rumour mill has it. The Gunners departed a battlefield leaving their field-pieces behind. (I'll use the word departed because they may have just gone for a brew...).

The Engineers took over the guns and stopped the rout (sounds good stuff doesn't it... especially if you're a Sapper or ex-Sapper. Not so good if you're a Gunner).

For this act of gallantry (allegedly) the Sappers were awarded the right to wear the blue Artillery lanyard as a battle honour. This is of course propaganda, because the Royal Signals also wear a blue lanyard and I'm sure the Gunners never ran off twice; the second time leaving the guns to the 'Scaly Backs'... (Nick-name of the Royal Signals).

I must add at this point, there is serious rivalry between the Sappers and Gunners, and whether they meet on the football field, rugger field, or in the boxing ring it is a no-holds barred battle.

As I said, this was the word as given to us Sprogs in the first few days at Old Park. For the true explanation please see the Gunners website).

Just a bit of needle – no hard feelings Gunners, let's move on...

Our final item of kit issue was a set of what was referred to as 37 pattern webbing; 37 being the first year of introduction; ammo pouches, shoulder straps, small pack, water bottle, ground sheet and steel helmet otherwise known as the piss-pot.

This kit like most of the other stuff we were issued was completely outdated and lacking any in form of ease-of-use.

It was hard and awkward to put together, hard and uncomfortable to wear, and it had the flexibility of plywood. Again, how British and Commonwealth troops won the Second World War wearing it heaven only knows.

Military clothing and equipment was improving, but oh so slowly. It wouldn't be until 1982 when British troops sailed 8000 miles and fought a gruesomely bloody ground war in the Falkland Islands that military heads would realize just how bad and outdated the armies kit really was and from that point equipment would change, be it slowly, for the better.

For regular troops and probably the Junior Infantry, Para's, and Marines a better and reasonably modern set of webbing was available; the 58 pattern.

Following successful completion of our first two Courses, Smudge told us, we would be allowed to buy and use certain items of kit at our own expense – ammo boots these are leather soled, studded boots that preceded the DMS boot. As best boots they looked far smarter than the DMS and having layered leather soles meant the edges could also be bulled to a mirror finish. We could also purchase and wear the 58 pattern webbing and in Course 8, Puttee's to replace our canvas gaiters. I will come back to the kit purchase later in the book.

So, a few short hours into our new and voluntarily adopted military life we... well 'we' as in everybody but me, had a whole new wardrobe to prepare and process. Daunting was an understatement.

Day 2

I was dreaming, in the dream I was falling - tumbling down a hill and woke up with a mighty banging and crashing going on around me.

To say this was disorientating and somewhat frightening would be an understatement.

My bed was on its side and I was trapped between the bed frame and the wall with the mattress and bed clothes on top of me.

All of us in the room were in the same boat – every bed had been tipped over and all of us were lying on the floor.

When I eventually found my way out of my predicament there was our Junior Lance Corporal Smudge Smith at the end of his bed laughing.

Course 8, the most senior Course in the Squadron had woken early to rampage through our lines and tip all the new-boys out of bed; apparently this was tradition; it was 0530 - day number two had begun...

'Ok, let's get to it' said Smudge.

'Everyone ok?'

Nobody answered.

'Right, get those beds back up the right way; don't worry this won't happen again, it's a first morning thing. Get to the wash rooms, don't piss around, you'll need every minute this morning. Get washed and get back here to get your bed packs made. Dress in your civi's; you'll be on the landing in half an hour to begin your cleaning tasks. You've got an hour before breakfast kicks-off and you don't go down to breakfast before your duties are done; not done – no breakie. You'll be parading at 0830 and following parade your Troop Officer will be talking to you. Today's' a big day lads, you've got a fucking heap to get through, now get going.'

I righted my bed, grabbed my wash bag and made for the door – no hang-on a massive queue - I'll make up my bed pack and then wash.

I turned back, in doing so bumping into a couple of my roommates who were following me through the door.

'Bathrooms full.' I said.

I started to get dressed, at least from the waist down and make up my bed. It wasn't so difficult, just a case of making sure the folds were all exactly the same size, then bumping down the pillows and turning the open end underneath.

Job done it was back to the ablutions. I waited my turn for a place at one of the three rows of five sinks.

While I waited I looked around me again, for a brief moment I had time to take in and register where I was. The washrooms were ok, the floor was of reddish paint, at least it was not polished, the walls were painted the same as all the other walls a dark gloss grey up to waist height with a lighter paint from waist to ceiling. From the washrooms you took a step up to the shower area and two bathrooms. Although it doesn't seem that many showers and baths for so many boys in the early seventies we never bathed or showered as often, so it didn't seem unusual.

I quickly took my place by a vacant sink cleaned my teeth and ran a flannel over my face and under my arms. Ablutions complete I went back to my room and finished dressing.

All my mates were doing the same – shouting was coming from the corridor and the JNCOs were strutting up and down getting us to 'get-a-move-on' and get on with our chores.

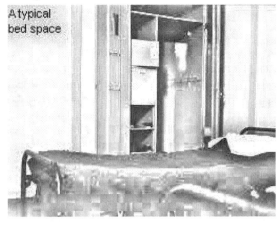

A typical bed space

I had been tasked with Paul Dodwell (Doddy) to clean the washing room – that was the clothes washing room. As it was the first morning and no one had done any washing we were pretty lucky. The unfortunate boys were those who had to clean the ablutions and toilets. They were stood waiting for lads to finish; but this would be the first and only time. In future any late comers were told to fuck-off; you got up, got washed, and got out double quick; the only late comers could, and would be the JNCOs; they of course were a rule to themselves.

Having cleaned the clothes-washroom, Paul and I returned to tidy our bed space.

Smudge was there issuing orders.

'Dust your bed space everywhere – bedside light, skirting board, under your bed legs (*under the bed legs? Is he serious? Yes he was! Jesus*), top of your lockers, there mustn't be a speck anywhere. Sweep out your area into the middle of the room then dustpan it into the bin. We'll do the bumping when we get back from breakfast.'

Smudge started walking round inspecting our open lockers and bed areas. Nothing was to be visible on the bedside locker and the inside of our lockers had to be laid out to perfection even our soap, toothbrush, paste and razor had to be in a neat line. One by one he released us for breakfast.

'Get down there before 'C' Squadron arrive,' he said.

'And don't fucking hang about - eat and get back up here pronto. Ok?'

'Yes Corporal.'

It was around 0645 we had half an hour maximum.

We headed for the top of the stairs and were pleased to see no queue, there was a short one but only for the last set of stairs and we were soon at the hot plate. The breakfast looked lovely; there was a major fry up – sausage, bacon, mushrooms, beans, tomato and all types of eggs. Cereal, toast and fruit.

'Bloody hell' said Les 'it's like a fucking hotel.'

He spoke the truth; I don't think any of us had ever seen a spread like it.

As we stood there once again we could hear shouting booing and laughter coming from the quad.

Once again it was 'C' Squadron Intake being marched over for breakfast. 'Poor sods,' said Ray.

'Fuckem – don't feel sorry for them,' said Les.

'Why man they're in the same boat as weh.' Said Ray in his strong Geordie accent.

'What the fuck was that,' said Les 'For God's sake, we're going to have to teach you English.'

Les was grinning while he said this which was a good thing; I could see Ray didn't take kindly to having his dialect knocked by a Mancunian who really didn't have room to talk.

'You've hardly got room te taak hev yee with a bloody accent of yours.' retaliated Ray.

'Move it!' Came a voice from behind the hot plate.

'Yeah, get a fucking move on Sprogs!' Came a voice from further back down the queue.

This broke up our impending argument on regional differences and we moved forward quietly with our plates.

Breakfast over and climbing the stairs we were told in no uncertain terms to keep to the sides, they've been swept and bumped.

Some of our lines were still on their way down.

We went through the fire doors to still more shouting and the sight of three lads swinging bumpers from side to side in the corridor.

'Had your breakfast have you', shouted Mick Foster.

'Good get on this bumper and let these lads go – come on move it!'

I pushed my irons in my pocket and took over. I soon got in the rhythm but realised that it was quite a tiring job. Up and down I went.

Slowly things were getting sorted; lads were returning from breakfast, most of the chores had been done and it was only a few minor things needed doing.

I was dismissed with my bumper back to my room where Smudge got Gerald Dickerson to take over and do our room floor.

J/Sgt Perry stuck his head through the door.

'Smudge, Ned Batley's starting on this side of the block in ten minutes. Stand them by their beds.'

'Right,' said Smudge. 'Sergeant Batley is one of your Troop Permanent Staff Sergeants the other is Staff Shaw. Sergeant Batley will be walking round each room on this side of the block this morning on a lockers-closed inspection. I will stand by the door and as he approaches I will call the room to attention, I'll shout - Room - Room, Shun! You'll stand at the foot of your bed and bring your feet together like this. Then he'll most probably tell you to stand at ease – stand easy. When he leaves I'll call Room Shun again and you bring your feet together – this is what you do (he then gave us a demonstration of the movements and the difference between standing at ease and standing easy).

'Get it?'

'Yes Corporal,' we said.

'Ok stand by your beds.'

The fire doors were open through to the main staircase and we could hear the other Room-jacks bringing their rooms to some sort of attention.

Sgt Batley seemed to spend a quick five minutes in each room.

Then it was our turn...

'Room – Roooom – SHUN!' Ordered Smudge.

We preformed quite well under the circumstances. Les as an ex-cadet doing a proper job; bringing his knee up and slamming his foot down hard.

This would be typical Les for the two years I knew him, a cheeky, exuberant, outgoing and likeable kid one of the best friends I would ever make.

Sgt Batley marched in, standing tall, back straight - we were told he'd had a serious injury which accounted for his very upright stance. Behind him came Johnny Spriggs and J/Sgt Perry.

'Stand easy,' ordered Batley.

He then walked round the room looking at each bed space and asking our names.

When he asked mine I said 'Burt - Sergeant, Steven Burt.'

Spriggsy chipped in...

'This is the lad I was telling you about Sarg, turned up here yesterday unannounced.'

I saw J/Sgt Perry glance enquiringly at Smudge...

'Well we've found you a home Burt, now we'll have to work on keeping you here, unless of course you'd rather join another Junior Regiment? Which I'm sure you wouldn't. It'll get resolved today, don't worry.'

I didn't get a chance to answer before he turned to address the room.

'A good presentation for your first morning, well done. You'll all parade outside shortly and your Troop Officer will address you. Today, tomorrow and Sunday will be full on – no break. By Monday morning you'll know how to service your kit and also how to put it on and present yourselves as soldiers. Monday morning you'll join the rest of the Squadron in uniform on parade. Tomorrow and Sunday you'll parade on your landing where your Junior NCOs will fill you in what will happen during the day.'

He turned to leave...

'Room - room Shun!' ordered Smudge and we came to attention as Batley, Spriggsy and Perry walked out.

'Stay where you are,' ordered Smudge.

'Well done. Ok, this is what will happen next, when Sergeant Batley has finished the big end room he'll go down and tell your Troop Officer - your Troopy.'

We'll call you out to the quad and size you off in three ranks, Dixon, you'll know what that is having been a cadet... you'll get into one long line all ninety whatever of you by size... tallest on the left through to shortest on the right; with me so far?'

We all nodded.

'Good, when you're all in this long line you'll number down tallest to shortest from one to whatever. Then - and for fuck sake get this right and do not forget your number; you'll be ordered - odd numbers take one step forward, even numbers take one step back, march. Ok? Odd numbers only will step forward even numbers will step back; its that simple lads... who doesn't know odd from even?'

We were all quiet.

'Good, I'll take that as a positive then. Don't let me down, someone down there will fuck-up, they'll either forget their number or don't know odds from evens – don't let it be anyone from this room.'

He said this while looking across at Steve Cottle the lad from Tilbury who the previous day when asked whether he was Co or Cu (we had Gary Cutting - Cu and Steve Cottle – Co, in our room) had replied 'I'm neither Corporal I'm C of E.'

This would have been funny if Steve had made this comment as a joke, but sadly he was serious. He never had a clue what the NCO had meant when he said this; it done Steve no favours in the 'on the ball department' and his reply would stay with him throughout his time at Dover. *'Oh yeah, you're Steve C of E aren't you?'*

We most definitely had to have our wits about us.

Smudge carried on with his instruction... 'Once in a line you'll be ordered - front rank turn to the left and rear rank turn to the right. Listen to me closely, the first guy on the left in the front rank won't move, he'll stand still looking forward, you'll all march round onto his position and form up – middle, rear, front, middle, rear, one, two, three, one, two, three, get it?'

'Yes Corporal,' we collectively replied.

'Good; we - your Junior NCOs will of course guide you the first time. Remember where you are and who's around you because when you form up the next time you'll take up the same positions. We don't want you milling around like lost sheep.'

While this explanation had been going on Sgt Batley had moved into the other room over the other side of the landing through the swing fire doors and on into the 'big end room', so called because it was twice the size of the rooms off the corridor. By rights I should have been in this room with my surname starting with 'B' but fortunately I wasn't and I'm eternally thankful that the cards fell the way they did for me. The BER as I'll refer to it from here on, was an awful room; crowded with around fourteen to sixteen beds, and noisy with very little in the way of privacy.

I'd got really lucky with my room, my Room-jack Smudge, room-mates and bed space inside and behind the door on the right. I would have hated the BER.

Batley and Spriggsy were heading down the stairs.

The Squadron morning parade that we had heard taking place in the quad two floors below was being dismissed, all the other Courses heading off to the tasks they were so familiar with.

Now it was our turn.

Kevin Perry was at the top of the stairs on our landing that we would come to know so well and hate.

'Right! Let's have you out here on the landing.' Shouted Perry.

We piled out almost tripping over each other our lovely polished corridor wreaked in the melee.

Our Junior NCOs were gathered together against the banister.

'Ok, you've been briefed by your room NCOs on what will happen next – downstairs, one long line tallest on the left, shortest on the right; you'll be joined by your mates from the far side of the block, then we'll start sizing off. Ok let's go!'

We cascaded down the two floors of stairs and out through the swing doors onto the quad, our colleagues from the far side of the block upper floor were also spilling out from the doors opposite, the doors that led to the offices where I'd been taken by Johnny Spriggs the previous day.

Junior Lance Corporals (JLcpl) and Corporals (J/Cpl) were pacing up and down shouting for us to form into a single line; there must have been fifteen of them in all.

Eventually we got there, the line stretching from the road across the quad to the big main doors leading to the canteen and cookhouse entrance; it was quite a squeeze. One by one with the aid of our JNCOs we changed places and shuffled left and right till we were sized-off; tallest by the roadway shortest by the cookhouse door.

'Ok – now you're sized-off I want you to call numbers from left to right – that's your left – that's you there,' he said pointing to the very tall lad almost in the road. 'You're number one. I want volume no mumbling ok – right lets go.'

There was silence...

Kev Perry walked over to the lad on the end.

'Are you fucking deaf or what!?' He shouted into the lads face.

'I told you to shout your number – if you hadn't noticed you're on the end of the line, you're number fucking ONE! Got it!?'

The lad must have been shitting himself...

'Yes Sergeant,' he said.

'LOUDER!'

'YES SERGEANT,' he repeated on the top of his voice.

'Good, we haven't got all fucking day. Now shout out your number.'

'ONE!'

'TWO!'

'THREE'... and so it went down to the end of the line, ninety seven in total. Not a bad effort really once it got going.

'Good – now – odd numbers one step forward even numbers one step back, MARCH!'

Almost - most had got it right, some had got it wrong and our JNCOs were pushing and pulling boys into the correct line.

'Sharpen-up you lot, you were picked for the Sappers because you're fuckin brighter than the fuckin rest, start showing it!'

He then explained how we were going to march our way into three ranks, which we did relatively easily.

'Remember where you stand and who's around you, these are the positions you'll return to on all future parades. Now, when your Troop Officer comes on to the quad in a moment I'll call parade, parade, SHUN! You'll bring your feet together and stand tall just like you did upstairs in your rooms. Got it?'

Silence...

'Am I talking to myself again – I said GOT IT!'

'YES SERGEANT!' We hollered in return.

I think it was dawning on us that when he asked a question he expected not only an answer but a loud answer.

Our Room-jacks were standing in a line and Kev Perry was stood at the top of the steps leading from the offices.

Suddenly the door swung open; Perry came to attention as Batley, Spriggsy, and our Troop Officer came onto the Quad.

Troop! Trooop! SHUN!

We done that quite well I thought.

'Stand them easy Sergeant Perry,' said our Troopy.

'Troop stand at EASE!' Ordered Perry. 'Stand easy!' We relaxed our shoulders as we'd been shown earlier that morning in our rooms.

'Good morning lads, I'm your Troop Officer, Lieutenant Rogers I will be your Troop Officer for your first three terms at Dover that equates to the next twelve months. You have chosen to become Royal Engineers –

40

Sappers - members of the finest Corps in the British Army whose Colonel-in-Chief is none other than Her Majesty the Queen; *pause for effect* - we have standards and traditions in the Corps to which you will become acquainted and adopt with pride. You have also been fortunate enough to start your career, not only as a Junior Leader, but in 'A' Squadron, the best Squadron in the Regiment.

Your first three terms here will run similar to those at school with set daily time tables; however your subjects in the majority will be in no way similar. Apart from your continuing education, which will decrease as the terms pass, you will be entering an adult world of serious training and we will be expecting you to take your training seriously.

During your first three terms you will be concentrating on foot drill, small arms drill, weapons training, field craft and physical fitness. In later courses you'll be learning Combat Engineering B3 and B2. Courses one to three, seven and eight would be the minimum Courses you would do here at Dover, you may however be fortunate enough to do trade training and some outward bound Courses. So, as you can see, your life here can be very interesting, it can be great fun and very rewarding with the opportunity to progress through the junior rank structure. But you need to work hard and work together. Your first thirteen weeks will be tough – very tough; but if you come through it and most of you will, you'll find life falls into routine and gets easier every day. If you don't play ball, if you don't sign-up for the team, I promise you nothing other than a very rough ride.

When the time comes you will leave Old Park as fully trained professional soldiers, most of you will hold a B2 Combat Engineering qualification as well as the first grounding in a separate trade. You will be streaks ahead of your contemporaries in adult service and you will stand head and shoulders above others when it comes to promotion.

I wish you all good luck; I'm sure I will get to know you all over the coming months and I'll now hand you back to Junior Sergeant Perry who'll explain your itinerary to you.'

'Troop! Trooop! SHUN!' Commanded Perry.

This took us slightly by surprise; some had drifted off into dream land while stood there, so our response was slow.

Perry saluted our Troopy.

'Carry on Sergeant Perry,' said Rogers.

'Thank you sir,' replied Perry as our Troopy turned and left the quad.

We were now all stood rigidly in what we thought was the 'attention' position.

'Right, stand easy again – you will now return to your rooms where you will continue to prepare your kit with your room NCO. They will go through all aspects of kit preparation with you. During the day you will be escorted by room to the barbers where you will receive a free haircut. You will also be given the opportunity to go to the 'NAAFI' to stock up on any items you don't have or failed to bring with you. We will arrange for any kit issue that is unusually large or small to be taken to the QM store and changed.

(I fail to remember how we came to get our kit... I believe I'm correct in saying the only item that was given out by size was our boots, berets and No2 dress hat; the rest of kit was just stuffed into a case and kitbag and handed over. What didn't fit and frankly most of the stuff didn't because it was made for men not for boys, we had to swap among ourselves, either lads in our own room or those next door. Only the bigger lads had kit that remotely fitted).

This evening you will get the opportunity to write or telephone home if you wish to. There are two telephones at the guardroom barrier.

When walking around the barracks you will walk upright in a soldierly manner, you will not put your hands in your pockets; you will not walk over the grassed areas. If you are more than one in number you'll walk together side by side with a third or fourth person behind, in a small squad like formation. Do I make myself clear?'

'YES SERGEANT,' we bellowed.

'Ok, I will call you to attention again, I will then shout parade dismissed. You'll uniformly as possible turn to the right, and make your way back to your rooms.

'Troop! Trooop! SHUN!' – We became rigid with feet together. 'Troop FALLLL OUT!' We all turned to the right, well most of us, and made our way upstairs to our lines.

Within minutes of being in our room J/Sgt Perry walked in.

Les our keen-as-mustard ex-cadet shouted 'Room Shun!'

We all jumped to our feet and this impressed Perry no end, it also earned Les his first set of 'Brownie points'; although Les would be one of those kids that would lose his credit rating as fast as he made it.

J/Sgt Perry had come in to see me and find out what the story was with my unscheduled - and to those at Dover, unexpected arrival at Old Park.

I had to go through the whole story again.

'Come with me Burt, we'll go and see the Chief Clerk.'

I followed him out of the room, down the stairs and into the office area.

Each door had a mounted plaque with the title of the person inside. AO (Admin Officer), SSM (Squadron Sergeant Major), and others.

'Ah, you again,' I was greeted by the Chief.

'I take it you're here to enquire after this lads position Sergeant Perry?' Asked the Chief.

'Yes Chief, I only got to hear of this mix up this morning, it's a bit odd; ok we've got him a bed but nothing else; we really need to get this sorted. Plans have changed and Intake are on the parade ground first thing in the morning drilling, how's he going to drill with no kit? At least if we issue him a set of kit he can join in. If he leaves us either he can take it with him or return it.'

'Good point Sergeant Perry, leave it with me, I'll do my best to be back to you before lunch time.'

Perry thanked the Chief Clerk and I followed him out of the office area.

Instead of going across the quad we went up the stairs directly from the offices, we were now on the far side of the building.

On the third level landing I realised we'd entered the other side of our Intake lines. On this side of the block the room allocations were alphabetical from 'M' to 'T'. From 'T' the remainder of lads were billeted on the bridge lines over the cook house. I walked behind Kev Perry while we made our way back to my room. He stuck his head in every room as we passed. Each room was a hive of activity.

When I got back my room mates were at the point of leaving for the barbers' shop – I joined them and again descended to the quad. My head was spinning, it wasn't yet lunch time and I felt I'd been awake forever.

It was less than a hundred yards to the barbers shop on the side of the building housing the NAAFI shop and JNCOs club; we joined a queue of roughly thirty others, I thought to myself this is going to take ages; but no, it definitely was not.

The early seventies was still the hippy era. The era of long or at least shoulder length hair. This was our first military haircut and 'Bert the Butcher', as our Regimental hairdresser was affectionately nick-named, was having a hay-day. He must have thought all his Christmases had come at once.

Almost three hundred haircuts to get through in a day didn't give him any time for - *'Would you like a little more off the back and sides Sir?'* It was straight in with the clippers – up the back - up the sides and 'next!'

Watching my unfortunate comrades going through the door to the chair with, in most cases long stylish locks, and then coming out almost bald, took me back to our village barber in Winsley.

Mr Scadden the unofficial village barber, who would sit us on a box in his green house, put a basin on our heads and trim round the edge for a shilling.

Today was production line cutting for Bert and in no time I was in the chair – zip up the sides – zip up the back, scissors across the fringe and done. It was truly a desperately hideous haircut, but at least we were all in the same boat.

I was out the door and 'Bert' was one boy closer to drowning in an ever rising tide of hair.

Smudge was waiting to collect our room together and we walked as a squad the stones throw back to our block.

The rest of the morning continued with kit preparation.

Those who were unfortunate enough to have been issued with new belt and new gaiters had to blacken them with boot polish. Some were lucky enough to have been issued with pre-used kit that had been blackened and only need polishing.

We were shown how to thread and secure the single run of bootlace, how to polish and shine our work boots, how to press our KF shirt and denims; at the end of the room was a metal framed-wooden topped trestle table which had to serve us all for ironing our clothes, Smudge included.

We had an iron issued to the room, not a steam iron, just a normal flat iron.

This we also had to share; and we would discover that these irons would be forever going wrong. Out of the five rooms on our side of the lines we generally only had three irons working at any one time. It was a nightmare with lads trying to press their kit in the dark after lights out at 2200.

Following our return after mid-term break many lads brought their own iron back with them. The use of a private iron could then be bartered for cigarettes or money... money to buy cigarettes which then be bartered again.

We were taken into the washrooms with our berets and Smudge showed us how to soak them and mould them into shape with the cap-badge over the left eye. Next term he told us you can cut out the lining and you'll get a better shape to the headwear; but for the present we had to leave our kit unaltered. After Course 3 we'd be able to mould in a two-way stretch and wear the badge closer to the centre of the forehead, Engineer style. Every subsequent term we were cut a little more slack and given more respect, but as Smudge had told us the evening before at dinner - we had to earn it every step of the way.

The preparation time flew by until we heard the jeering and laughter echoing once again around the quad. It was 'C' Squadron Intake arriving for lunch and once again getting the brunt of 'A' Squadrons 'Micky-take'.

'Ok, grab your mugs and rods and get in the lunch queue,' said Smudge.

We had an hour, and following our meal could relax on our beds until the next round started.

We lay there talking among ourselves, finding out about each other's pre-Dover lives – how we got to Old Park and why we wanted to leave home.

Les had always wanted to join the army, right from a small child. He'd joined the army cadets at thirteen years old; he was good academically but didn't want to stay on at school he chose the Engineers because of the trade potential. The same story applied to most of us Ray, Steve Cottle, Doddy and I. We couldn't get much of a story out of Gerald; he came from the Midlands and lived with relatives not his parents. He was a sad case and wouldn't be with us long. Gary Cutting came from a pretty well-to-do family and really wanted to be a soldier but his mum had created merry-hell about him joining up. During our second term after Christmas his mum would have a (supposed) break-down due to her son training to be a soldier and on recommendation of her doctor Gary would be released back to civi-street. It was pretty unfair on Gary because he was a nice lad and was doing as well as the rest of us. He really didn't want to go.

Lunch over we again returned to kit preparation. Smudge got them all to dress in each part of their uniform while I stood by and watched. The BDs, the denim work wear and combats; then he took Steve Cottle on his own and showed us how to assemble the webbing; belt with ammo pouches, small pack and water bottle.

'That's all you need to know for now,' said Smudge. 'We'll come on to how and what to pack another time, there's a method to everything.'

This we were rapidly beginning to realize.

J/Sgt Perry once again made an appearance, Smudge called us up and once again we stood smartly to attention. During our Intake term this would happen constantly every time an NCO or JNCO entered the room.

In our following terms it slowly began to drop off for all but Permanent Staff NCOs and JNCOs above the rank of Corporal.

'Smudge I'm taking Burt up the QM, RHQ have given the go-ahead to issue him with kit regardless.'

This was music to my ears; I'd have my own gear and at last be able to join in with the others preparing for the morning.

Off I went trying to keep in step with Kevin Perry.

Walking in step is not that easy unless you've been trained to do it as we would find out over the coming couple of days.

On reaching the Quarter Master stores we went in through the main door. Off to the right was a small office and in front of me was a long grey Formica topped counter. Behind this counter stood rows of racking containing every item of kit I'd been introduced to over the last 24 hours.

'Hello Q!' Shouted Kev. 'Anyone about!?'

The office door opened and a Permanent Staff Corporal came out.

'Hi Sergeant Perry and what can I do for you?' He asked.

Got a guy here who turned up somewhat unexpectedly,' said Kev. 'We've no record of him on the Intake radar and he may not even belong to us but RHQ are looking into it and until a decision is made he's to be made welcome and kitted out like the rest of them. Can we sort him this afternoon?'

'You're lucky mate, I was just on the point of shutting up shop for the afternoon. (I was to learn over the years that the QM stores in whatever Squadron or Regiment you went to were a rule unto themselves. Those privileged enough to be chosen to work within the kit distribution business never really put themselves out or broke into a

46

sweat). Ok, let's get you kitted out. I take it it's a full set of everything Kev?'

Yeah, the whole works,' said Kev taking a seat in the corner.

At this point of the day my unexpected arrival at Old Park would again work in my favour. I would be kitted out as an individual.

The corporal on the other side of the counter had the time to issue me kit that would fit me and also with items like belts gaiters and webbing, he found me items of kit that had been previously worn and used by others.

The gaiters and work belt were already blackened the belt had gunmetal buckles and sliders; this meant they were not brass and did not require polishing; my No2 belt had already been blanco'd and was nice and supple with the sliders already squared-off. I'll explain this later.

The clothing was picked to fit me and best of all I was given a triple 'B' Beret; a prized item of kit Kev Perry told me. Apparently all junior squaddies wanted to get their hands on one of these, the triple 'B' or BBB beret was smaller than some of the other makes and moulded better to your head; the overhang of the material from the edge was smaller in diameter so when pulled down on one side it didn't come so far down the ear. This is hard to explain but any ex-squaddie who reads this and was around at the time will know exactly what I mean.

Kev Perry said I was a lucky fucker to get the kit I did. I was just thankful I now had my own KFS set and mug, I could return the set I borrowed to their rightful owner.

I also had a rather unusual suitcase. All the issue suitcases I'd seen of my roommates were typical of the time. Brown, sturdy, with the solid leather handle and leather over the corners.

The case I'd been issued with was very similar to the one I'd arrived with only not so big. It was the cardboard plastic veneered type, not at all robust and looked as if it would fall apart with the amount of kit loaded into it. It was dark blue. The Corporal explained that they'd run out of military suitcases due to the

Intake numbers. The army… or at least in this case the Junior Leaders at Dover had to buy in civilian type cases to make up the shortfall.

Anyway, kit bag in one hand and case in another and watched over but not assisted by Kev Perry I staggered back to my block.

Things were still buzzing; my mates were now going through ironing tuition. Smudge had his own clothing on the bed and was demonstration how to press the different clothing using a wet hanky to get perfect creases.

We were told that the following morning, following the rest of the Squadrons departure to Regimental Parade, we would parade in our work dress; 'shirt sleeve order'. Which meant our shirts had to be pressed to perfection with the sleeves rolled up above the elbow, the turn up on the sleeve two inches. This was dress code for summer; April to October, or from when the order was published by RHQ on Part 1 orders. The whole Regiment dressed the same way; there was no – *'Oh, it's a bit chilly this morning I think I'll wear a coat or a jumper'*. Oh no, we froze or sweated together subject to orders from above.

Dependant on the weather in the morning, we'd be inspected either in our room or in the quad and it would be a meticulous inspection; we could expect to be standing in three ranks for some time. Then we would rectify the mistakes and be inspected again. This would continue until we got it right. Then we'd do the whole thing again with the uniform for education, the BDs.

I started to put away my kit; I had the advantage of having helped my new room-mates do this. At last I had my own stuff to work on and prepare.

Dinner, or tea as we called it then came and we went down to join the queue, before leaving we were told that there would be another parade on the landing at 1800 – this time we'd better be there ready and waiting.

We came up from our meal and sat on our beds talking and smoking, it didn't seem to make any difference that we were so young, if you smoked you smoked and that was it.

At 1755 we were all on the landing, our JNCOs with us.

We were informed of our itinerary for the following day.

'Tomorrow morning's room inspection will take place in works dress. Your lockers will be inspected so make sure they are laid out exactly as they should be, your room NCOs will check your lockers tonight. Your cleaning routine will be just as it was this morning; we expect the standards to be as good if not better than they were today. Do I make myself clear?'

'YES SERGEANT!' We loudly responded. Perry was grinning...

'Following locker and lines inspection you will parade outside, you'll adopt the same positions in three ranks as you did this morning. Do I make myself clear?'

'YES SERGEANT!' We loudly responded for a second time.

'You will then be inspected by your Troop Permanent Staff. Following inspection you will begin foot drill. God help us all.'

Again he was grinning.

'Following this meeting return to your rooms; when your room NCOs are satisfied with your lockers and your kit presentation for tomorrow you may, if you want to, go to the guardroom and telephone home. You will go in groups of two or more and return in the same groups walking smartly and in a soldier-like manner. If you don't want to phone mummy or daddy you can write or do as you wish in your rooms. The NAAFI sells stamps. Your room NCOs will explain how your first week will work – it will work somewhat differently to the following weeks because we need to get you from a fucking disorganised pile of shit into something resembling a troop of men that resemble soldiers; and I use the word 'men' very loosely. You will be working through the weekend. Depending on how you perform tomorrow we may allow you a semi-relaxing Sunday afternoon.

One further piece of information – sickness; you do not, regardless of whether you feel groggy with a cold, suffer from malaria, yellow fever, cholera or any other ailment large or small, stay in bed.

You get up, get dressed, and carry out your general cleaning duties.

You will then parade with all the other sick, lame and lazy fuckers in the quad in front of Course eight windows, that's to the left of the doors at the bottom of the stairs. Regardless of whether you're dying or suffering from a boil on the back of your neck you WILL always parade with small pack containing, pyjamas, pumps, towel, and wash kit. Following parade you will then march your way to the M.R.S where you'll queue to see the Quack. He will either pronounce you dead, unfit, light duties, or put you out of your misery forever. That gentlemen is how sickness works in the army.'

Seemed a bit harsh to me...

'Any questions?'

'NO SERGEANT!' We shouted.

'Ok, dismissed.'

We went back to our rooms.

Telephoning home was not something a person done in 1971. Telephones were red boxes on street corners; there were no mobile phones. God forbid; it was rare enough to have a telephone in your house let alone in your pocket. If you phoned home you were considered a bit of a mammies-boy. When I'd gone to Jersey for a week with my school in the final term none of us phoned home. And it never entered my head on my second night at Dover. Only Gary Cutting from our room went to the phone and this would set the scene for Gary until he left us in Course 2. His departure to the army had apparently left his mum an emotional basket case and he had to talk to her every day. Eventually it would prove too much and he would be discharged back to his parents; sad, as he made a good Junior Soldier - smart, sharp, he'd have gone far.

The rest of the evening continued in locker and kit preparation. My new mates had almost finished their gear and so chipped in to help me. All the time Smudge was telling us the score.

How the Regiment and Squadrons operated were published on daily orders - Part 1 Regimental and Part 2 Squadron. They were posted on the office notice board and must be read every day. The reading of orders became as engrained in our routine as polishing boots or pressing clothes. They told you what was happening at both levels.

We would spend all the first week doing foot drill and fitness training, we would be tried out for numerous sports; all geared toward representing 'A Sqn' 'Shiny A'; in inter-Squadron and Regiment competitions. We would attend the M.R.S (the Regimental Medical Unit) to have a medical and a set of inoculations. We would also be marched to the QM to be issued our No2 dress.

Within a few weekends we would be proficient enough at marching as a troop to be able to join Saturday morning Regimental parade, although without a weapon.

Our itinerary for the rest of the term telling us where to be and at what time every day would be published on the notice board alongside daily orders.

As we chatted we began to realize that this room was now our home, and our bed space with bedside and standing locker was where we kept our life's possessions; not one of us had thought to bring a transistor radio or a tape player. There was no television in the rooms although there was a common room or if you like a TV room round the other side of the lines.

A year from now we would have a replacement OC (Officer Commanding the Squadron) a Major Durey who had returned from a six month expedition taking two of the newly introduced 'Range Rover' four wheel drive vehicles down the Trans-America highway and across or through the Darien Gap between Panama and Columbia

The expedition started on the December 3rd 1971 from Anchorage in Alaska and ended at the southernmost tip of Terra del Fuego in Southern America.

The two Range Rovers supplied by Rover Ltd and crewed with men from the 17th/21st Lancers. The British Trans-America expedition was led by Major John Blashford-Snell, who had Blue Nile and Red Sea expedition experiences behind him.

The route was along the 18,000 mile long Pan-American Highway, with 3 months in the middle crossing the road-less part within the Darien Gap jungle isthmus.

The Darien Gap or El Tapon - "The Stopper" is swamp and rain forest jungle of 250 miles (400 kilometres), until that moment never crossed by vehicle.

There are no roads, no bridges, no continuous tracks other than those known by the local indigenous Indians. The whole area is jungle, swamp and river, inhabited by a selection of objectionable mammals, reptiles and insects. The expedition was supported by generous sponsor companies in Britain and America. Duckhams supplied the oil. Tirfor and Mayflower supplied hand winches and recovery gear. Marks and Spencer gave the clothing, and the food company Heinz supplied the expedition with no less than 3 tonnes with food.

A reconnaissance team decided the best possible route. Then came the main team which cleared the jungle, then 30 horses carrying the packs. Finally the two Range Rover's; the Range Rovers were guided by Bob Russell from the Royal Engineers, who walked in front of the vehicles for the whole route, guiding them in the right direction.

With each of the vehicles, also walked a crew of eight Royal Engineers who were responsible for the digging, laying ladders, cutting trees, winching, etc to keep the Range Rover's moving through the jungle.

The speed of the expedition was slow, some days only a mile covered, if they were lucky.

The Engineers were armed with machetes and power saws, everywhere were severe obstacles like huge trees and ruts.

The expedition carried with them solid aluminium ladders which could carry the whole weight of the fully laden Range Rover, but weighed

only 100lb each. They were invaluable as bridges in crossing the different obstacles like gullies, ditches, slopes, trees etc. The ladders were also used as platforms on the inflatable Avon rafts to cross rivers and other water obstacles. The rafts were driven by 20 hp Johnson outboard motors or pulled across by the vehicles own Fairey capstan winches.

Major Durey gave us a presentation on this epic journey when he joined us in September 1972. It was without doubt a mammoth undertaking.

He was a great bloke, progressive - a moderniser; and on his arrival some real changes were made for the good of the men, or should I say boys, because that's what we technically still were.

Having practiced getting dressed, buckling our gaiters and seating our beret's; our works kit for the following morning all prepared and our lockers spick and span, we went downstairs for a cup of tea or a slice of bread and soup; supper.

Both the bread, soup and tea were left in the foyer in front of the main dining room door on a trolley; you went and took what you wanted. I suppose the same happened at the other end of the cookhouse in the 'B' Squadron foyer; what 'C' Squadron done over the far side of the barracks for supper I don't know, they probably had a collection rota.

Smoking, eating and drinking we lay on our beds talking until it was time to turn in.

Already we were discussing among ourselves what we would bring back from our first weekend at home, six weeks hence.

I had a radio at home, not a transistor but a valve operated am/lw radio in a square box it was powered by a six volt battery the size of a house brick and came on via a switch operated by the lid. This was our technology of the time.

Les said he'd bring back his reel-to-reel tape machine and microphone; the idea being that at 5pm on a Sunday we could set up the tape with the microphone against the radio speaker and record Alan Freeman's 'Pick of the Pops'.

One or two of us would bring back another flat or steam iron.

Our second day ended.

Although I was still not yet officially a Junior Sapper at least I had a set of kit which meant I blended in. I would know for sure whether I was staying or going on Monday.

Our first weekend

The duty Corporal woke the Squadron six days of the week.

The duty roster changed nightly with a Senior and Junior Corporal on duty sleeping in the duty office. At 0630 they would do the rounds banging on doors and banging on lockers. I would defy anyone to sleep through the racket.

Today was our first day at being soldiers. We bounced out of bed and into the washrooms. Grabbed a sink, had a wash and back to the room to get dressed; not just dressed but militarily dressed – there's a BIG difference.

Vest and pants khaki, cellular (to give them their official name), army issue underwear; followed by shirt KF, (not cut to fit, the excess material would balloon out of the top of our denim trousers like froth spilling out of the top of a beer bottle).

Then came another tricky part of the procedure - securing the lace at the top of the boot and tucking the trouser into the gaiter.

Laces were not criss-crossed; a knot was tied on the thick end of a leather lace and it was fed from lace-hole to lace-hole up the boot. Laces must not be twisted; the leather lace was square cut from a piece of hide and died black. The smooth outer of the lace had to be facing upward with the visible part of the lace remaining parallel all the way to the top. The lace then goes round the top of the boot under itself pulled tightly back. You're now holding a short end of a lace positioned on the inner side of the ankle; the remaining action is to wind the left over end around and around the lace that goes around the boot. Get it? Great...

Sorry, it was hard to explain, but I needed to do that just so the reader can get an idea of the oddities we had to learn. Some kids took days to learn how to get this right and as we were marching in a squad you'd see boot laces drifting out from underneath gaiters along the way.

The gaiters were another nightmare. They were handed – left and right. The difference between the two was a semi-circular cut out in the front of each gaiter that goes over the top of the foot. Have a look at the picture and you'll get the idea. (Not the way the boots are laced, which is incorrect). The buckles of the gaiters go on the outside of the ankle. Amazingly lots of lads just didn't get it and for a couple of weeks into our new profession you'd hear some poor lad being screamed at on parade because his gaiters were on the wrong way round or the buckles weren't tight enough so the gaiter would drop to the point where it was almost scrapping the ground at the heel while the trouser legs would spill from the top.

What this picture doesn't show is how the trousers marry with the gaiters. We had to tuck the bottom of our trousers into the gaiters - then pull the trouser up slightly so they 'ballooned' over the top. This was an exasperating exercise; we could never do this in such a way that we looked smart.

We looked like a bag of shit with a belt round the middle. The only kids who looked half good were the ex-cadet kids.

Later in the Course, after our half term break we were allowed to use elastic bands (Lacky's, as we called them) in the bottom of our trousers. The trouser would then be pulled over the top of, and half way down the gaiter, nipped in tight by the band. It looked a lot smarter.

Finally with our bed packs made and half dressed, we had a hurried breakfast, shot back upstairs and got on with our chores.

All the time our JNCOs were strutting around the corridors shouting orders, calling lads back to do a better job, threatening us with hours of extra cleaning and God knows what.

Eventually we were at our lockers tidying them and making sure they were neat enough to pass the coming inspection.

J/Sgt Perry stuck his head through the door. 'Smudge, it'll be a joint locker and dress inspection ok? Be prepared for a long wait.'

There was a shout from the washrooms.

'Who's fucking responsible for the sinks?! Get your ass in here! Come on MOVE IT!'

It wasn't anyone from our room but we could hear a couple of lads getting a prize bollocking for leaving hair in a plug hole.

We looked in terror at each other.

Smudge came round looking at us all and sorting out our dress also pointing out defects with our locker layout.

He looked at Steve Cottle who was as thin as a bean-pole, his dress was shambolic. His shirt was twenty sizes too big for his emaciated frame, his beret was pulled down over his right ear till it almost touched his collar and his boots and gaiters were just all over the place.

'Fucking hell Cottle you're a mess, for Christ sake let's try and sort you out.'

Smudge knelt down and adjusted Steve's gaiters, then he tried to make his shirt look a bit more presentable, but he was fighting a losing battle with Steve.

Throughout our two or more years at Dover, uniform of any type would never look good on Steve and he'd be hounded mercilessly over it. He was one of these lads who was all fingers and thumbs, a bit kack-handed but very easy going, for these reasons his time at Dover would not be easy. However he was a really nice lad and became a good friend.

I would end up leaving Dover one term before Steve but he did hang-in-there through all the flack thrown in his direction and as far as I'm aware he passed out into adult service December 1973.

At this point in time the rest of the Squadron had collected weapons and were parading in the quadrangle for Regimental parade. This took place every Saturday morning and was a dry run for the end of term Course 8 passing out parade. For the majority of Regimental parades during the term we would practice in standard works dress, for the final three weeks it would be full dress rehearsal in No2s before the big day when parents, girlfriends and other family turned up to watch Course 8 on their final day as Junior Soldiers.

In our room overlooking the quad we could hear all the shouted words of command as each Course or Troop shouldered arms for the march around the barrack road to the East Square.

'Right, get stood by your beds,' said Smudge. The inspection was approaching.

We heard J/Cpl Martin Hill bring his room next door to attention. Hill would be promoted Junior Sergeant at the end of this term and when we returned after the Christmas break he would take over from Kev Perry as Course 2 Junior Sergeant in charge of us.

Then it was our turn.

'Room – rooom – SHUN!' Ordered Smudge.

We banged our feet to the floor and straightened our backs.

At this point at least we knew how to stand to attention properly; Hands in fists down the creases of our trousers, heels together with feet angled outward, back straight, head looking slightly up and ahead. On no account should we move our eyes or head. Even if spoken to we should just maintain the same stance.

In walked Sgt Batley followed by Kev Perry and Spriggsy.

One by one they went round the room starting with Paul. They looked over his bed space in his locker and then at his presentation in uniform. Paul got a well done.

Gary was next and he also got a well done. Then it was Gerald's turn. Spriggsy was looking Gerald over while Kev Perry pulled a pair of socks out of the bottom of his locker.

'Name?'

'Dickerson Sergeant.'

'Your locker smells of socks Dickerson; that's not a good start is it?'

'No Sergeant.'

Nothing else was said at that point; our leaders continued on around the room pointing out failings in our dress and locker layout. We were still stood rigidly at attention.

When finished Batley and Spriggsy left the room.

Kev Perry having remained behind turned to Smudge.

'Following inspection they'll parade outside for drill, there will probably be more drill after lunch. When they've finished later this afternoon we'll have a meeting on the landing. This evening we'll have another locker and dress inspection, they'll continue on into the evening until they get it right.'

He walked out.

We moved to stand down.

'I haven't said move,' said Smudge angrily. 'Stay where you are.' Smudge was not amused, he walked over to Gerald.

'Socks? Dirty fucking socks lying in the bottom of your locker for the whole world not only to see, but fucking well smell as well! *This would be the first step toward Gerald's Permanent departure.*

Ok this how it works – you're all responsible for each other; I seem to recall having told you this already. One of you fucks up, all of you suffer. So it pays for you all to work together and sort each other out. Dirty laundry – we all have dirty laundry, but you keep it in a plastic bag in the bottom at the back of your locker, when we have locker inspections stick it in your suitcase out of the way. Don't leave it where it can be seen by the whole fucking world and its mother, and you do your dhobi as soon as you get the opportunity; don't let it build up. Have you got that?'

'Yes Corporal,' we rigidly replied.

Smudge continued; 'You keep your kit and your lockers spotless at all times, if you don't it'll be inspection after inspection all night bloody long if necessary.'

We could hear shouting coming from the quad; Smudge looked out of the window.

'Get yourself down stairs and formed up, your first drill session is about to start.'

For the first hour we didn't leave the quad.

We formed up all ninety whatever of us and started with the basic foot drill movements. Attention, stand at ease, stand easy, left turn, right turn, about turn. Over and over again we practiced these six basic movements by numbers till we were perfect... well let's say better.

We had been moved into 'Open Order' – a drill movement where the front rank takes one step forward and the rear rank one step back. This movement along with 'Dressing' was also practiced again and again.

'Front rank one step forward, rear rank one step back - In open order... Right dress!'

These were drill movements that required no marching we remained on the spot; *bang, bang,* you took the step either forward or back then swivel the head, fist up to the shoulder of the person next to you and shuffled outward until spacing's were almost equal.

We remained like this looking to the right until the command was given; *'Eyes front!'* Arm comes down to the side, head is now snapped forward.

This spacing allowed our instructors to walk through the ranks.

Over and over we practiced these half dozen simple movements.

Many of us were slow or made mistakes and the instructors bellowed at those unfortunate enough to have balls'd it up.

With our complete troop on parade and in open order the size of our Course took up the whole of the quad. I believe at this point our Permanent Staff group decided that we needed to be split into two groups. In future we would parade in two squads and drill in two squads unless told otherwise. But for this afternoon at least we'd be as one.

Regimental parade had finished and the other troops were returning to the quad. They marched in, halted and were fallen out to return weapons to the armoury. It must've been getting close to lunch time.

Eventually we were dismissed and cascaded back to our rooms, having been told to form-up again at 1330 for more drill in the afternoon.

Once more we were in three ranks awaiting our orders.

Quickly Staff Sergeant Martin took us through a recap of what we'd learnt during the morning session; far from perfect but workable.

We were told we would march to the 'West Square', the square behind ours and 'B' Squadron block.

The left foot, right arm thing was explained again. Alarming recollections came flooding back of my assessment weekend in Corsham earlier in the year. *Oh God here we go again!* I thought.

Me and my comrades for that assessment weekend in March had received the basic first steps into the art of marching and it had been nothing short of an epic disaster with bodies tripping over one another and bodies literally sprawling in the road. That weekend there had only been around twenty four of us... today there were ninety plus. I knew what was going to happen...

Marching in step like anything else is easy once you get the hang of it... in fact you scratch your head and wonder why it seemed so difficult. It's the coordination thing. Your left leg moves forward with the right arm and via-versa. Sounds easy doesn't it? It is when you <u>don't</u> think about it. However, as soon as you're told you've got to do it that way, and you think about doing it that way, it all goes out the window.

Of all the drill movements we were to learn over the next three Courses – foot and weapons drill, I really believe getting the hang of marching in step was the most difficult.

To explain the fiasco that took place trying to get almost a hundred thick, tired and brain-dead civilian kids marching in step from the quad to the square, a mere one hundred yards away would take pages.

We were hopeless – it was the left and right thing.

So many of us just couldn't get the fact that you start with your left foot. Some didn't even know left from right. Some swung the left arm while putting the left foot forward. Have you ever tried that? It's almost impossible to do this unless some hardnosed, unforgiving, shaven headed Drill Sergeant is watching your every move.

The first part however, the turn was ok.

'Squad will move to the left in three's... Left TURN!' Not half bad, we were pointing the right way.

Then came the actual marching order.

It had to happen, like a little bird we had to take that first fledging flight or in our case step, as a group – a squad – a body of men (slight overstatement there).

'By the left.... Quick MARCH!'

We stumbled tripped and kicked each other.

To the left onto the road we shambled out of the quad and up the short ramp onto the square. All the time Staff Martin was keeping time with 'Left-Right-Left-Right-Left-Right-Left…SQUAAAD HALT!

We stopped. That just about sums it up. A more unmilitary movement you would never witness. Our three ranks had no shape; our columns were all over the place. Staff Martin was surprising nice about it.

'Turn and face me,' he ordered. 'Get yourselves back in three ranks.'

But from here on we had an afternoon of hell.

The start - Quick march! Once going we'd march to the end of the square. Then halt.

We didn't about-turn. We'd 'Halt'. Then left turn and left turn again, and then march back. All these movements were practiced by shouted numbers and broken down into parts.

The about-turn on the march, which is a five part movement along with the halt which was a three part movement, our Drill NCO considered was just too much for one afternoon. The about-turn would wait for another day.

We weren't the only ones on the square, 'B' Squadron Intake were out doing exactly the same drill.

We stopped and were allowed to relax against the wall for a ten minute break and then we were back at it again.

By the time we finished we actually marched pretty reasonably back to the quad; halted and left turned.

I considered we'd done pretty well.

We were only back in our room minutes before we were called on the landing to be told we would be having a further room and locker inspection at 1930 and if things weren't perfect we'd have another one at 2100.

Sunday we'd be trialled for different sports.

I hate to think how many times during our first term at Dover we were called onto that landing. It must've been close to every evening. Something or someone had been found lacking and when that happened we all suffered. Not the individual, not even the room concerned but the whole Course; although our Junior NCOs did differentiate between the two sides of the block. If we screwed up on our side, the other side weren't punished for our failings and visa-versa.

Some evenings we would be bumping the corridor in teams of five, six or seven lads, one behind the other for hours, once or twice in just underpants and boots! This was only one of various quirky and sometimes pretty nasty punishments dished out in the name of progressive training. These I'll filter in as we go along.

Sunday breakfast went on longer – till 0900; although this made no difference to the Intake Course, at least not on our first Sunday. Our first Sunday begun at the same hour with the same cleaning routine as the previous two days.

We were on parade today in our PT kit – red vest, dark blue incredibly baggy shorts and black lace up daps/pumps whatever you want to call them, the word trainers or runners wasn't even on the horizon in 1971.

We formed up in the quad and were given our instructions beneath windows full of jeering lads who had a whole day off. They would have a leisurely breakfast, followed by a walk into town or some sport. No room inspection, no bed-pack and no parade. We would probably not have that luxury until after our first half-term break and then only if we were progressing well with our training.

For the next six weeks at least, the WRVS and NAAFI would be our only areas for recreation.

We were told that from the following morning Monday we would parade in two groups. Bridge lines would parade with our side as they did when called to the landing. Only when instructed would we form up as a single troop.

We would warm up this morning with two circuits of the perimeter road ending up on the concreate area between the two gymnasiums. Then we'd be paired off and 'Box'.

Smudge had warned us. 'If you don't box and you don't want to be a part of the boxing club play dead.'

Apparently 'A' Sqn were very proud of their boxing team and any lad with even the remotest glimmer of boxing potential would be dragged off to the club to undertake further assessment. I had no intention of being one. I had my good looks to consider!

We were paired off by the PTI's (Physical Training Instructors or Prize Bastards as they were more commonly known). We stood there in our two's waiting to enter the ring. It was one round of 3 minutes and while one pair of lads was slogging it out or running round avoiding the blows another pair were getting gloved-up. We had to be quick 'B' and 'C'

Squadrons had to go through the same routine; the day had been planned out with both Gym's in use and the sports fields over the back of Old Park between the trade training wings and the perimeter fence and what was then a minor road going in a semi-circle around the hill and coming out in Buckland at the head of the Dover valley.

In the mid-late-seventies a new road was ploughed through this area as far as the cliffs with a sweeping elevated section completing a short cut from the A2 directly into the eastern docks; Jubilee Way took the traffic away from Buckland, and the main thoroughfare into the centre of town.

I fought a lad called Giles; that was his surname. He must have heard the same boxing-recruitment rumour as me; he too had no intention of showing the slightest flair for punching the shit out of someone.

Consequently we ended up dancing around each other fainting left and right without landing a punch.

'Get fucking stuck-in!' The PTI's shouted.

'Hit him for fuck-sake, it's a boxing bout not a fucking Tango!'

Their reference to 'him' was of course a generalisation; both of us required the same abusive-laden encouragement.

This two or three minute bout felt like half an hour, when the whistle blew we hadn't laid a glove on each other. We were whistled and boo'd out of the ring – not just by the Permanent Staff but our own comrades as well! Just went to show how pathetic we'd been...

'If we had time you'd stay in there till one of you dropped,' balled the PTI. 'Bloody Nancy's the pair of you.'

I didn't care I was in one piece with good looks intact.

Others took it far more seriously and pummelled the crap out of each other. Blood flowed, a few hit the mat, some shed tears, no mercy was shown.

We did however have more than a few potential Cassius Clay's among us (you'll know him more famously as Mohammad Ali – Clay before he became a Muslim and changed his name).

Dave Hopwood from the room next door to us; a small lad from Doncaster whose dad was on the professional Snooker circuit, he was a killer in the ring. He too would become a good friend over the coming two years. He'd end up going to 28 Amphibious Regiment in Hamelin at the same time I was posted to Osnabruck. Davey would fight in the Inter-Squadron boxing competitions and I don't think he ever lost. Another lad called Frazer, he and Dave were in the same room next door to mine (J/Cpl Hills room) he was a heavy weight and again a really good boxer, obviously his nick-name became 'Joe'. I crossed swords with him later on during the term; I accused him of nicking a pair of my socks from the drying room, he lifted me of the floor one handed by the scruff of the neck and held me against the wall. I said sorry I was mistaken...

Boxing finished we were marched back to the block for a tea break and told to report after fifteen minutes.

Cup of tea and cigarette later we were being jogged to the sports field for field events. Shot, javelin, etc, also the one, two, four and eight hundred yards on the oval circuit. We spent the rest of the morning proving ourselves.

All in all it had proved a pretty good day. We had heard nothing to indicate that we would have an evening of chores and that proved to be the case.

We were marched back to our block on the road past the WRVS and through the dip. This circular road around the inside of the barracks was roughly half mile in circumference. We would as the weeks went by often run round and round this circle beginning in gym kit, we'd progress to denims vest and boots and then fighting order and marching order.

Later, when in Course 7 we'd be running this circuit carrying a wooden telephone pole on our shoulders practicing for the Inter-Squadron assault course competition. Previously the competition was held between the three Course 8s, but the system would change in September 1972 and all three Course 8s would separate from Squadrons and form a single troop to be based above the education block. Course 8 would still take part in Regimental Parades but other than that single inclusion, would remain separate, concentrating solely on their B2 Combat Engineering qualification. Squadron allegiance would still remain but the red, green, and blue cravat we'd all worn with Squadron pride would disappear and we would be considered on the road to being adult soldiers. Some of us would be barely seventeen years old.

On the march back to our block we were halted and different areas pointed out; The education block, the almost new indoor swimming pool backing onto the new-gym, RHQ, the Church, and further down the hill or 'back hill' as it would be commonly called, were the stables with around ten horses. The Officers' quarters were set among the trees opposite to the stables.

It was in truth a very lovely barracks and today on a Sunday in the late September sunshine with the trees still in full leaf it really was attractive and peaceful. If you had to be in the army and had to be in a barrack somewhere this was not such a bad place to end up.

Twenty five years on in late September 1997 I would return to Old Park as a civilian. After completing a Yachtmaster Sailing Course I would take a spur-of-the-moment detour south from Ramsgate to look again at my old barracks.

On that day I would find the entrance barriered and guarded by a civilian security officer.

The barracks had been sold and were due for demolition. The whole area would be turned into industrial units and housing. I was gob-smacked. How could they?

The security guard on the gate let me in to look around and for two hours I walked the roads and paths that had been so familiar to me. I looked in windows – the Signals training room, the Combat Engineer wing, the QM stores and the gyms, everything was standing, everything was exactly as I remembered it. I walked to the end of the greens behind 'B' Squadron, high on this promontory you could see the harbour and town hundreds of feet below and in the distance the coast of France.

I walked back to 'A' Squadron and tried all the lower floor sash windows till I found one open, I lifted the lower frame and climbed inside.

It was deathly silent and eerie.

As I walked back through those corridors of my mid-teens I could again hear the laughter the shouting and the clatter of footsteps on the corridors and stairs. The buzz in those corridors only ever ceased after lights out.

I walked through the offices, the cook house and up the main staircase with its hard wood capped bannister to the first room I'd ever slept in, room 96 on the top floor overlooking the quad. Nothing had changed. The walls were still the same colour, the floors were still the same colour, the washrooms and showers still contained the same sinks and the bedside light above where my bed was placed was still exactly the same. It brought a lump to my throat. How I would have loved to be there once more with Les, Steve, Doddy, and Ray Dakers .

Sadly the mid-nineties were not yet the years of 'camera phones'. I had a mobile by that time, a Nokia 3110 with a pull-up antenna, a good phone, modern for the time, but alas no camera. So I left and returned to the gate and my car without any sentimental photos.

Sadly very few photos remain of the barracks and apart from my passing out parade attended by mum and dad in August 1973 and the few meagre photos they took on the day I have but half a dozen.

I returned home that day and wrote a long letter to 'The Sapper' magazine telling of my visit to Old Park and the news I had been told of the pending demolition. I of course asked why. Why should such a lovely well laid out barracks containing such great amenities be trashed; surely there must be a use for it. I never got an answer.

What I did get however was a bag full of mail from ex-Junior Leaders who had done their time at Dover. Let's start a group... let's start an association, let's have a reunion. I was at the point of leaving for Thailand, to a job that involved me being away for an unspecified length of time, maybe years. So after a few telephone calls with a guy named Tom Graham he agreed to start the ball rolling to organise and recruit for a Junior Leaders Association and I promised my support.

This is the story of how the Branch of the Junior Leaders Regiment Royal Engineers Association came into being. Initially it required twenty persons this was the required number for an official association. However when we held our first reunion in Dover in 1999 the attendance was around one hundred and eighty. It has met every year since.

We returned to the quad and we were given details for the following day. In the morning we would begin education. We would be marched to the education block following 0830 parade in the morning in our Battle Dress. After lunch we would continue drill.

'Squad SHUN!'

'Squad Disssmissed!' We turned to the right, marched 3 paces and went upstairs to our rooms.

It was 1600 Sunday. The evening, apart from kit preparation would be our own.

We could visit the NAAFI, write letters and listen to music if we had a radio.

However Smudge informed us - Monday would be the start of a new week, it would begin with a room inspection which would also include inspection of our dress, if we were found wanting it would be a long and heavy Monday evening. I suppose this pep-talk went on in all rooms not just ours. That evening although supposed to be relaxing would still be a busy one.

We came back upstairs from our meal and in turns used the room issue iron to press our hideous BD's. To get a crease in the wool serge was almost impossible. Getting dressed in them was almost as bad. Fortunately we were still in 'shirt sleeve order' which meant we didn't have to wear the jacket, we wore a belt with the trousers; but a few weeks on when 'pullover order' was introduced we had to wear the full uniform, BD jacket as well. That really was a killer.

This evening I decided to give mum and dad a quick call. I had some money that I'd brought with me and it would last until Wednesday which was pay day; at lunch time on parade the little brown envelopes were dished out.

We were not on bad money really, I recall it was around £15.00 per week when we started and it went up quite rapidly; I was on around £22.00 a week when I left Dover in 1973.

We could elect to draw either one or two pounds every week. If you were a smoker you were best to draw two; cigarettes were ten pence for a pack of ten 'Sovereign'.

One pound a week seems a very meagre amount of money considering we had to buy all our personal stuff like soap, toothpaste, shampoo, as well as boot polish and dusters as well.

In the future all those items would be brought with me at the start of a new term.

To give you an idea of costs - a can of Coke at the time was five pence. A packet of peanuts two pence, a sausage roll or a pasty with a cup of tea in the NAAFI around six or seven pence. Not expensive but also there was no room for rash spending.

To give you an example of our money compared to an apprentice who left school the same time as me. Jeff my mate took an apprenticeship at Dotesio Printers in Bradford-on Avon; he brought home £7.00 per week.

After deductions for bed and board the rest of our weekly wage was saved for us by the pay office and it was given to us in a lump sum at the end of every term.

Obviously those drawing one pound per week went home with up to £15.00 more at end of the term than those drawing two.

Whether we drew two pounds or one, none of us ever seemed to have any money. Some lads would be on the scrounge continually, especially smokers who were forever wandering through the rooms like vultures trying to cadge fags, or if you lit a fag they would be round you in an instant begging a drag or a dogend (the last quarter inch of the cigarette before the filter).

I can see the faces of those kids to this day, bloody miserly pain in the asses; always on the scrounge for something.

When we broke up at Christmas I took the train to Wiltshire to spend a couple of days with my Gran prior to going home. I had taken an instant dislike to the place where dad and mum had moved our family a few weeks before my departure to Dover.

Norfolk - or at least the bit we were in, was like living on the Russian Steppes, miles from bloody anywhere. The sign at Thetford that now reads 'Welcome to Norfolk – Nelsons County' in 1971 just read *'Beware! Beyond, there be Dragons'*. People didn't seem to own belts... trousers were held up and coats were held closed with string, best shoes was a pair of clean wellies, people would brag about having a flushing toilet and most could only count to twelve using the fingers and thumbs of both hands.

I'd resented the move and let my parents know in no uncertain terms. My going 'On Leave' train warrants issued by the army would generally be made-out, Dover – Bath Spa return, not Dover - Gt Yarmouth. If my parents wanted me in Norfolk they could pay to get me there. My preference was always the train to see my mates, westbound from Paddington. Mum and dad cottoned on to this and eventually phoned my Squadron office and said on no account should the warrant be made out to Bath Spa, they had to be made out to Great Yarmouth. No problem I just bought my own, Bath Spa, Paddington return it was £4.75.

However I must say now 45 years on that I have, over the years, fallen in love with the county and have many good friends here. The seven or eight months of the year when we're tourist free it is a very lovely county to live in.

Gran and I were very close throughout my childhood I always got a little extra something from her, sixpence here or a shilling there. When I'd been naughty it was gran's I'd run to for sanctuary. I loved her dearly.

While I was at hers answering questions by the million and telling her how things worked in the army I mentioned how hard we found it to live on the weekly allowance given to us by our paymasters. From that moment on until the time I was posted to Germany in November 1973 gran sent me twenty five pence every week to subsidise my weekly income. She would send this in the form of a postal order bought at Mrs Evans Post Office in Winsley village and popped directly in the post-box at the same time; it always arrived with me on Monday and would be handed to me at mail-call during our post lunch time parade. This 25p was just magic; ten Sovereign for 10p which I could ration through till Wednesday; a bar of chocolate, a can of drink or a tea in the NAAFI in the evening; a sticky bun in the WRVS while we played bar-billiards. A small amount of money but oh so important, I couldn't thank gran enough; by the time I got to Course 8 it was 50p.

Anyway I sat down to write letters. As well as gran and parents I had a few girls who I'd left behind and who'd asked me to write to them. Angela my childhood girlfriend in Winsley through my school years , Clare a girl who I'd taken out a couple of times in the fourth year of my secondary school Nelson Haden in Trowbridge. And Monika a girl from Munich in Germany that I'd met while on holiday at my aunts Christmas 1968. She was a lovely girl who'd become a special friend; she had visited us in Winsley at Whitsun the year before and I hoped it wouldn't be too long before we met again.

I had with me a black writing case with matching address book that had been given to me as a parting gift from mum and dad; in it I had a supply of writing paper and envelopes. I didn't mind writing and throughout my years away from home, in the army and beyond I would always regularly write to my parents, grandmother, friends and girlfriends.

My mum kept every single letter I wrote and gave them to me in 2001. They have been invaluable in writing this memoir.

Short and sweet and all very similar I sealed, addressed and stamped my letters. Later I would take them to the guard room for posting.

I went to tell Smudge I was going to the phone and mail box.

'You don't need to tell me Steve your evening is your own, you know what's what, just keep off the grass and don't put your bloody hands in your pockets. You can expect a whopping queue and a bloody long wait.'

I asked if anyone wanted to join me but ended up going on my own.

At the guardroom I posted my letters and joined the queue for the phone. I was there an age before getting in the booth; dialling the number I heard the beep, beep, beep and pushed my first two pence piece into the slot followed by a second and a third.

My mum was on the end of the phone, dad never answered the phone, or for that matter wrote letters.

'Mum it's me, quick take this number, my money will run out, you'll have to phone me back.'

I gave her the number that was written across the middle of the dial.

Two pence went quite a long way, you got roughly 3 minutes for two pence so I had nine minutes.

There was no speaker phone so mum had to relay questions from my dad and brother and pass on my news to them. I gave them my news told them my story of being homeless without going into too much detail. I told them I'd put it all in a letter. Then I asked how they all were and how they were surviving on cabbage and potatoes.

Yes I know – odd eh? Well there was a reason for this. Our family arrived in Norfolk a week before the end of August, mum and dad started their new job as Broiler farm managers with Buxted Chickens on the 1st September.

Guardroom at Old Park Barracks.

They - we, arrived in Norfolk with no money. My mum and dad had no savings. They only ever saved money for the good things in life and when they had enough saved they spent it. Cars, caravans and holidays were my mum and dads priorities.

Prior to leaving for Norfolk we had taken a brief holiday with my German grandmother in Mulheim.

The moving of our furniture to Norfolk had to be paid for, bills had to be settled, other financial odds and ends taken care of such as some new clothes for me leaving home and a new school uniform for my brother.

Mum and dad were working as a man and wife team in their new job. It was a monthly paid salary job, so, no money till the end of September.

They were indeed flat broke. They'd blown the lot including the month's rental deposit from our Landlord farmer Vic Turner.

So from the moment we'd arrived in Norfolk we'd been on a cabbage and potato diet. I'd been on it almost a month, the rest of my family still had two weeks till mum and dads payday at the end of the September; they were paid of course in arrears.

We had a good laugh about this, mum saying she'll never eat cabbage again, while dad, who grew up on home grown cabbage loved it and could eat it for England.

Nine minutes was enough, other kids were waiting to use the phone, shuffling their feet and looking daggers through the glass.

I walked in a soldier-like manner back to my room, it was supper time, a few of us went down to the dining room foyer for a mug of tea; on my return I made a last check of my kit and settled myself down for the night.

Course 1 September 1971

This was the beginning of week one of a thirteen week term which would finish for our Christmas leave on Saturday 18th December. In the coming weeks we would experience diversity in our young lives that we or our parents could never have comprehended. We would grow in stature and confidence; we would become fit and sharp. Those, and there were only a minority, that couldn't keep up for one reason or another would fall by the wayside and find themselves on the train north bound out of Dover. And these first weeks were only the beginning as the terms went by our knowledge base for all things military would just keep growing.

The Monday morning was not a good start.

We all struggled with the BDs our bed-packs and our cleaning chores. A couple of us never got down to breakfast. We formed up in the quad and had an inspection by Sgt Batley. Our turn-out we were informed was not acceptable, we'd parade again that evening at 1900hr in BD order.

J/Sgt Perry took over where Sgt Batley left-off informing us that he'd walked the lines and that our bed-packs, rooms, and lines in general were not up to standard so following the 1900 BD parade, at 2100 we'd have our rooms and lines inspected again.

After giving us this information we were marched in two separate squads to the education block and halted outside. We were told that we would be divided into classes and our morning would be spent working on 'modules', these were the army education tests based loosely on the secondary school 'O' Level qualification. We needed to obtain certain levels to achieve a placement in our chosen trade.

How we were all catered for with classrooms and teachers I do not know, as well as the new Intake, the education block and instructors had to also cater for Courses 2 and 3, both these Courses were completing their modules, although not so many.

At break times it was impossible to get into either the WRVS or the NAAFI, they were both full to bursting. We would take our mugs with us and two urns of tea were delivered over to the education wing from the cookhouse, even then trying to get a drink and a bun was a shit-fight.

We had a time table for classes; I remember doing English, Math and Tech-Drawing, we also learnt battlefield first-aid; how to use the compass; working out magnetic north and grid north; how to work out bearings taking into account the magnetic variation (mag to grid get rid – grid to mag add, this I'm sure was the formula taught to us providing you're east of the Greenwich Meridian).

Also the primary theory of field craft was taught in the education block. The Sappers – The Engineers, are part of what was called 'The Teeth Arms' the forward fighting units of the army. Whether they're called by the same name in 2016 I don't know, but that's what we were a part of in the seventies. Before we ventured into the world of shaped charges, water supply and improvised bridging - the world of the Military Engineer, we had to learn how to be infantry soldiers and all the intricate skills that went with it.

We started with the basics of movement over terrain in both daylight and at night, we'd put this into practice, firstly over the playing fields behind 'B' squadron then in the fields around Whitfield and Temple Ewell.

Maths and English, you could keep em. We hated doing the stuff we'd left school to get away from. But patrols and field craft – moving in formation – the Column, the 'V', Wedge and File - the art of the seven 'S's, Shape, Shine, Shadow, Silhouette, Spacing, Skyline and one other Sharp-movement. These were all the things you had to be aware of when moving tactically across country.

There were others as well such as noise and how to prevent it; nothing in your kit should rattle and your clothing shouldn't rustle.

We would learn how to dig ourselves in defensive positions, where to site our section machine gun. Back up plans for pulling out, how to call down fire orders. We would take turns in being patrol or section commander, planning not only on paper, but using on-the-ground modelling giving a far greater perspective to the job we had to do.

This was 'Boy's Own' stuff, war games we'd played in the woods as kids we were doing for real and we came to love it; if you didn't love it you shouldn't have been there.

Education only lasted till lunch time and then we were marched back to the block where we were dismissed.

In a mad rush we went through the swing doors and upstairs for our nosh rods, then straight down for lunch.

Following lunch we had to parade in gym-kit. We were being marched to the M.R.S for jabs.

Before we left the room Kev Perry came in.

'Room SHUN!' We sprang to attention.

'Stand easy, sit down' said Perry.

He came directly to my bed space.

'Well I've got some news for you Burt. It might be good it might be bad – that depends on how you like being a Junior Sapper in 'A' Squadron?' In his hand he held a slip of paper.

I looked at him a bit lost; I'd clean forgotten that I still hadn't heard from records as to where I was supposed to be. With all that had been going on it had gone clean out of my head.

'Fuck sake, you're forgetting that you're still technically fucking homeless aren't you...? Well you're not anymore. Like it or not you're staying here and with a bit of luck we'll turn you into a Sapper.'

I never said anything; I was a bit dumb struck.

'Well? What do think of that? Good or not?'

I started grinning. 'Yes Sergeant, very good, I'm happy about that thanks.'

'Great, well done, if you'd said no you would've stayed here anyway and I'd have made yur life a bloody misery.' He was grinning as he said this.

'Here's your number Burt, this really makes it official. You're a two four two five, all your opo's are two four two four, but then they didn't get lost in the system did they...'

I looked down at my number, 24251061 a number that I would end up remembering all my life. I was grinning. *Sorted, thank God for that.*

'Don't get up,' said Perry as he walked out.

My new room-mates were as pleased as me, they came over, patted me on the back and gave me the well done's. Ray rattled of a speech in Geordie which I didn't understand a word of, but I got the picture it went something like this... '*Well mate that's fucking canny good news, Ahm glad you're staying, well Ah reckon we're aal glad you're staying. Yee divvnae want te be a bloody paratrooper anyways did yee .*' Like someone talking with a gobstopper in their mouth.

So here I am and here I stay – that was a relief.

We changed into our PT kit and left our BDs lying on our beds, we would be putting them on for another inspection at 7pm. We formed up in the quad in one single squad for our march to the Medical Room.

We had to line up for the usual, touch your toes, open your mouth reflex under the knees caps and cough. To this day I don't understand

72

why a bloke in a white coat has to hold your balls while you cough? If the Doc had a fetish for little boys all his Christmases had come at once that day.

Having gone through the first routine it was on to the injections, two or three different types but I can't remember what they were, tetanus was one but the others... liquid in a tube... Also blood was taken to determine our blood group for our ID card and dog tags.

At this point kids were dropping like flies. Some really had a needle phobia.

Having gone through the first process one after the other we queued for the jabs.

As some kids walked up to the Doctor who was administering the needle they just keeled over, it was almost every seventh lad.

Some went down before they even got to the Doc, like Davie Hopwood (the boxer) who was in front of me; he just crumbled in a heap.

Me and a roommate of his from Beverly in Humberside, Mog (Maurice) Fawsett carried him outside where a row of seats had been placed just for the recovery purpose, fainting must be a regular occurrence – most of these seats were occupied.

Others kids went down as soon as the needle touched the skin. Sensibly they had asked us to sit before administering the jab. It was quite funny really.

I remember going through the TB inoculation while at secondary school; we had a five needle puncture in the lower arm, if the spot became red and angry you had immunity and didn't need the TB jab; if nothing happened you required the full immunisation (it could possibly have been the other way round), anyway only a few kids were immune, most had to have the jab and we queued up outside the school medical room. I don't remember one kid whining about it and I don't remember any child fainting. They breed them tough in West Wiltshire.

The next check was dental - mouth open, a quick check for gaps, old fillings, rotten teeth. With future dental work noted, we'd be told when to return; out we went job done. There were over ninety of us so it was not a quick process.

We were marched back to the quad and halted.

In a short space of time most of us had got the marching sussed, those that still screwed up really got roared at.

It was around 1530 and our Permanent Staff took some time to fill us in on what we'd be doing the rest of the week. Tuesday we'd start the day being introduced to the Regimental cross country track, a two and a half mile circuit of Old Park Hill. We would do this in the company of our PTIs; we'd do a second circuit on our own.

Return to the block, get changed and parade again in our two squads for drill and swimming; one squad going to the pool to undertake swimming ability tests and the other doing further foot drill training. After lunch the squads would swap. Wednesday morning we'd be back to education in the morning and in the afternoon we'd pick a sport which we would continue to play throughout the term. Wednesday was Regimental sport afternoon. Thursday drill and field craft practice, again in two squads and swap. Friday would be education morning and drill in the afternoon.

Foot and rifle drill, fitness and basic field craft would take the majority of Course 1.

One item of our equipment that as yet we hadn't seen or touched was the SLR, the Self Loading Rifle the weapon that would become our personnel firearm. We were told we wouldn't get our hands on this, or any other weapon before completion of our first six weeks. There was a hell of a lot of other stuff to get through first.

Our wages were explained to us; we were also told that we could draw down on our savings if we needed to buy an item of clothing, a present for someone at home etc. However to obtain a withdrawal from our savings entailed a third degree grilling by the AO (Admin Officer). We had to go the Chiefs office and collect a form that questioned how much we wanted to withdraw and what we wanted it for. This we had to fill out and return to the CC who passed it first to our Troop Officer who had to sign and agree it, then after a time it was passed on to the AO, sometimes it could take three weeks!

We would be called into his office for a verbal explanation as to why we wanted a new pair of shoes, why we couldn't wait till half, or end of term to buy them. Like, 'Why now'?

In most all cases we had to show the old item to satisfy the AO that they were beyond repair and required replacing.

I remember wanting a pair of shoes and Les said he'd get a new pair as well, I think we were in Course 3 by this time, both of us filled in the form and both of us were called into – or should I say marched into, the AOs office together. I had my old shoes with me and Les didn't. The AO I must admit was quite a genial fellow, tubby with a large moustache - he was a bit of a softy.

He looked at my footwear and agreed to let me have my money. Then he said 'Dixon, where are your old shoes?'

Les said, 'I never brought them Sir.'

'Why not, I need to see what condition they are in.'

Les replied, 'they're in good condition Sir.'

'Then why do you want a pair of new shoes?'

''Cause Burt's having a new pair Sir.'

'Because Burt's having a new pair..? If Burt jumped off a wall would you follow him?'

'Depends how high it was Sir?'

I don't know how I kept a straight face. Les meanwhile was staring straight ahead poker faced into the distance.

The AO just looked at him, shook his head and signed both chits. As we were leaving he said...

'Dixon.'

'Yes Sir.'

'I shall expect to see the new shoes.'

We were both laughing our heads off as we walked back across the quad. But this was the Mancunian side of Les all over and I wasn't much different, throughout my army career I got away with blue murder; Corporal Sally Trotter of the WRMP (Women's Royal Military Police) a lovely girl five years my senior who would enter my life early in my first tour of Northern Ireland in 1974 (and by tour I mean active service during the troubles not a cycling holiday), would tell me one evening while she let me clip her stockings to her suspender belt in her room in Ebrington Barracks, Londonderry - 'it's your smile that does it Steve.' More of Sally in volume three.

The rest of the week's actives and training imparted in full we headed upstairs knowing we had a shitty evening ahead of us.

Our training took many forms and was passed on to us in many different places, in the classroom or on the parade ground, in the gym, in our rooms and of course on the landing. I really ought to write this word with a capital 'L' because 'The Landing' was a very important place.

During our first thirteen weeks we came to hate the Landing because this was where all the crap was dealt out to us; either as an individual, or all of us collectively.

We'd be shouted at, shown up, ridiculed, made to perform press-ups, sit-ups and other stunts, till we dropped with exhaustion; given orders, given chores, given punishment and very occasionally complemented and praised; but also and finally the place where basic things got explained to us.

Make no bones about it if you fucked-up you <u>were</u> singled out.

If you wet the bed – and one or two did; or your locker stank, or you were found on parade to have a dirty neck, the Landing was where it would be made known to all your comrades. A 'quite word in your ear' was not the way - public humiliation was common place. On one occasion a bed wetter was made to wrap the wet bottom sheet around himself like a diaper and naked apart from this garment stand in front of the whole Landing sucking his thumb while reciting 'I'm sorry I wet my bed, I'm sorry I wet my bed'... while we all laughed and jeered. Absolutely ruthless.

We couldn't please – during the first thirteen weeks the idea was to break us. No matter how perfect we got it, it was never enough. What could we take, when would we break, who would break first?

But as we progressed through Courses two and three, episodes like these became less and visits to the Landing became less and less.

Life settled down.

Oddly if a person was singled out and given some crap for whatever, it was shrugged off – you'd go back to the room and your mates would pat you on the back and tell you not to worry about it. Unless of course you didn't mend your ways – if that was the case the outcome would be somewhat different; which you'll see further on.

That particular Monday night was another late night. Following the BD inspection we quickly got changed and started our cleaning routine for J/Sgt Perry's room and lines inspection at 2100. By the time we got to bed we were all in.

We were being tested and pushed. We just had to grin and bear-it. Watching our peers in the higher Courses we knew it would ease up eventually.

'RIGHT! Get fell in, one single squad!'

We stood there in our gym kit. It was Tuesday morning and we were starting the day with a five mile cross country run – twice round our barrack perimeter.

'We will be starting,' shouted Spriggsy, 'from the far side of the square. PTI's Bakewell, Rawlings and Phelps will be running with you. They will shepherd you round the course for the first circuit and will position themselves strategically as an aid to your memory for the second circuit. We expect you to complete both circuits within an hour maximum. You will on completion of the second circuit go to your lines shower and change. After break at 1030 Intake two will parade with towel and swimming trunks. Intake one (*our side of the block*) will parade for drill. We want maximum effort. You all had to pass a fitness test during your assessment to get here and fitness is what we want to see. Those who don't perform will find themselves doing another two circuits this evening.

Ok, settle down –

TROOP! – TROOOP! - SHUN!

Troop with turn to the left in threes – LEFT TURN!

By the left QUICK MARCH!

And as right as you like off we went - simples.

We marched over the square and past the assault course. As we went past we couldn't help looking. The six-foot wall, the twelve-foot wall and the scramble-net were obvious, there was probably another dozen obstacles to cross as well.

EYES FRONT! You'll get to see the assault course soon enough don't you worry, shouted one of the PTI's.

'And once you're on it you'll fucking well wish you weren't.' shouted a second.

Very heartening.

We arrived at the perimeter and in our three ranks carried out some warm up exercises.

'Listen in!' Commanded Bakewell. 'I will lead you round setting a reasonable pace, one you should all be able to maintain. Corporal Phelps will bring up the rear with Corporal Rawlings bringing home any stragglers. I don't want stragglers on the first circuit. I will not be amused if there are any. Give it your all.'

This didn't bother me in the slightest; I'd run cross country for my school.

We were all running on the spot, Our room had already discussed this run together, Smudge had filled us in on the cross country track which ran through the woods on a very narrow footpath above the village of Temple Ewell, then around the side of the hill and down to the minor road we called 'The back hill' across the road and up the footpath which brought the runner out onto the road on the far side of the officers mess. Here we turned left and ran back along the side of what was then a very minor 'B' class road until we got to the main gate.

From here we would normally run around the circular roadway through the dip and back to the quad; as I've written previously a run of just over two miles. In gym kit this was not difficult, however as the weeks went by our dress for running would rapidly move from gym kit to boots, denims and tee-shirt, then fighting order (ammo pouches and water bottle). Today it was explained on our first circuit we would not turn left through the dip but run down round the back of the QM stores, right around the edge of the square, (Holy ground – you did not walk or run on the drill square) and back to the starting point; without stopping we'd launch straight into a second circuit.

Suddenly we were off.

In a large group we headed into the trees but the track rapidly narrowed and we formed a line formation, space was limited even for overtaking, we were literally running on a narrow path worn in the side of a very steep slope.

Some lads were lagging and others were trying to overtake, some slipped, lost footing and stumbled, some were already walking. By the time we got to the back hill a group were already pulling away with PTI Bakewell, that was ok, we had two circuits to complete. By the time we'd completed circuit one I was in the top 25%, Bakewell had stopped and was waving us through shouting encouragement. Now the front runners had room to stretch their legs and those behind room to overtake. We had adopted the important rhythm needed for cross country running. 'Get into the grove' or mind-set and it becomes almost automatic. In no time we were back in the Quad. I didn't know where I'd come because as we came in our names were taken and we were sent straight off for a shower, we'd be told later. I took off my top grabbed my towel and went to the wash room. I was the first back from our room.

Slowly the washroom filled up with laughing lads some happier I might add than others, there would always be some that were fitter and faster even in the army.

We did have some heavyweights among us and they weren't as quick on their feet but they had other qualities. I can't remember anyone getting crapped on because they were last on a run or didn't do so well in the gym or pool, as long as you were seen to be doing your best; that was the important bit. Our instructors would push us and scream at us to keep going and they had a canny knack of spotting those that weren't really trying.

We got dressed, had a mug of tea and paraded for drill. We would be beating the tarmac for the next two hours.

Basic foot drill would take up a great deal of our time during the first 6 weeks. Already we could form-up, march, turn left and right and halt; oh, and dress-off in open and close order.

Our next session carried on with marching on the spot, about turns, breaking into and out of double time (going from marching into a fast jog while remaining in step), going into and out of slow march and saluting as a squad.

The reader at this point will be wondering just how many drill movements there are; well there's a hell of a bloody lot I can tell you; I would say, at a guess, there's around twenty five foot drill commands and these we would practice over and over again within our first half term. Then on return from our short weekend break we would start drilling with the SLR - rifle drill. Around another twenty movements without including the more complex movements of firing a volley and fixing bayonets all which had to be practiced by numbers; first shouting one – two - three - one - two - three – one! Then doing the numbers in your head until it becomes second nature. All drill movements were learned this way.

It was actually quite fun and the better we got at it the more we enjoyed it because we were all drilling in union and there's a sense of exhilaration when a body of men can perform in such a manner.

We would become proud of our ability to act as a troop – as one.

Now and again one of us would fuck-up and get roared at. We had one lad called Jones, he was Welsh; he dropped his weapon during rifle drill a fuck-up like this you could put on par with dropping the Holy Grail or a coffin at a funeral or worse!

Dropping a weapon any time anywhere was the ultimate sin!

Our Drill Sergeant, Staff Sergeant Martin went ballistic with Jones…

'YOU SON! WHAT'S YOUR FUCKING NAME!' He balled about two inches from Jones face.

'Jones Sergeant.' Jones replied.

'Pick that weapon up Jones! I might have guessed you're a fucking Jock, you're a disgrace to the Scottish fucking nation!'

'Welsh Sergeant'. Jones replied while picking up his rifle.

We were all staring straight ahead biting our lips trying not to laugh.

'WHAT?!...' *Our instructor was going blue in the face.*

'Welsh Sergeant, I'm Welsh.'

'Don't you fucking argue with me Jones, if I say you're fucking Scottish you're fucking Scottish, if I say you're a fucking Pigmy from Borneo you're a fucking Pigmy from Borneo. Do I make myself CLEAR!

Shut-up you lot! EYES FRONT! He shouted at the rest of us.

'Jones fall out and come round here.'

Jones duly shouldered his weapon fell out of the ranks and marched smartly to the front of the squad.

'Now Jones, hold that weapon above your head and double round the outside of the square until I tell you otherwise. GO!'

Agony – we'd all done this at some point, either as an individual or as a group because we'd screwed up; the SLR weighed in at around 11 lbs (5kg) and very soon felt a great deal heavier. Your Biceps would be screaming.

Off Jones went while we carried on drilling.

Jones completed three circuits before he was allowed to fall back in the ranks.

Sweating and panting he stood there.

'Jones!'

'Yes Sergeant.'

'As loud as you can, tell me and your comrades what you are!?'

'I'M SCOTTISH SERGEANT!'

'Well done Jones, you see, you knew I was right all along. The squad will turn to the right in threes, Righttt TURN!'

It just does not pay to open your mouth. Of course Staff Martin knew Jones was Welsh, but it was lesson to all – keep your mouth shut.

From that moment on Taff Jones was known as Jock – such is life in the army.

Getting back to the present...

We were still on basic foot drill but getting better; the rest of the morning we covered miles over the drill square, doing all the quick marching movements, we returned to the quad, got dismissed and went for lunch.

In the afternoon our side of the block paraded for swimming. As well as finding out who could and who couldn't swim we were put against each other competitively to see just who the best swimmers were. The Squadron needed new blood for the swimming team and also the water polo team. There were tests we had to take such as swimming in our boots, shirt and trousers. Boots we were allowed to untie before jumping in.

We had to jump from the side and swim two lengths, then remove our boots and throw them to the side of the pool. Then remove our trousers, (all this while treading water), tie a knot in the bottom of the legs and from behind your head quickly flick the trouser over so air was trapped in the two knotted legs. If it had all gone to plan and you hadn't drowned on the way, you had in front of you a float... at least for a while. It was bloody knackering. Some lads were mortified of the water and had to be practically thrown in. The expression 'I can't swim' stood for nothing. Get in there and work it out.

Swimming became part of our physical training curriculum and was an enjoyable part of the training day. Pete Bedigan from Newcastle I remember as an outstanding swimmer; he made the water-polo team and throughout our time at Old Park played for both the Squadron and Regiment.

The following day; the Wednesday we had education all morning.

We paraded in BDs and with relief passed our inspection. After lunch our pay was handed out; for me a smoker it was the princely sum of two pounds. I've explained previously how the pay system worked.

Following pay parade we were allocated our sports or clubs for the afternoon.

A list of choices had been circulated, and requests had been submitted. We had quite a variety of choice unless of course you had excelled at a sport during the trials on the Sunday; if so you became an automatic contender for that particular sport – you had no choice; Dave Hopwood and Joe Frazer for instance ended up doing boxing, Pete Bedigan – water-polo, they didn't get a say in it.

I had decided to go for the saddle club. The Regiment had its own riding stable with around ten or twelve horses and I put my name down and got it.

I'd done some horse riding; while we lived in North Bradley I'd gone horse trekking on Salisbury Plain with my parents, their friends and my brother. I'd also rode for a while with my secondary school; similar to Dover we'd had a club and sport afternoon on a Wednesday and I'd ridden, be it briefly, at Widbrook Grange, a stable just outside Bradford-on-Avon on the Trowbridge road. At the time I'd picked this as a sport hoping I could meet up with Angela who went to Trinity School in Bradford. Both Nelson Haden and Trinity rode there on the same day. It never panned out so I ended up changing my Wednesday afternoon activity to work on the Kennet and Avon canal restoration project.

But I did enjoy horse riding and was pretty good at it. I also knew a kid at school who lived just down the road from us in Yarnbrook, he had a horse and for a couple of months or so he'd kept it in our paddock on the farm. We'd ride it with and without saddle and bridle around the local fields. So I saw myself fitting in nicely.

One other reason for picking the saddle club and this was to be honest the overriding reason, was girls.

Smudge had told me that girls while at Dover were not in abundance. In fact that's an understatement, they were almost non-existent.

'Don't for one minute think you'll end up with a girlfriend while at Dover, they just aren't interested in poor one-quid-a-week 'Freds.' He said. *('Fred's' being the nickname for us JLs. Why? Haven't a clue – never knew the answer then and don't know it now).*

'You better just bottle it up till you go on leave or fall in love with your hand. The girls round here apart from a few, and they're pretty fucking desperate, just don't want to know.'

However he was wrong on this score because we ended up after our first six weeks being allowed to go to the once a week NAAFI disco and I did get off with a lass from Whitfield only a couple of hundred yards up the road. I also met a lass in town who took me back to hers for tea… twice… maybe she felt sorry for me.

I'll come back to this later.

'But,' said Smudge. 'If you join the saddle club you'll at least get to spend an afternoon in the company of some girls. The Regiment lets local schools use the club and I think there's a naughty girl's institution out on the Folkestone road that also uses the club. So that's about the only female company you're likely to get during term time. I don't know how easy it is to get in, horses have never interested me. But you'll definitely get a ride one way or another.' He finished with a grin.

Well I was interested in horses and more to the point I was interested in girls. I may have only been fifteen but I'd had my bite of the cherry while living on the farm at North Bradley and found it very nice thank you.

I would give it a go.

Sure enough I got lucky and I started with the saddle club on a Wednesday afternoon and on a Saturday when I heard we may have some female company.

The days moved on and things got slightly easier.

Our No2 dress returned from tailoring and with that came more bullshit.

How to 'ring' our hat, 'bull' our boots, 'blanco' our belt, bayonet scabbard holder and rifle sling and of course press the clothing that went with the accessories.

Without, I hope, boring the reader I'm going to go through some of this preparation procedure because it does take some believing.

To start with, everything brass had to be cleaned with Brasso, this included the backing plate to our collar bombs; oddly the bombs themselves, the bit on the front of the collar that was visible were 'stay-bright' brass and didn't need cleaning, as were the jacket buttons, yet the belt hook stitched into the side of the jacket was real brass and again had very, very carefully to be cleaned; as did the ends of our rifle sling and best belt. The belt had to be stripped down and the webbing blanco'd before work could commence on the brasses.

A great deal of care had to be taken cleaning the brass work attached to the sling and belt, these were the bits that couldn't be removed; the buckles on the back and the adjusting hooks and plates on the inside. We had to be careful not to get a spot of Brasso on the blancoing.

The picture shows the brass clips on the inside of the belt which provide the adjustment. Then you have the sliders to the left and right of the actual buckle which keep the whole belt tidy and smart. The sliders in the picture are not positioned correctly, they had to be tight up against the buckle not 2" away as the picture depicts.

The buckle itself interlocks; a solid side and an open side - solid side goes through the open side; solid side is always to the right-hand-side of the belt as you're wearing it.

The way we were told to remember this was, 'cock on the right' – 'fanny on the left'. This applies to any belt and I still thread my belt onto my trousers this way to this day; when I see belts buckled the other way (the female way) I always feel like telling the bloke to sort himself out!

We were told – you're only half dressed if you haven't got a belt on your trousers. It was a part of our presentation I've never forgotten and tend to agree with; a bloke only looks half-dressed wearing trousers with no belt.

Anyway I'm ranting on here; let's get back on track...

Our belt brasses would be kept separate from the belt, each piece wrapped separately in a yellow duster. When we first got the belt (not me because I was issued a previously used one) the sliders and buckle needed to be buffed to a mirror finish. This was done using a piece of felt, or a piece of soft wood, like cork or balsa soaked with Brasso; or a very hard piece of sponge like material was even better. The same needed to be done with the sliders, but first they had to be squared off. If you look closely at the picture you'll see an indentation in the top of the slider, also note that the vertical edges are rounded at the top and turned in. This is fine for a work-belt, the sliders are shaped to the webbing, but for a best belt the Junior Leaders demanded a smarter set of brasses.

To achieve this we needed to gently knock out the crease on the top and bottom of the slider, square-off the corners and get rid of the bevel. Our room screw Lance Corporal Smudge Smith who knew all and had all, showed us how to do this with a piece of rectangular metal bar around 4 inches long 3/8 inch thick and about a 1 inch wide. This piece of metal was his own, probably scrounged from the trade wing, not any form of army issue.

Of course being an Intake Room-jack he needed it to help his flock of new recruits sort out their kit.

Once you'd gone through the process of shaping your brasses you never needed it again so it was pointless everyone having a piece of metal like this. I'm guessing when Smudge gave up being an Intake Room-jack or moved up to Course 8 he would've handed it down to another Intake JNCO, and I suppose other Room-jacks would've done the same.

Two bed-ends would be dragged together leaving a gap that could be spanned by the piece of metal; the slider would then be slipped over the metal which was supported between the two bed ends. Then, using a metal foot from the base of another bed (cause we didn't have a hammer – at least not in our room; probably Martin Hill next door had one because he was the type of keen shit that would) we would gently tap the sliders into shape. It was not a quick process we couldn't afford to get deep indentations in the brass, you wouldn't be able to get a mark like that out, and so we had to take great care.

We just took it in turns till the two little boxes for each belt were squared-off.

Boots – best boots had to be bulled; again a strict technique was used.

You needed and old yellow duster, a new fluffy one was no good, it needed to have been washed a few times.

A tin of 'Kiwi' polish. Only 'Kiwi' - 'Cherry Blossom' was, for some reason just no good for the job, also we needed a candle and a spoon.

Best, or No2 boots had to be bulled almost to the top and took hours of perseverance. However once you got going it became a bit of an obsession. Some lads with nothing better to do would just sit on their bed in the evening bulling away at their boots; lads would quietly try to get their boots better than their mates and bragging rights went to those that did.

How did we do this – well, firstly we had to remove the pimples; all new DMS boots were covered in these little pimples over the leather. To get rid of them we wrapped a sock around a spoon so as not to burn our hands and heated  the back of the spoon over a candle, when the spoon was almost red hot you'd put your free hand inside the boot and press the hot spoon on the pimples all over, other than the toecap and heel. (Boot-burning as it was known). After a few heat treatments the pimples would be gone. Pimples didn't matter on work boots because they were only highly polished using a polishing and shining brush – 'bulling' was a totally different method of getting an unbelievable shine that was literally a black mirror finish.

To start with we'd burn down the polish, this involved catching light to the polish in the tin and letting it burn for a few minutes. This was said to get rid of a great deal of the wax content and make bulling easier. The polish in this tin would only be kept for our best boots, not used on our work boots. After the polish in the tin had dried hard you put the duster over your index finger, wetted the tip of the duster on your tongue, got a tad of polish on the tip and start working in circles, every now and again adding a small gob of spit (hence the expression 'spit and polish') this method would slowly build up the layers to a brilliant finish; it took hours. The whole boot had to be done and as you were working you needed to flex the boot as if you were walking and then continue. If you didn't do this when you put the boot on and started walking lumps of polish would break-off.

Slowly you'd witness the boot turning into what I can only call a work of art. When you had brought your boots to the maximum finish you'd be left with polish rings or swirls on the surface. These were not really obvious on the boot shell overall but were plainly obvious on the toe and heel caps. To get rid of these rings we would hold the boots under cold running water and bull again with cotton wool until the swirls disappeared and you were left with a gleaming mirror finish. We did exactly the same exercise on the black rim of our peaked No2 dress hat.

You probably wonder where was Health and Safety..? You've got to be joking! It was non-existent; half a dozen kids sitting round with boot polish tins on fire and red hot spoons, and that was just in one room alone, didn't seem to bring anyone out in a sweat. We got on with it.

Using common sense and initiative was what was expected of us as Junior Leaders. If we'd damaged ourselves we'd have been on orders for being negligent.

It's hard to get your head round the extremes of bullshit. You may think there weren't enough hours in the day for us to complete all this stuff? Believe me we thought the bloody same!

The thing is we didn't just do it during the day; we worked on the stuff into the night.

Inspection after inspection and if it wasn't right we were punished.

To give you an example – one evening we had a best boot inspection followed by a second and a third. Our Troop NCOs did not consider that the standard was high enough overall. Ok some lads may have had the perfect boot but it cut no ice – the troop suffered en-masse.

So the following evening found all of us sitting along the corridor naked, except for our underpants, on our steel helmets with all the windows open bulling our boots. This was I'd like to add, in late November with a fucking gale blowing outside.

Another example – locker inspection, Gerald Dickerson in our room was the cause of every single item of kit being thrown from every locker in our room out of the top floor window into the quad below. Why? Because he had 'gungy' smelly gear in the bottom of his locker. We – his roommates hadn't dealt with it so we all suffered. The only saving grace here was it was only our army kit that was thrown out not our civilian clothing. We had to go down to the quad and chuck it all into our suitcases and kit bags bring it back up and try sorting who owned what. This was the first of a couple of incidents brought on by Gerald's inability to keep himself or his kit clean and eventually led to his leaving but I'll come to the why's and wherefores later. We weren't the only room to have our kit thrown out of the window. It happened to most rooms once or twice during our Intake Course.

We were all aware of the continuing problems in Northern Ireland; rioting, stoning's and shootings were becoming common place in the daily newspapers, as well as bombings. It began with civil rights demonstrations by the Catholic community who demanded equality within the British Counties in Northern Island. At the time equality was sourly lacking; inferior housing, inferior job prospects and hardly any representation in government or government services created a boiling pot which was ignited in the first instance in June 1968 by an incident over who got a council house. From this point things went downhill and went downhill rapidly; shootings, bombings, murders and rioting.

In August 1969 troops were deployed on the streets to maintain law and order. By this time the body count in death and injury had gone way up into the hundreds and the violence had crossed the Irish Sea to the British mainland. Two bombs had been used to try and kill Lord Carr the Employment Minister with a car bomb outside his house.

Bomb scares were becoming common place in railway stations and other public places. To define bomb scares to those who may never have heard or been involved in one – an anonymous caller telephones either the police or an institution such as an airport or factory, to report a bomb being planted in a certain location, they may or may not also state that it will go off at such and such a time; in our case it was our barracks. How good of them to let us know...

We had been told within the first few days of our arrival that bomb scares had occurred at Old Park and we were warned that they would inevitably happen again. The fire alarms would go off and we would carry out the drill; leave the building immediately by the nearest staircase and parade by troop on the West Square where the roll would be called. Leave quickly, do not pass go and do not collect two hundred pounds, as the Monopoly saying goes.

We would stand in our three ranks shivering in our pyjamas, great coats, and boots and after a period of time delegated persons would be dispatched to search allocated areas for anything unusual. Then eventually on the brink of freezing to death we would be sent back in.

In reality the chances of anything or anyone being inside one of our barrack blocks would be highly remote. Any stranger would be spotted and questioned in an instant and to be honest no fool would try to waltz into a block housing two hundred and fifty lads only to keen to punch the living daylights out of someone not supposed to be there. They would also have to look like a squaddie be it a Fred or a member of Permanent Staff.

No, none of us was unduly worried about a bomb under the bed. In other areas of the barracks... well maybe; but then we didn't sleep in the gym or the QM stores.

The bomb scares and evacuations we went through were hoaxes. The telephone calls made by some drunken civi who thought it would be a great idea to disrupt the bed-time of the squaddies living above them on the hill. The reason I blame drunken civi's is because when they happened, and it was quite often, the alarm always went at pub kicking-out time which in those days was half past ten to eleven.

If by any trick of fate we'd have got our hands on the culprits they would have been torn limb from fucking limb.

The first bomb scare for us happened within our first couple of weeks, it was around 2130 and we were all winding down, some lads were in bed, others in the shower or bath.

A mad dash to grab some warm clothing then down the stairs. You can see why I say if we'd got hold of them they'd have wished they hadn't been born.

Education, fitness, field craft and drill followed in the evening by more kit preparation. This was our first six weeks. Once we'd learnt our basic foot drill we were a part of Saturday morning Regimental parade; marching round to line-up with the other three Squadrons in front of the trade training wing. Then Squadron by Squadron we marched onto the East Square to practice the drill routine that would become the end of term passing-out parade for Course 8.

At this point our participation was without weapon. When we returned after half term we would be issued with an SLR that would be our own personnel weapon with bayonet. This weapon would be zeroed and used only by the person to whom it was allocated.

We couldn't wait to get our grubby little hands on one, however before we could shoot with it we had to learn how to drill with it, strip it, clean it and put it back together with our eyes closed. It would become an extension of your own anatomy.

(*Zeroing a weapon is the adjustment of the forward sight on the end of the barrel and rear sight on the back of the breach mechanism to compensate for the shooters own shooting style. You aim for the tightest grouping possible on the target with five rounds over one hundred yards. Then adjustments are made to the sights to bring the group to dead-centre of the target*).

Another shock to the system - well to some anyway was church parade. We had a really lovely garrison church next to RHQ. As well as continuing our RE (religious education) as part of our academic studies we would attend church by Squadrons every 4th Sunday. It went something like this A, B, C, then the 4th week was Regimental church parade... however, and here's the catch, the church wasn't big enough to sit the whole Regiment. So over the preceding three weeks prior to Regimental church any Fred who had been picked-up or found lacking would be added to the Regimental church parade list; in short a punishment parade. (I wonder if the Padre knew this happened). So you

Our lovely Church within Old Park.
Following the closure of the barracks
this became the Dover Harbour Board Social Club.

found yourself with probably thirty others parading in the quad on a Sunday morning while your opo's jeered at you from the surrounding windows. You would then be marched down to the church with the same number of lads from B & C Squadrons, also Officers with families who had to be seen attending. This would be classified as a Regimental church parade.

The church was a 'Church of England' church; of course other denominations were not excluded. If you were RC, Jewish, Muslim, whatever... you were welcome. However if you wanted to attend your own denomination church you had to go into Dover. I don't know if Dover had a Synagogue or a Mosque for what was referred to in 1971 as the minority faiths, I suppose they were there somewhere.

But the Roman Catholic Church was the 'Our Lady of Dover' RC church at the bottom of the back hill and unlike the lads attending our CE church they had to go every Sunday; compulsory! I'm sure they were only too willing to turn-out every Sunday come sun, rain, or snow, secure in the knowledge that when their time came they would go to heaven – on arrival at the pearly gates their church attendance figures would be checked and with a smile they'd be allowed in. Whereas, us lowly Anglicans would have to beg entry. We didn't care, two Sunday's out of four we could stay in bed.

The time was approaching our first 'Camp'. 'A' Squadron would spend a week in Norfolk at Thetford in the Stanford training area. We would embark by chartered train from Dover and disembark at Brandon; the station closest to the Stanford training area. Somehow the train was directed around London, we didn't need to change trains.

Over the preceding weeks we'd practiced and trained in our field craft. We'd spent a couple of nights under canvas in Bivouac's (Bivi's) over behind the assault course on the edge of the wood that led into the cross country course.

Bivi's are small two man tents made from heavy canvas; another bit of kit left over from a bygone military era. When rolled up with wooden pegs and poles one tent weighed a bloody ton. When I look now at all the lightweight kit available from camping shops I wonder why on earth the military weren't involved in modernising their own equipment. It was without doubt only one small step removed from what had been used and worn at Waterloo. This massive failing and wakeup call only came to light as I've previously stated when the army was called to fight a war in the appalling conditions of the Falkland Islands in 1982. Even after this bloody and grim conflict that was only won through the shear skill, guts and determination of our brilliant Armed Forces the improvements were not fully committed to. Men still bought their own gear and are still buying their own gear in 2016. Also the world of armament and personnel weapons had moved on and a single shot long barrelled rifle was no longer a practical option. The military procurement system came up with a new weapon - the SA80. Now a great deal has been written about this weapon most of it non-complimentary so wanting to get first-hand information I questioned friends and friend's kids who are soldiers, or who recently were soldiers; men who've used, and are still using the SA80. I won't repeat what they said but I will add that non-complimentary may be an understatement.

We were marched over to the Squadron G1098 store (*in BAOR I was to find each troop had their own G1098 general purpose store containing everything a Sapper troop in the field needs*) next to the Combat Engineering wing to sign for the necessary kit and be given a demonstration on how to erect the tent. We unpacked our 'Small Kit', this was the everyday essentials such as mess tins, nosh-rods, socks, sewing kit, boot kit, pants, shirt and food.

Inside your square mess tin would be a hexamine cooker containing hexamine blocks; these are blocks similar to the fire lighters sold today to light fires or barbeques.

Our rations were either 24 hour packs or food issued from larger ten man packs both known by the slang term of 'Compo' rations; short for composition, a composition of different meals and sweets to keep a man alive in the field. Good wholesome stuff and unless you were a real picky eater, not bad at all. The food only required heating not cooking, chicken supreme, stew, treacle pudding, all could be eaten cold and often were. Tea powder... yes tea powder, a bit like coffee granules, condensed milk in a tube, sugar and a thing called an oatmeal block.

This oatmeal block could be eaten cold like a biscuit or if you were patient and could afford to spend time heating two lots of water one boil-up for a brew the other for the block, you could make a form of porridge.

Boil the water, float in the biscuit till it dissolves then squirt in a shot of condensed milk and stir the whole thing round with a dash of sugar; a right mix-up but warm and sustaining.

A few years into the future I would be the driver for Major BCA Lee Officer Commanding 16 Field Squadron in Osnabruck BAOR. When on exercise I'd do a fair amount of cooking from 'Compo' rations in the back of a Land-Rover and I done a pretty good job of it. Although I hasten to add I had a double ring portable camping gas cooker, which was a sight easier than using a single hexamine block.

So this was our first taste of roughing it. We were allocated guard rota's which went through the night; we 'Stood-To' in morning and evening. This is a manoeuvre that goes on throughout all military units in the field, where at dusk and dawn all personnel (except for the cooks where you have centralised field kitchens) move out of the camp to a marked perimeter and lay in cover for an impending attack. Again a continuing hang-over from an earlier era…

Short for 'Stand-to-Arms', the process of Stand-To was observed morning and evening by both sides most notably on the Western Front. The war in the trenches.

Each man would be expected to stand on the trench fire step, rifle loaded, bayonet fixed. The theory ran that most enemy attacks were mounted either before dawn or shortly after dusk under cover of darkness. Consequently both sides took care to ensure adequate preparation at such times, manning the fire step an hour before dawn and dusk.

There was an obvious irony in that both sides took such elaborate precautions against the eventuality of an attack despite the fact that each would be engaged in Stand-To at exactly the same time. Nevertheless attacks were indeed launched at either dawn or dusk, particularly once it became clear to one side that the trench opposite was manned by relatively inexperienced troops.

Both sides would often relieve the tension of the early hours with machine gun fire, shelling and small arms fire, directed into the mist to their front: this made doubly sure of safety at dawn.

'Stand-To' lasted between half an hour and an hour. The whispered word would go out, 'Stand-To' and we would silently move out into our pre-allocated perimeter positions; after which each man would be ordered quietly to 'Stand-Down'; breakfast would follow in the morning.

What I didn't get was – if both sides knew that each other Stood-To at the same time, then Stood-Down at the same time, how come one side didn't wait until the other side Stood-Down and either went to sleep or had breakfast and then attacked? I suppose it had been proved to work, I still thought it was a bit of a waste of time. I was still doing Stand-To right up till the day I left the army… only on exercise of course.

During the day instead of going back to the cookhouse for lunch we prepared our own compo food and practiced patrols, camouflage, and movement over and through terrain.

We had an exciting display in the use of training pyrotechnics. I write that as plural when I probably should write it in the singular as I can only remember the one item. A 'Thunder-flash'!

This was a stick roughly a foot long and an inch in diameter that simulated a hand grenade. Explosive value was that of about twenty crow-scarer's bound together. It was a lethal aid to training that we were seriously informed would blow your hand off if we were unfortunate enough to be holding one when it went off; or your foot if you stood on one.

Bloody Brilliant!

We were told that if someone threw one at you during an exercise, DON'T on any account pick it up to throw it back. *I made a mental note to run.*

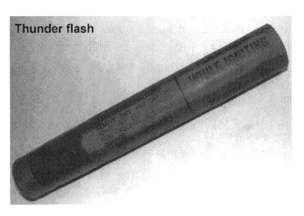
Thunder flash

To demonstrate the power of this stick of gun-powder Staff Shaw, (Permanent Staff Sergeant for the other half of our Intake) brought out an old steel helmet; he showed us how to initiate the fuse and then placed the thunder-flash under the steel helmet.

Five seconds is all you get and BANG! The fucking helmet disappeared upward like a bloody rocket; must've gone at least a hundred foot in the air. When it landed and was handed round to us the ferocity of this training aid became clear – there was a crack clean across the top.

We all thought this was a 'well-cool' bit of kit and couldn't wait to get out on patrol exercises with a few of these stuffed in our belt. Havoc!

Those couple of nights under canvas we had to share a Bivi and we buddied up with a pal from our own room. I ended up sharing with Doddy, but in truth it didn't matter, all the lads in our room were ok but for one; Gerald.

Gerald was a pain in the ass and becoming a bit of a thorn in our side. He just couldn't get the 'looking after yourself' bit.

He was continually bollock'd by Smudge for being scruffy, his clothes were unclean and unpressed, his locker untidy and smelly.

We, his roommates, had given up on him as he was continually dropping us in the shit. We'd sent him to Coventry as the expression goes and as nasty as it sounds none of us wanted to share a tent with him.

So Gerald ended up the odd one out. He ended up sharing a tent with a lad from another room and this boy was also not impressed. After our 48 hour mini expedition under canvas he reported Gerald to his Room-jack who then had a word with Smudge.

This had dragged on for weeks now and there was no improvement in Gerald's turn-out or hygiene.

Following this report about Gerald from another room JNCO, Smudge was livid and held a snap locker inspection in our room; he requested Kev Perry to join him. Gerald's locker was ripped to pieces; it was in a disgusting state with filthy clothes, towels that hadn't been washed and an open razor that chocked full of yuk.

Gerald was taken out of the room and down to the offices.

Meanwhile… while he was gone, Smudge got us together and told us that as a room we collectively had to dish out the punishment. It was a fire hose job.

We'd heard about this and other forms of punishment for different misdemeanours. For those who were unclean the punishment was the fire hose.

On his return from the office we were to grab him and drag him into the shower. We then had to turn the fire hose on him for a good five minutes or until we were told to stop.

I don't think any of us saw this as an enjoyable exercise but we had little choice. It was the way things worked and this was a direct order.

We waited a good half hour before Gerald mooched back into the room…

'Get stuck in,' said Smudge. We hesitated while Gerald looked round wondering what was going on.

'I said get on with it!' said Smudge with voice raised.

Collectively we dived on Gerald grabbing his arms. Before he realised what was going on we had pulled him to the floor.

He'd clicked what was happening or about to happen to him and was struggling violently trying to break free and lashing out with his legs. He was quite a big lad standing over 6 feet.

'Grab his legs!' Shouted Smudge. 'Come on for fuck sake, there's enough of you!'

Eventually we had all four limbs contained. Others were looking in the doorway and we bowled them clear as we half dragged, half carried Gerald to the showers. Steve Cottle the lightweight of the room had unwound the fire hose and was following us through the wash room.

'Hold that fucking nozzle tight Cottle I'm turning it on, if you don't it'll blow you off your feet;' this coming from Smudge on the Landing. Smudge didn't give us a chance to get clear – an almighty jet of ice cold water came streaming through the gap in the wall between the wash and shower rooms. The five of us struggling with our poor roommate gave a last shove and sent Gerald staggering back against the wall, his feet went from under him and he crumbled in a heap in the corner – the pressure of the hose holding him there. One by one we were obliged to take the hose and hold it on this forlorn figure. We – his so called room-mates took it in turn to keep the hose on him until we were told to pass it on. Once we'd all taken our share of dishing out the punishment the hose was turned off. Gerald was just slumped in the corner of the shower soaking wet and not moving. We left him there, rolled up the hose and went back to our room. The sentence had been carried out; it had been witnessed by many from the other rooms and was a grim reminder that lack of discipline or hygiene would not be tolerated.

'Stay there I'll get you a towel I don't want your sodden fucking clothes on the floor in my room,' growled Smudge.

The rest of us had also got pretty wet and we were changing our clothes when Gerald came in naked with just a towel round him, he was openly crying, none of us said a word.

He dressed and went into the dhobi room to wring-out and hang up his clothes.

'Don't dwell on it,' Smudge was in no mood to have us get all weak on him. 'He had it coming and in the morning he's gone.'

We looked up surprised.

'Sergeant Perry took him down the office, he was informed he was not considered JL material, this room will be better off without him. The hosing was unavoidable, it's what happens, it's what's expected. I had no choice. I'm in charge of this room and bad discipline is reflected in my end of term report. I want promotion at the end of this term and Dickerson was on the point of jeopardising that promotion. The rest of you - you're a good set of guys, you're doing well. He'll pack first thing in the morning, hand in his kit and be on the train by mid-morning, you won't see him again once you've left the room to parade. In fact I'll tell him to stay in the TV room when he comes up after breakfast. He's no less capable then any of you, if you could do it so could he and he didn't. Now I want you all to forget it and to move on.'

We all felt pretty bad about what happened. I'd travelled down on the train with Gerald – at least from Canterbury; but even then all those weeks ago I'd looked at him and wondered if he'd make a soldier.

The sad fact was that the system wasn't prepared to release lads lightly. You really had to fuck-up big time to get chucked out; it wasn't a case of – 'well he'll never get there so bye bye'. It was a case of persevere - of 'knock him into shape', he'll get there eventually.

The army, or, Junior Leaders Regiment Royal Engineers as Smudge had told us on our first day, were not going to let us go easily.

We got the chance to apologise to Gerald in the morning while Smudge went to the ablutions. He understood it wasn't personal. We all shook hands and said goodbye.

Smudge was right. When we got in lunch time his bed space was empty of bedding and his locker empty of kit.

We pushed the locker and bed up against the wall which made Ray, Les and Steve's bed spaces bigger and we threw a lot of our surplus gear into the now spare locker.

We soon got over Gerald's departure and frankly our room was better for his leaving. He was never replaced in our room; we were down to six in number.

We were briefed on our movement to Thetford and what we needed to take with us.

Following the exercise we would have a 48 hour leave. This would be our first break, our first trip home after six long and difficult weeks. We were all looking forward to the break.

However some of those lads that lived in the north of the country and in Scotland didn't think it was worth going home for 48 hours; they remained in Dover and for the first time were able to leave the barracks over the weekend and explore the town.

I lived, or at least my parents did, in between Norwich and Great Yarmouth, an hour by car from Brandon Station, the station from where we would arrive and depart. It seemed a waste of time for me to go all the way back to Dover to climb on a train and return along the same route I'd just come down. Unlike the other Courses, Intake troop had no weapon to hand in on return. We had no reason to return to the barracks.

My journey down to the tip of Kent seemed pointless and I wondered if I could pull a fast one and leave my troop at Brandon, rather than going all the way back to Dover; I spoke to Smudge about it...

'I thought you didn't like Norfolk?' He jokingly said.

'You told me you were heading down to your grans in Winsley for your time off? I was going to travel with you.'

'This is my first leave and I'm on my parents door step,' I replied, 'if we were on Salisbury Plain I'd probably go to my grans, but I suppose being my first leave from the army my parents would be well miffed if I didn't go home; anyway I'm looking forward to telling them how life has been down here. I'll travel down to Bath with you when we break up for Christmas. What should I do about getting picked up in Brandon?'

'I'll speak to Sergeant Batley about it, leave it with me.'

Smudge was good to his word and the next time Sgt Batley saw me he told me he'd spoken to Lt Rogers and I should go and see the Chief.

My ticket would be made out as standard, Dover - Gt Yarmouth – Dover; but if my parents wanted to pick me up at Brandon station Sgt Batley said fine, the Squadron had no issue with that. All warrants and pay would be handed out before we left from Brandon anyway so it was no big deal. It just goes to show that outside of our pretty strict training regime our Officers and Senior NCO instructors were really a decent bunch. They could have very easily said 'no you come back to Dover with the rest of the troop'.

The day came for us to leave for Stanford.

Bedford RL four ton trucks pulled up outside the Quad for the Squadron to load cases and kit-bags. Dressed in our combat gear, by truck and coach load we went down the hill and through the town to Dover Priory station. This was our first time out the barracks in five weeks. I felt, and I'm pretty sure my entire Intake troop felt, that this was a milestone.

We disembarked the buses and trucks at the station. The truck drivers and assistants were unloading kit onto the station platform ready for cross-loading into the goods carriage; we wouldn't touch our kit again until we arrived at Brandon station in the Stanford training area.

We formed up in our three ranks waiting to embark the train; around us the other Courses were doing the same.

We were to embark by Courses and as we fell out and made our way onto the station platform we were given a packed lunch, a brown paper bag with a couple of sandwiches, a drink and a piece of fruit in it. The catering staff jokingly told us not to eat it all at once. This was a chartered train – it had no buffet car.

Following a pretty uneventful journey we arrived at Brandon station and the whole rigmarole started again.

We were billeted in long Nissan huts, huts left over from the Second World War, around 20 bed spaces up the sides of the hut with lockers and bedside lockers.

Half a dozen trestle tables with chairs ran the length of the room with a big coal burning pot belly stove in the centre. This monster we had to light, fill, empty and clean-out ourselves, we also of course had to bring in the coal.

Our kit-bags and cases were off-loaded outside the huts and we scrabbled through the pile sorting out whose was whose.

Our section during chopper drills. Stanford Oct 71.
Taddy (with the stripe) and me at the back of the group.

We had JNCOs in the rooms with us but they were placed at random and the two in our hut I didn't know, they were there as authority figures and to make sure the hut ran smoothly and was kept clean.

During our week in the Thetford battle area we continued to practice the skills we'd learnt at and around Old Park – patrols, using cover, movement etc. We dressed in our battle order and applied camouflage to our webbing, steel helmets, hands and faces. We learnt how to strap and pack our gear so it wouldn't rattle or glint from the sun.

We were given compass routes to follow for miles – a form of orienteering exercise moving from one point to another, both at night and during daylight.

One of the most enjoyable and exciting elements of the week was helicopter training embarking and disembarking; forming a cordon perimeter around the chopper as we bailed out the door and for some of us helicopter landing drills – how to recognise, mark-out and bring the chopper into a safe clearing and land it using the correct arm signals.

Not all of us had a go at this, as you can appreciate it wouldn't have been practical to have the chopper landing and taking of ninety odd times. But for around ten of us it did happen and was great fun.

We formed listening patrols at night in hides, while the senior Courses had to Recce us (Reconnaissance), then record our strength position and move through us without us spotting them.

If we spotted them we had to blow a whistle.

We never blew the whistle… the blunt truth was we were to bloody scared, it had been leaked to us the if the Recce patrol was spotted and the whistle blown the patrol would have no option but to overrun our position, as well as being bombarded with thunder-flashes, which none of us fancied the idea of; in the melee a few boots would go in and a few rifle butts would get thrown about; no one really worried where they landed… well we did - on the receiving end; so we just kept quiet and let the Recce patrol gather whatever information it wanted.

It was an enjoyable week, we got dirty, we didn't wash every day, we crawled through bushes and over scrubland in the dead of night, we put into practice the theory we'd learned in the classroom or over the back of 'B' Squadron block. We may not have had weapons, but that would come after our return to Old Park, we felt we were on the way to being soldiers.

On the Thursday evening our train warrants were handed out, it was an officially stamped military movement order which allowed the person named there-on to exchange the warrant for a ticket as stated on the order. My ticket was Dover – Great Yarmouth return, but I'd only be using the one way.

That evening we had to pack up and clean-up, leaving the huts in the morning as we found them. Twelve months up the road from now we'd be returning for another camp at Stanford. I'd be in Course 7.

I went to the phone box and telephoned home giving my parents instructions and timings; they should be at Brandon station for 1000 at the latest.

And they were.

Prior to mounting our transport we were given our little brown envelope with our weekly wage. Due to our going on 48 hour leave we were allowed to draw up to twenty pounds. This was no small amount of money. We were banking around twelve pounds a week after deductions

– food and board; so over the thirteen week term that's £156.00, take off the two pounds per week plus the twenty for the 48 hour mid-term leave and we were still left with £110.00 for our Christmas leave. A great deal of money, my dad was only clearing around twenty eight pounds a week for Buxted Poultry, although house and heating were free.

Unlike our trip up to Norfolk when our gear was loaded and unloaded for us, we were now lugging our own gear around. We piled into a fleet of trucks; those who couldn't get a seat on a bench had to stand among the kit bags and cases.

We were driven from the camp into Brandon railway station where the train was already waiting.

I'd spotted my dad's car as we pulled into the station with my family sitting inside. I'd given them strict orders on the phone that they were not to come running over hugging and kissing me. I would meet them at the car; that's exactly what I done. I reported to Spriggsy that my parents were here and waiting, he picked up my kit-bag and walked with me across to the car.

'Mister and Missus Burt? Hello – I'm Corporal Spriggs; I'm one of your son's instructors, nice to meet you.'

My mum and dad shook hands with Spriggsy and after a few words with them he gave me a cheery fair-well see you Monday morning turned and left.

Spriggsy was a good bloke and during my time at Dover he would be a great mentor coaching me in my shooting and encouraging me during Course 7 when I found things difficult. He stood by me on that first very difficult day and stands out in my memory as a top bloke at Dover.

I dragged my kit to the car.

Dad got out and with a smile gave me a pat on the back and opened the boot for me to chuck in my stuff. We were back in the car and away. My first six weeks of army life completed.

The final weeks of Course 1

The trip home in the car passed quickly but very noisily. Mum, dad and Pete all throwing questions in my direction which I done my best to answer.

'Woo, woo, slow down,' I said. 'We have plenty of time for all these questions.' But it was no good they kept it up all the way home.

One of the first things mum and dad done when getting in a car – any car, whether their own or someone else's was to light a cigarette. Habit, just like after a meal the first thing was to push back the chair from the table and light up. My parents both smoked like chimney's and their smoking without any shadow of a doubt was what started me smoking at eleven years old; my brother also.

Friends of mine whose parents didn't smoke, didn't smoke and don't smoke to this day.

I could go on about this for pages but I won't. Let's just say that I followed – until the age of twenty in my parent's footsteps. A spell in a military hospital written into my future would educate me otherwise but until then I, like many others of my age thought smoking was cool; gold coloured packets of 'B&H' or 'Cool Green Menthol' were an indication of what you were and what you earned... sad but true.

I'd never smoked in front of my parents, but today in the car when my mum and dad lit-up so did I. I saw my dad look in the rear view mirror and his jaw drop.

'Eh, what on earth are you doing? Elsa he's smoking!' Said dad looking at my mum.

By now the car interior was a thick cigarette smog; I could barely see my brother across the back seat.

Before mum could say anything I decided to end this conversation for once and for all.

'Yes I'm smoking, I've smoked for years, just like you have, I'm smoking because I've watched you – my parents smoke since I was a little boy. I'm no longer at home, I'm living in a block with two hundred and fifty kids, of which the majority smoke. Perhaps we should all give up or open a window before we choke Pete to death?'

Nothing else was said.

I was extremely lucky I was home by midday and mum was sorting through my dirty clothing. I was horrified to see mum still had the twin-tub in which to do the family washing, I asked her when she intended to 'get modern' with a front loading automatic? Yes, of course she wanted one, but they were very, very, expensive. What we now see as an almost disposable appliance, was, in 1971 almost a month's salary to most families. The same applied to any other household appliance; they cost a great deal and if they packed up, unlike today where you just throw it the bin, you'd take your 'whatever' to an electrical appliance repair shop and it would be mended.

Anyway back to doing the family washing... Mr Fletchers shop in Ormesby had a laundrette with coin operated washing machines and dryers; mum was still quite willing to go to the village and sit for two hours reading while the family dhobi washed, rinsed, spun and dried.

A very odd thing happened as I got out the car and went through into the garden. Our oldest German Shepherd dog 'Gina' that we'd adopted as a very sickly puppy while living in Poston Way six years before, looked round the corner at me and barked...

This was an amazing turn-up; she had never barked once in all the years we'd owned her, it wasn't that we'd prevented her barking or reprimanded her for barking, it's just she had never done this most natural of doggy things. This peculiar and somewhat out of doggy character behaviour had been commented on often by our family and by others. Ball chasing, other dogs, cats, strangers coming in the gate, even when rabbiting on the 'Common' – never a murmur.

But today on my return to the family home I was greeted with a joyful bark and a wagging tail. We were all dumb-struck and after a few seconds burst out laughing. Of course Gina had never been without me round the house; yes, we went as a family on holiday and the dogs when that happened went in the kennels. But during the years she'd lived with us I'd always been at home; in fact when we lived in Poston Way, before we had our second German Shepherd Rosko; Gina had slept most nights on the foot of my bed. As well as my brother and parents our dog was obviously pleased to see me home.

I didn't mind when this 48 hour interlude at home came to an end.

You see I had no friends in Ormesby – in fact I had no friends in the whole of East Anglia. My friends were in the West Country. Unlike my brother who had started school locally and had made friends in his year at school, I'd more or less left Norfolk as soon as I'd arrived.

So following an early Sunday lunch; kit from our exercise scrubbed, clothes washed, ironed and packed; a packet of sturdy elastic bands for my gaiters and my valve driven radio, my parents drove me for a second time to Great Yarmouth station.

As odd as it may seem to the reader I had no reservations of going.

This time I didn't go to Ramsgate, I sat in the correct half of the train.

At Dover Priory station there was a fleet of RL trucks from the motor pool. Transport sent down a constant stream throughout the day to meet each train and take lads up to Old Park; remember the whole of the Regiment had been stood down for the 48 hour break, not just 'A' Squadron. Around six hundred kids minimum were returning from home; crowds of us arriving on every train throughout the day.

We were dropped at the guardroom and under the ever watchful eye of the Provost Sergeant formed up in ranks of three and made our way as smartly as it was possible with our kitbags and cases back to our blocks.

Slowly over the course of the afternoon and evening we were all reinstalled in room 96.

Those of us that returned pre-evening meal wandered down together, grabbed our grub and sat talking about our weekend at home, what we'd done and what we'd brought back with us.

Smudge sat and spoke to us; he too had enjoyed his weekend in Westbury.

'Did you know there were others from down our way Steve? I travelled down from Paddington with a couple of other lads from this Intake - from round the other side of the block? Alan Tadd and Gerry Merrett, one's from Bath and the others from Melksham... Gerry's from Melksham if I remember, Tadd got off with me at Bath, I asked if they'd spoken to you and they said they hadn't, anyway I told them both where you came from and what room you're in so I expect they'll look you up at some point.'

I said thanks and that I'd walk round and say hello one evening. One lad I had met from Swindon, Tony Cook in the room across the Landing but I didn't know the two guys Smudge referred to. For the first six weeks life had been too hectic for socialising; our side of the block had formed pretty much a separate troop except for Saturday Regimental Parade.

'Who's been down and read orders?' Smudge asked us.

We all looked a bit sheepish – of course we'd forgotten.

'None of you? Well it didn't take you long to forget that golden rule did it. Ok so what's changed in the last week? You'd know if you'd read them… we're now in Jumper order or as we tend to call it 'woolly-pulley order, that's what's changed. This means for you poor Sprog's doing education tomorrow, BD jackets. Get them out, make sure they're pressed.'

The last to return from our room was Steve Cottle; he got back around 1900, returned by car from Tilbury by his mum and dad. By then the rest of us had unpacked refilled our lockers with all the stuff we'd dragged up to Stanford and prepared our kit for the morning.

'So when are we going to be called onto the Landing Corporal?' Les asked Smudge while setting up his reel-to-reel tape recorder.

'That won't happen this evening Les, I don't expect for a minute that all the Room-jacks are back and technically we're still on leave till 0800 tomorrow morning. There's a bit of a trust issue going on here. We may not even have a room inspection tomorrow morning, just parade at half eight. But you can bet Sergeant Perry will be looking round the rooms and ablutions and if they're not spot on you know what you'll be doing tomorrow night. Hit the fucking floor running tomorrow morning and give it the same as you do every other morning and things will be ok. You've crossed a big milestone, providing you keep your standards up things will be a little easier this half.'

Once our kit was prepared and it didn't take much as we'd all made sure the ground work such as boots, belts, gaiters, and work clothing had been prepared before returning; we sat my little radio on the table next to Les's reel-to-reel, tuned it into radio 1 and done a test recording; we all had to be dead quite, the reel-to-reel had a separate 'mic' that stood next to the radio speaker and every sound from elsewhere in the room would be recorded. On Sundays when we recorded Pick-of-the-Pops we'd put a keep out sign on the door and lay on our beds either reading, writing or bulling boots while 'Maggie May', 'Gypsy's Tramps and Thieves' and Alan Freeman was captured on tape.

There would be hell to pay if anyone came barging in making a racket.

Monday morning and the Squadron were once again on parade. Although the present dress mode was referred to as 'woolly-pulley order', quite a few of the Courses were wearing denim type jackets. With the denim work trousers they looked very 'cool' and soldierish, whereas we in our full BDs with black lace-up shoes looked like extras from a John Mills war movie.

We were addressed by our Troopy...

'Well done all of you. It was a successful week in Norfolk and you all put into practice what you've learnt here in Old Park over the last six weeks; I've heard good reports from your training NCOs.

The second half of your course will continue in the same vein – you'll further hone the skills you've learnt and you'll learn new ones. This afternoon for the first time you'll draw from the armoury a weapon; the SLR. The weapon will have a number; you'll remember the number because this weapon will remain your personnel weapon during your time here at Dover.

Over the next six weeks you'll learn to strip it, clean it, shoot with it and drill with it. It will become as much a part of you as your boots and beret.

I trust you all had a good weekend and I'm pleased to hear you all made it back, that doesn't always happen – but we're now back to work... which I believe this morning starts with education. Well done. Carry on Staff.'

We were brought to attention and marched to our lessons.

After lunch we changed into our denims and following parade marched to the armoury, we fell out and formed a queue by the door. The moment most of us had been longing for had arrived; we would get our own gun! I say gun loosely, of course it was a weapon and a very serious one at that. But we were fifteen years old, still kids really and the word gun at that moment seemed to suit.

The armoury was big – huge in fact. It held weapons for the whole Regiment. Not only rifles but the LMG, the SMG, pistols for the Officers, bayonets, racks of magazines (not the ones you read, the ones that hold bullets or rounds as they're correctly referred to) and probably more besides. It also had a workshop to carry out repairs.

A corridor ran along the wall to the left as you went through the door with a counter top opposite. A metal mesh went from two feet above the counter to the ceiling and the weapons were stored by Squadron in sections behind this mesh; the three areas of counter top coloured red, blue and green. This was to speed up distribution on days such as Regimental parade days when the whole Regiment needed to draw a weapon in a short space of time.

My SLR along with a cleaning kit and a pair of ear plugs in a little plastic box was slid under the mesh toward me; number 111 an easy number to remember. I signed for this work of art, was told to keep the cleaning kit and plugs, they formed part of my permanent kit. I moved along the corridor and out through the exit at the far end.

My SLR, during my time at Dover, was a walnut stock and walnut butt model, with a recess in the butt under a flip cap to hold an oil bottle. My reason for explaining this is because not all the SLRs were the same; some had black plastic stocks and wood butts, others had both plastic stock and butt. The plastic models were newer and lighter in weight. I was quite happy with what I'd been issued – now I just wanted to shoot it and sitting writing this in 2016 and looking at the photo, I would just love to get back on the range and shoot that weapon again. I loved it and I was a very good shot.

That afternoon again we were divided into groups, one group going to the Square to start rifle drill, the other group again split into two went into two rooms within the block and started learning the drills associated with loading, unloading and making ready the weapon, also the mechanics of the weapon; stripping, cleaning and reassembly with both Spriggy and Sergeant Paggetti our senior weapons instructor of Italian descent, who delighted in telling us of his many battles in Aden, Kenya, and other far flung corners of the Empire. (We called him Sergeant Spatts, I seem to remember him being a member of the boxing club as well; he had the face for it).

We would drill, with arms at the same intensity as we had our first six weeks of foot drill until they became second nature.

Range drills we would practice in lines in the classroom over and over again.

LOAD – Safety catch on, pouch open, magazine on. Do not cock the weapon.

READY – Weapon pointed down range, weapon cocked, safety remains on. Followed by – *'In your own time carry on.'*

UNLOAD – Safety catch on, magazine off and into pouch, weapon cocked – round from the chamber is discharged from the breach, look inside the breach – all clear let the working parts forward, safety off, pull trigger while mussel is pointing at the ground. Well after forty five years that's how I remember it. I'm pretty certain that sequence is correct.

Weapons maintenance, we would practice until we could literally do it in the dark or with our eyes closed. We would hold blindfold stripping and reassembling races over and over again. Breaking down the rifle into its six working parts, the gas plug mechanism and the breach mechanism before anyone say's I'm incorrect with the number, that's without breaking down the firing pin).

We would take the magazine apart and also practice loading the mag from bandoliers of one hundred rounds. Who could pump in the twenty rounds in the shortest possible time.

For fifteen, sixteen year olds this was mega stuff.

We also had an intensive fitness regime. Cross country runs took place at least twice a week; also route marches where we'd dress in boots, denims, red vest and battle order. In three ranks as two squads we'd speed-march round the roads of Whitfield, Temple Ewell and Buckland. PT, swimming and the assault course, not a day went past without some form of physical training in our schedule. We would return exhausted, kick off our boots, rip of socks and lay back on the bed for a couple of minutes to ease our throbbing and often blistered feet. However every day we were becoming fitter and stronger, our scrawny frames filling out with good food and exercise, well most were, I seemed to be growing in height but not in girth, I was beginning to resemble a bean pole; nevertheless I had amazing stamina and was up there on the leader-board when it came to any form of running.

Our routine was becoming ingrained. Although our evening call-outs to the Landing continued they were now far more relaxed and we even exchanged some banter and laughs with our JNCOs which in all honesty we held in awe.

On that first evening back from our mid-term leave, the Monday, we were called out. It wasn't to get a bollocking but to fill us in on some further details.

'You're in the second half of your first Course now.' Kevin Perry informed us (a fact we were all too well aware of).

'Those of you that are still here, and I'm pleased to say that is very much the majority, have done very well. But we don't slacken off. The pressure is on through this Course and into Course two. Some of you wankers will no doubt have aspirations of becoming JNCOs yourselves? God help us. I've seen nothing to inspire me as yet (he said this with a smile) but keep at it you never know, stranger things have happened.

I'm sure this lecture had been passed down from one Junior Sergeant to another since Old Park opened its doors.

Ok, here's some changes to the rules.

You are now allowed into town, book out in the duty office and book back in by 2100. Don't get into fights with local kids. They will try and egg you on, – there are a couple of groups in town that make a point of shouting crap and provoking a fight. However if you do find yourself in a fisty-cuff situation don't fucking loose. You may as well get hung for a sheep as a lamb. And if you're up in front of the OC or God-forbid the CO because of fighting with locals they'd rather hear you won than lost; army logic... winning may reduce your sentence.

You can also go to the NAAFI Disco, where if you're really unlucky you'll pick a local girl. Just be careful at full moon as she's likely to grow a tail and rip your throat out.

So did anyone get lucky at the weekend? Dixon, how about you? Those girls up your way, I heard you only have to whistle and their knickers fall down?'

Les was looking down and shuffling his feet – unusual for Les.

'No not this weekend Sergeant.'

'You disappoint me Dixon, I can see you're embarrassed so I won't pick on you anymore. Look up Dixon there's no money on the floor.' We were all laughing...

'Where was I? Oh yes, you can now, if you wish decorate the inside of your lockers. Photos of mum and dad, your dog the one with the tail and the one without (laugh again from us all); page three pin ups and pages from dirty magazines providing all JNCOs have had a chance to read em before you cut em up. Not sharing your wanking material with JNCOs is a 'behind the guard offence'. I will be holding a locker inspection in the next week to view the standard of totty you fuckers hang around with when you're at home. Dodwell I hear yours is pretty hot?'

'Anything you say Sergeant,' replied Paul grinning.

Kev Perry was referring to a friend of Pauls from Cheltenham. It wasn't his girlfriend as such, but a friend of the family a girl called Lorraine Doe, she was bloody gorgeous, a model, and I ended up writing to her the following year when in Course 7; I'd been given the boot by Angie and Doddy thought it would cheer me up; that's a good mate for you! At the time I couldn't believe my luck!

'As you know,' continued on Kev, 'we also have a Barrack cinema over behind the Combat Engineering wing. Films are there for all to enjoy but I don't want to hear back that any of you lot have been spotted cuddled up side by side in the back row. We'll leave that shit to 'B' & 'C' Squadrons (another laugh). Oh, and there's no fucking choc-ices either.

And finally your Room-jacks have told me, and this is also hard to believe, they think you're worthy of calling them Corp instead of Corporal. Against my better judgement I'll also relax the Sergeant thing. What do you say?'

We were all quiet...

'How about as loud as you can; thank you Sarg.'

'THANK YOU SARG!' We all bellowed.

'Ok get out of here.'

We made our way back to our rooms in good spirts.

Obviously we couldn't wait to get into town and one of our first free nights we got dressed into our civi's and headed down to the duty office, signed out, and following a five minute lecture on behaviour expected of a JL and the avoidance of a fight with local youth, we headed down past RHQ and the stables for the back hill. It's a long walk from 'Buckland' the area at the bottom of the back hill to Dover seafront proper; around two miles; but we were all keen to go and those first couple of weeks back following half term break we were dying to spread our wings, and by all I include 'B' & 'C' Squadron Intakes; to pursue our new found freedom, explore the town and if possible – even though we'd been told over and over again there was no chance - meet some girls.

When the gang of us first arrived at Dover we looked like any other bunch of young mid-teen kids you'd see anywhere in any town, village, or coffee bar. However following our 'Bert the Butcher' haircut and our now instilled military style of walking, or should I say marching, rather than slouching; we all stood out a mile from our civilian peers. Also in-keeping with our walking-in-smart-squad style adopted in the confines of the barracks, this habit was also carried over on our forays into town.

Shoulders back, no hands in pockets and in even numbered groups we were like mini SAS units walking round the town... no actually we weren't like SAS units at all – what am I on about? Anyway moving on...

Dover was not an attractive town.

As a town in 1971 it was drab, boring, and without any form of attraction except perhaps the Castle.

In 1971 people tended to pass through Dover, it wasn't a town that people visited to stay; it was a port of entry and exit.

Coming off the A2 from London, the main street called London Road runs from the bottom of Whitfield Hill down the middle of the valley toward the sea, where it then becomes the interestingly named - 'High Street' it then carries on a few more hundred yards changing names as it progresses toward the promenade.

After passing through Market Square and the Monument you end up at the 'T' junction on Waterloo Crescent. You can go no further.

To the left of you is a huge slab of what were then council flats, this slab of typical fifties, sixties, appalling architecture done the most fantastic job of blocking out everything scenically available to the person heading toward the beach; pebble beach I might add. Whoever came up with the idea of plonking this block of flats in what must be the worse position possible for enhancing the small amount of attractive seafront Dover has, well, all I can say is the council must've been on a whopping back hander from somewhere... However if you were fortunate enough to be housed by Dover or Kent County Council in one of these flats you had the most fantastic view over the harbour and English Channel as far as the French coast. No doubt today they've all been sold off as private dwellings and I would guess they're worth a bundle.

At this 'T' junction you turned left for the eastern dock and right for western dock and that just about sums it up.

Three hundred yards back from this junction would be what was then referred to as the epi-centre of the town; consisting of a couple of pubs and a Wimpy burger bar... much like today actually... Today though, Dover has the addition of a yacht marina, should you be wealthy enough to own a boat and a clothes retail outlet selling brands nobody recognises. Oh, and it still has its saving grace, the lovely castle.

It didn't take long to dawn on us that the reports passed down from our Room-jacks and other longer serving peers were indeed correct.

Not a lot happened in Dover and there was not a great deal of anything of interest.

There was a cinema half way down Castle street, the last remaining flix in the town; but why pay to go to the town flix when we had a free picture house in Old Park showing the latest movies... unless of course you wanted to see something X-rated. These films had an admittance age of eighteen (it had been raised in 1970 from sixteen) and I doubt there was one Fred in Old Park of that age. So our little cinema, as nice as it was only showed 'U', 'A' and newly introduced 'AA' rated movies. Except on one occasion when a film rated X actually slipped through the net and was shown every night for a week, a film that had been released in 1968 starring Jane Fonda a film that every hot blooded adolescent boy wanted to see... Guessed it? 'Barbarella'. Oh yes! Barbarella the Queen of the Galaxy. This film was based on the French 'Barbarella' comics and shows the rather delectable Jane Fonda in some pretty scantily clad costumes. A brief summary of the film follows...

In an unspecified future, Barbarella is assigned by the President of Earth to retrieve Doctor Durand Durand from the Tau Cetiregion. Durand Durand is the inventor of the Positronic Ray, a weapon that Earth Leaders fear will fall into the wrong hands. Barbarella crashes on the 16th planet of Tau Ceti and is soon knocked unconscious by two mysterious girls, who take Barbarella to the wreckage of a spaceship. Inside the wreckage, she is tied up and several children emerge from within the ship. They set out several dolls which have razor sharp teeth. As the dolls begin to bite her, Barbarella faints but is rescued by Mark Hand, the Catchman, who patrols the ice looking for errant children. While Hand takes her back to her ship, Barbarella offers to reward Mark and he suggests sex. She says that people on Earth no longer have penetrative intercourse but consume exaltation transference pills and press their palms together when their "psychocardiograms are in perfect harmony". Hand prefers the bed, and Barbarella agrees. Hand's vessel makes long loops around Barbarella's crashed vessel while the two have sex, and when it finally comes to a stop, Barbarella is blissfully humming. After Hand repairs her ship, Barbarella departs and promises to return, agreeing that doing things the old-fashioned way is best.

So that's Barbarella in a nut-shell and at some point in the movie she ends up being strapped to an orgasmatron machine which she thoroughly enjoys – God bless her.

Of course us fifteen and sixteen year olds had no idea about sex we just went along for the special effects... and if you believe that you'll believe anything. Oh, and now you know where the eighties band fronted by Simon Le Bon got their name from.

A walk across to our cinema was a pretty regular event for us poor Fred's with no money; on a couple of occasions I visited the cinema in town but I'll come to those trips later.

Our next trip into town was on a Saturday afternoon; we optimistically held onto the belief that something grand could happen to us in Dover, that maybe as we walked down the street a party of pretty girls would invite us to a party or some sultry lonely housewife may call us in to give her a good seeing-to. It didn't take long for these hopes to be dashed.

The highlight of our first afternoon into town was a trip to a special point on the seafront railings; well to me anyway, to show my mates where seven years earlier I'd nearly killed myself running across the road into the safety railings.

As a room we checked out; we tended to do things as a room. If you were planning on doing anything, you'd ask your own room-mates before going next door asking less familiar colleagues and more often than not if no one from your own room would join you, you wouldn't bother going at all.

As we progressed through the Courses and you got to know lads from other rooms better this shyness tended to disappear.

A motley lot in an assortment of motley clothing we wandered into town arriving finally at the seafront, it was now late in the year – November - cold and overcast; the sea was grey and even with the massive breakwater walls surrounding the harbour a huge swell crashed on the beach causing the pebbles to rattle as they were rolled with the outgoing surf. I was wearing a lumber-jack coat; it was multi-colour check with an artificial fur collar. We all wore this odd clothing. Doddy who arrived at Old Park sporting long brown hair and an Afghan coat looked a right hippy; he still had the coat and not the hair, now he just looked plain odd. The smartest among us was Gary who looked a real MOD in his Levi Stay-press trousers, Loafers, Ben Sherman shirt and a Crombie coat. He looked a real cool dude and if anyone could pull a bird, in his trendy on-the-button rig-out it would be him. A wool Crombie coat was £20.00 none of us could afford one. Gary came from a well-to-do family and was I guess slightly spoilt by his mum. I loved his coat; evenings he decided not to come into town he'd lend it to me for a couple of fags. I thought I looked real cool in the Crombie... I was so wrong. When I wore it home on leave the following term (Gary passed it on to me) my dad said I looked like a chief mourner in a funeral procession.

We turned to walk toward the eastern dock past the block of flats to our left.

The duelled Town Wall Street behind 'The Gateway' as it is today was only a single carriage in 1971; Marine Parade and Waterloo Crescent were the main thoroughfares passing in front of the flats and sweeping round to the docks where the Premier Inn now stands.

As we walked I'd been chatting to my mates of the many times we as a family had passed through the docks on our way to visit my German family in the Ruhr area of Mulheim, Duisburg and Dusseldorf.

I held their attention with my stories; not one of my room-mates had ever left the UK and my talking of our family adventures all over Europe since I was a toddler held their interest and prompted many questions.

Lots of the lads hoped that their step into army life would lead to world travel and a life of adventure.

I told them of the morning we'd arrived in Dover to catch the 6am ferry to Oostende; we'd left as usual from Winsley before midnight heading up the A4 round the London south circular road and down the A2; a long journey.

It was a lovely early summer morning with the sun rising almost directly over the harbour. Dad decided to pull up on Maine Parade and we'd all get out to stretch our legs and open a Thermos before heading into the dock. The car was on the left hand side of the road pointing toward the docks and to get to the esplanade we had to cross the road.

Pete and I asked if we could go down onto the beach and mum gave us the ok.

In our excitement we ran across the road, me directly into the railing that separated the promenade from the road, it caught me across the bridge of the nose and the force of the impact lifted me off my feet; my body carried on with the forward momentum and I landed horizontally, the back of my head smashing into the concrete.

It was an accident that could have killed me or caused me long term impairment. I was unconscious - out cold for a few minutes. I came too in great pain, a massive lump on both the front and back of my head.

My parents consoled me but even with the mess I was in didn't believe I warranted a trip to the hospital. It took me quite a few days to recover and I had a whopping bruise on my face, both eyes were black and over the next few days went yellow, I looked horrendous all holiday and was thoroughly miserable.

The railings are still there to this day. Bollards painted white and the rail yellow; (so young kids running across the road can see them and don't mortally wound themselves) in 1965 they were grey and with the rising sun in my eye's I just didn't see them.

Hunched in the strong wind under leaden skies I stood with my mates at the point where this - 'could've-been-a-life-changing-incident' took place and recounted the tale.

Soberly we moved on to a dingy café for a grotty cup of instant coffee before the long trek back up London road and the back hill.

In reality the barracks were far more happening place; in the evenings we could, as I've already recounted, go to the cinema or the NAAFI or the WRVS; we had the sports clubs that we'd elected to join which were open to practice most evenings of the week and at weekends.

The fencing club of which Les was a member, the pool, gymnastics, boxing; all these pastimes and sports were there for the taking. We

Me showing of my locker pin-ups.

had rugby field and football fields, archery and tennis; the saddle club where I could just turn up on a Saturday afternoon or an evening during the summer. We had no reason to be bored.

The WRVS was run by the blue-rinse brigade and a lovelier bunch of biddy's you'd be hard pushed to find anywhere. They treated every lad that came through the door just like their own grandson.

The WRVS became a favourite hangout. The large room that had been so unwelcoming on our first afternoon became a hangout of choice, books, board games, bar-billiards and a game involving mini skittles. We could buy a cup of tea and a sticky bun for next to nothing and as the colder winter evening's set-in, with its soft seating it was a nice homely place to go.

Having been given the freedom to decorate our lockers, photos of girlfriends and family appeared Sellotaped alongside cuttings from girly-mags; all were plastered on the inside of the doors; no one seemed to bother how blue they were, we could display more or less what we liked and our NCOs both Junior and Senior would take time out to have a good look and pass comment during locker inspection.

At Nelson Haden, where I'd gone to school, the girls and boys were schooled separately; two schools in the same grounds. Our closest contact with the girls was chatting across a footpath that ran down the centre of the school; girls would sit on one side and boys the other. During my final year of secondary school a very attractive lass had started in our fourth year girls. Her name was Clare Sylvester and she befriended the bunch of girls that sat with my gang of boys. Clare came from Melksham, where she had gone to school until some misbehaviour had got her expelled. Her parents had found her a place at our school and so she spent all week living at her auntie's in Trowbridge and went back to Melksham at the weekend. Clare and I ended up being an item… or at least I was her item Monday till Friday. What I didn't know was on her return to Melksham at the weekend she became someone else's item. That lad just happened to be one - Gerry Merrett also from Melksham, a Junior Sapper in 'A' Squadron along with me.

A couple of weeks following our return from mid-term leave and Smudge's trip down west with Gerry on the train, Gerry decided to walk round my side of the lines and give me a look.

We were sat on my pit talking when he looked up and saw a picture of Clare in my locker.

'I know her!' He said in semi shock. 'That's Clare Sylvester from Melksham, what's she doing in your locker?'

'She's my girlfriend,' I replied. 'Do you know her?'

'Yes,' he said. 'It seems we must be sharing her, she's my girlfriend as well.'

As you can imagine this caused quite a laugh within, not only my room, but in the whole troop; Gerry and Steve going out with the same girl, one Monday to Friday, the other Saturday and Sunday. I can't remember if Gerry continued seeing her, I don't think he did. In truth I think he'd packed in with her some time before coming to Dover, but it was still very funny. I continued seeing Clare when I went down to Wiltshire during my time at Dover but when I went off to Germany she found someone else, a guy who was around far more permanently than me; I can't blame her really.

Our next major exciting moment was drawing our weapon for the ranges.

Hythe ranges are on the south coast. Hythe was on the far side of Folkestone and we got there by truck; the present fast road across the cliffs had not been built, it was a twisty single carriageway which took us right through the middle of both Dover and Folkestone, about an hour in the back of the four tonner.

After breakfast we went to draw our weapon which we locked in our lockers until our chores had been completed. The security of our weapon had been made clear to us – we take it everywhere, we never ever let it out of our sight not even to go to the toilet. You either lock it away or take it with you. A breach of this rule was a very serious offence and in a few years' time when serving in Northern Ireland a breach of this rule would land you in the slammer faster than almost anything else.

We dressed in our olive coloured combats, donned our 37 pattern webbing, ammo pouches and small pack containing our mess-tins and irons and formed up in the quad.

Three trucks arrived, our transport to Hythe.

The first truck loaded with around thirty five lads went round to the cookhouse where they loaded Hay-boxes of food for our lunch, flasks of tea and bags of buns for mid-morning break. The Hay-box is like a big thermos for keeping food hot... well warm anyway. I believe the very first Hay-boxes were actually boxes containing pots of food surrounded by straw or hay. As the design progressed the name stayed the same.

The second truck went to the ammo bunker which was located under an earth work near the assault course. A solid steel door led into a bunker lined with shelving containing metal ammo boxes.

Every round had to be accounted for and every empty case returned to the senior range coordinator, Officer, or Permanent Staff NCO.

Stocked up with ammunition and food, divided between three trucks we departed for Hythe.

We used two different ranges locally; Hythe and Lydd both are on the coast, I say 'are on the coast' because they are both still used to this day; they are extensive in size and play a big part in today's operational training program.

This was a whole new experience to us and as we jumped or clambered out of the truck we probably looked awkward and pretty unsoldierly; for a great many of us we had ill-fitting combats as well as incorrectly fitting webbing. To top of the whole sorry state we were responsible for this mighty gun that seemed; now we were in the field, to be big cumbersome lump of a thing.

'Come on you lot, sort yourselves out! Jump from the truck for fuck sake d'you think this is a Teddy Bears fucking picnic!? CUMON MOVE IT!' Hollered Spatts.

Then...

'YOU! - MORON!' He shouted pointing at one poor bastard.

'What the fuck are you doing!? Don't you ever let me see you using your weapon as a fucking walking stick again, I'll break both your fucking legs and you'll need crutches not a fucking stick. What's your fucking name? Remind me!?'

'Milburn Sarg.' Replied Bob.

Don't you fucking well Sarg me when I'm bollocking you Milburn, its Sergeant Paggetti, do I make myself clear!?'

'Yes Sergeant, sorry Sergeant it won't happen again,' stuttered Bob.

'To fucking right it won't; two nights behind the guard Milburn, same kit as you're wearing, fucking spotless.'

'Yes Sergeant.'

Bob desperately wanted to get out of the lime-light. He'd been walking along holding the barrel with the butt on the ground, just like a walking stick; no wonder Spatts went ballistic.

Two nights behind the guard.

Basically this was a punishment. The barrack duty guard paraded at 1800 in front of the guardroom. They were inspected by the duty Officer and Sergeant before being dismissed to the duty billet-room where there slept doing alternate guard duty through the night till 0600 the next morning. Normally eight Junior Sappers and a Junior Corporal formed the guard who also manned the fire picket trolley as well. You done two hour stints through the night in pairs, one person had to remain in the guard room to man the barrier. Those not patrolling slept in the duty bunk room, ready to spring into action if required...

You were inspected at 1800, started duty at 1830 and were fallen-out at 0630 when Permanent Staff RMP (Regimental Military Police) again took over the duties.

Parading behind the guard meant just that – the offender stood behind the guard and following the inspection of those on duty would also be inspected only far more rigorously.

You could get any number of nights and you could be told to turn up in any one of your uniforms but it was generally the uniform you were wearing when the offence occurred or No2 dress. Some duty Officers were decent and let you go directly following the inspection, providing your turn-out was up to muster; others could be a real pain keeping you there to clean the guardroom, polish brasses or sweep the guardroom frontage, in fact any number of chores.

The rest of us were hastily trying to get formed into three ranks, we'd all gone vacant on the truck and to be honest Spatts was right we'd gone into a - 'we're-on-a-jolly mode'.

We weren't making a very a very good job of it, for once we were all together, all ninety whatever was left of us and we weren't used to forming up in such a big group; eventually we got there.

'Troop! Trooop! SHUN!' Ordered Spatts.

'Right you lot, that was crap. In fact it was worse than crap it was sham-fucking-bolic! We do not fuck around like school kids on an outing especially when we're on the range, we're sharp, we're soldiers, we do things quickly and efficiently, if we had time I'd have you doubling up and down this track for an hour with your weapon above your head, but we haven't so starting from now shape up!

This is what's going to happen. You will split into two groups. Group one will go into the Butts, group two will begin zeroing their weapon.

Starting with the Butts - you are in a concrete corridor below the targets you see on that ridge in front of you.

The targets move up and down on a pulley system controlled by your lily-white hands. Each man will fire five shots from 100 yards. This will give us a group on the target; I will then order unload. We will inspect your unloaded weapon; we will then walk forward to inspect the target. Sgt Batley our two armourers and myself will adjust your sights based on your grouping. After they have inspected and adjusted the sight they will call down to you lot in the Butts to say they've finished. You'll then lower the target and put a patch of the same colour as the area the round has penetrated over the hole.

You'll raise the target; we'll return to the 100 yard mark and repeat the process. Corporal Spriggs will be a member of the Butt party and be in telephone contact with the firing point.

It's that simple gentlemen, do I make myself clear?... I said do I make myself CLEAR!'

'YES SERGEANT!'

'Good; you lot in group two. You will be firing from the prone position. What is the prone position Caldwell?'

'Flat on our stomach Sergeant.'

'Well done Caldwell, were getting things right at last.'

Spriggsy walked down the line counting the rows till he got to the middle.

'Ok, from here to the right listen in...

He brought us to attention and marched us to the Butts; halted and waited instruction.

'Ok, when I've fallen you out, pair off and take a target; check to make sure it's not holed, if it is repair it with the squares of paper and glue. Then raise the target, only one in the left hand slot; got it? Good. I want one of you with me on the phone. Burt, you'll do.

Hythe ranges.

Listen in; Squad – Squaddd – Shun! To the Butts - Dismiss! Burt come with me.

We went over to the corner where a green box sat on a shelf attached to two wires; a black handle stuck out the side.

Spriggsy opened the lid, where, inside sat a black telephone hand piece.

'Field telephone Burt, you've seen this before when we were in Stanford; now you'll get to use it. When all the targets are raised, I'll tell you to let the firing party know. Pick up the hand piece and wind the handle a dozen times quickly. Whoever picks up tell them Butt party ready. Think you can do that?'

'Yes Corp.'

'Good.'

I could see from my position at the end of the concrete corridor targets being lowered and targets being raised. Spriggsy walked along the long pathway talking to each pair of lads.

By each target a concrete seat backed onto the wall. Spriggsy returned and all the targets where raised.

Each metal frame could hold two wooden targets. Targets of a soldier, holding a rifle, running toward you. The centre of the chest had a white square approximately six inches by four.

'Ok Burt, give-em a bell, let them know we're ready.'

I lifted the receiver, wound the handle like mad and waited, a voice answered, 'just to let you know we're all ready down here Staff.'

'Thank you (polite), we're still loading magazines, tell Corporal Spriggs we'll commence firing when ready.'

I looked across at Spriggsy. 'They're still loading magazines Corp; they'll start firing as soon as they're done.'

It was quiet in the Butts, looking along the line, all the lads were sat back on the benches SLRs and small packs stood against the wall to the side of them; all targets were raised.

After a few minutes we could hear Spatts giving orders to the firing party.

'Prone position! Load! Keep those weapons pointed down the range! Ready!'

We could faintly hear the clatter of the working parts being cocked.

My heart, for some strange reason was beating faster, maybe it was because any second now a hundred plus rounds would be ploughing through the targets above our heads and into the embankment in front of us.

'Range 100 yards, five rounds - in your own time carry on!'

A split second of silence and then the firing began. Our lads had moved forward to look up at the rounds penetrating the flimsy ply target above them. Zip – zip - zip, they flew unseen through the cardboard and paper to send spurts of sand flying upward in the earthwork bank behind the Butts.

Slowly, after barely a minute the firing slowed down and then stopped all together.

I heard the order unload.

The next thing we heard was a great deal of excited chatter above us and looking up I saw Eric Skillen a Scottish lad looking at his target ten feet above us, the first target, the one closest to my telephone station. I could hear someone getting a bollocking for losing off six rounds instead of five.

The lads had now retreated back to the firing point and the targets were being dropped for repair.

The phone rang and I picked it up.

'Who's there,' said the voice, it was Spatts.

'Burt, Sarg'.

'Get Corporal Spriggs will you Burt'.

'Hang on Sarg I'll call him, he's right here. Corp! Corp! Sergeant Paggetti wants to talk to you.'

Spriggsy took the phone off me and talked a few seconds with Spatts. He put the phone down.

'They'll do another five rounds, the first five were apparently shit.' He walked up the line to tell the Butt crew.

Once again holes pasted over and targets raised, we waited and the whole rigmarole was repeated.

This time the targets were kept in place longer as the Permanent Staff team went along the line adjusting each lad's weapons sights.

Once again they shot. The results were viewed and the lads returned to the firing position.

The phone rang and Spriggsy stood next to me picked it up.

'Ok Staff that's what we'll do.' He put the phone down.

'Tea break; lower the targets!' He shouted. 'Pick-up your weapon and kit and fall-in on the track.'

The word was passed down the line; we walked to the end of the Butts and formed into three ranks to march the 100 yards back to the firing point.

The tea urns were stood on the edge of the truck tail-gate and one of the drivers was dishing out the buns. We found somewhere to sit down and enjoyed our break, life as a squaddie wasn't so bad really.

Following our break the second half of the first group came forward to repeat the zeroing procedure; we meanwhile returned to the Butts and continued on in the target repair role.

Group two finished, the phone rang and we returned to the firing point. It was lunch time.

We grabbed our mess tins and mugs and queued for a good solid stew from the Hay-boxes, with the stew came bread. Now this will bring back recollections to many. Not just any bread but army bread. Over the years I heard this story many times and I'm pretty sure it's true…

Army bread was made centrally in the army bakery in Aldershot in the UK and in Bielefeld in BAOR (Germany). It was made and packaged on the premises and distributed to all army units from these central locations. It was – white, medium sliced and always came slightly stale with a few blue spots in the middle. It came in a pinkish red waxed packaging (no doubt to protect it against damp in the field) with 'Baked by the 'RAOC', the RAOC badge and the word Tuesday on the package. (Royal Army Ordnance Corps).

This was a standing joke; as it never stated whether it should be eaten by Tuesday or whether it was baked last Tuesday; just Tuesday. It didn't matter when or where you got it, it was always Tuesday, slightly stale with its trademark couple of blue spots in the middle or on the crust. We didn't care; it mopped up the dregs of the stew in the mess-tin, filled up that small hunger gap and none of us, as far as I'm aware died of it.

We chatted away during our lunch; those who'd already shot filling the rest of us in on the details and recounting how well or how badly they'd fared…

Stew, bread and tea consumed, lunch over; at last our turn had come and we were swapped with the first group.

We formed a line to draw our ammunition and divided, as those who shot earlier, into two groups.

Our instructors had decided to issue us fifteen rounds, five to get the feel for shooting the weapon for the first time, five to zero and a further five to check we were on, or reasonably on, the centre of the target; basically to check our zero.

This was not my first time in control of a fire-arm. At home on the farm in North Bradley, prior to our moving to Norfolk I'd often shot with our farm managers 12-bore shot-gun. The previous Christmas, Christmas 1970, dad and mum had given me a 410 shotgun as a Christmas present. I was at ease with a fire-arm and knew the rules of safety very well.

However this was a different beast entirely and I'm sure we all had butterflies in our stomachs at that first introduction.

'Load your fifteen rounds into your magazine, DO NOT put the magazine into the weapon, put the magazine into your pouch,' said Spatts.

For me it was the left hand pouch – I was, and still am totally left handed.

This had caused some controversy during the pre-shooting weapons training. At first Spatts and Spriggsy had insisted that I shoot right handed. But I'd been all fingers and thumbs – I just couldn't do it. I'd explained that I'd shot before coming to Old Park, that I was a good shot left handed but there was no-way in the world I could shoot right handed. In fact I'd got quite stressed about it to the point where Spriggsy had given-in and spoken to Spatts. They relented and waited to see how I managed in a live firing situation.

The SLR isn't handed; it's made for right handed shooters only, the empty cases eject from the right hand side of the breech which means, if you're left handed, they fly across your field of vision (because the butt is tucked into your left shoulder). Also the safety catch is on the left hand side of the pistol grip which makes it awkward to access, having to literally bend your left thumb back around the grip or use the Index finger to flip the safety on and off.

These were the safety concerns the Spatts and Spriggsy had when they first insisted I shoot right handed. However neither were a bother to me, I soon got into my own style and never had a problem. In fact I shot and won medals for the Squadron and the Regiment while in Dover and also during my time in BAOR. My shooting ability and eagle-eyed reputation preceded me throughout my army career wherever I went. While at Dover I had serious competition from a lad in 'C' Squadron; he was also left handed and shot left shoulder. I was determined to be the best. Shooting had become a passion on the farm and I'd been good at it; I desperately wanted to carry that ability over to this weapon and show what I could do.

Again we were split into two groups, the group I was in to go first. The other group remained waiting near the trucks.

Before we dispersed to the firing points Spatts spoke to us.

'Remember your technique,' he reminded us. 'Breathing – breath in, hold and squeeze gently on the trigger; do not snatch the trigger. Hold the weapon tight into your shoulder; you should feel the same response from the weapon each time you fire. Relax slightly between each shot, move away from the sight. The first five shots will give you a feel for shooting the weapon. We will complete the zeroing after the first five round shoot, remember to check the setting on your rear sight – are there any questions?' There was no reply.

'If you have a problem with your weapon, lay the weapon down barrel pointing down range and put up your arm. We will see you and come to your assistance. Ok move to a firing position and await my orders.'

Leaving our small packs in a pile we moved out to a numbered firing position.

Spatts stood behind us half way along the group.

'If anyone has not got their ear defenders in put them in now, shouted Spatts.

'Adopt the prone position!'

We all lay flat; most on their left side giving access to the right hand ammo pouch, me slightly on my right side.

'LOAD!'

Sgt Batley and Staff Shaw where also stood behind us watching our range drill.

Safety catch on – pouch open – mag onto the weapon; this drill was running through my head.

'Take up the prone position as you've been instructed!' Shouted Spatts.

I rolled onto my front, splayed my legs and shuffled myself comfortable between the two ammo pouches on my belt. I made a bipod with my elbows and waited.

'READY!'

I cocked the weapon and tried to control my increased heart rate and breathing – *'calm down Steve, calm down,' I was telling myself.*

'Range one hundred yards, IN YOUR OWN TIME CARRY ON!'

Wow, this really was heady stuff.

I composed myself, raised the barrel, took a breath, held it and found the tip of the fore-sight in the centre of the hole in the rear sight and gently eased back the trigger.

I didn't know what to expect. That first shot was one of trepidation... CRACK! The butt of the weapon jerked in my shoulder but didn't hurt, it felt right.

First shot taken I calmed down, relaxed for a few seconds before bringing the gun back into alignment. I slowly loosed off my final four rounds.

The shots ringing out around me slowly died.

'UNLOAD!' Ordered Spatts

Safety on – mag off and into pouch – cock the weapon. A round was discharged in front of me.

Leave the discharged round on the ground; stand up keeping the weapon pointed down the range! We will pass-by and clear your weapon' ordered Spatts.

Working one from each end Staff Shaw and Sgt Batley came to each one of us to check the breech while we held the working parts back. After they'd passed we laid our weapon on the ground and replaced the discharged round back in the magazine.

All weapons checked we walked forward to the Butts.

We repeated the procedure to produce a grouping and I was very happy with my result.

Eventually we all shot and those who had been really so bad as not to have been able to zero at all had to go again.

Prior to departure we once again had our weapons checked and we formed a line to walk the hundred yard line to collect all spent cases. All done we wearily mounted the trucks and departed for Dover.

It had been a great day, most of us had had a successful shoot, a few hadn't; that's generally the case. There would be a great deal more shooting as the weeks and months went past.

Next time with our zero'd weapon we'd be shooting at distances ranging from two to six hundred yards. Personally I couldn't wait to return; I loved it.

It had been a long day and we returned after the evening meal had started. We were told to secure our weapons in our lockers, eat and return to our room to strip and clean the weapon. Each would be inspected by one of our Permanent Staff NCOs. Weapon inspection would begin at 1830; the armoury would reopen at 1900. Following a successful inspection the weapon could be reassembled and handed in.

We hurriedly ate, returned to our rooms broke down cleaned them and laid the working parts on one of our green army towels on the bed. The most difficult part to clean was the gas plug that had a 'U' shaped grove; if this was not cleaned spotlessly back to the metal, carbon would build up in the grove and in time could cause a misfire. We dealt with this by winding a bit of cotton wool round a match stick and dipping it in Brasso, this abrasive cleaning compound would remove the carbon easier than anything else.

Weapons inspection, as every other inspection we had was painstakingly meticulous; no quarter was given in these inspections and if it wasn't right you had to redo it. If time didn't allow, as this evening, because we were on a time frame for the armoury, you were given a verbal bollocking and ended up parading behind the guard. Get it right first time and all was well.

Today had been our first taste of the ranges, we had all waited in anticipation for this event, it was probably the one thing that we all looked forward to more than anything else – other than of course pay parade and leave.

We had, as the weeks went by, watched the other Courses going off to Hythe or Lydd.

There were also night shoots and night patrol exercises where the lads in the higher Courses got 'Cammed-up', donned their webbing most in 58 pattern and went off to play battle games.

One such night Course 7 had gone to Lydd for a night shoot.

Lydd range is right there on the beach, part of the reclaimed Romney Marsh. At night, at certain times of the year, the beach becomes alive with little crabs. This particular night the crabs were there and some joker thought it would be a right laugh to pick-up pockets full of the things, sneak into the rooms of the sleeping Intake troop and put crabs into the beds of those contentedly sleeping Sprogs. Of which I was one.

We had to give them credit – it was a raid carried out with no less then military timing and precision, nothing less than you would expect from men in the Royal Engineers; each room hit at exactly the same moment – with stealth!

It was like a scene out of a horror movie; they never switched on the lights, just sneaked in and placed a couple of crabs in each boy's bed… I'm sure you can imagine the scene.

We all came awake at much the same time, lads jumping out of bed shouting, even screaming, room and bedside lights came on; absolute pandemonium across the whole upper floor of the block. I'll never forget the image of lads stood there in underpants or PJs holding crabs and more crabs scuttling around on the floor, Course 7 were out in the corridor in stitches; of course they would be wouldn't they. It was bloody horrible and of course when our turn came and we were top dog we never done anything like that did we. No of course not.

Eventually things quietened down, crabs were all rounded up and either flushed down the toilets or thrown out of the windows. Sand, because they were covered in sand, had to be swept from the bed and then from the floor. I'm pretty sure I remember all my room-mates completely stripping their beds to make sure nothing was left undiscovered. Eventually we got back to bed and the lights were put out.

It was a great prank, one that of course was passed on from Course to Course.

We were now fast approaching the end of our first term. Life in room 96 was settled and running without a hitch. We all struggled with something, bulling, blancoing, or ironing, but mucking in we sorted it out between us. Gary was the only worry. Apparently his mum was still having wobbles about him being a soldier and he was at the phone nearly every night. It was sad for him; he was torn down the middle; knowing his mum was suffering so badly with him being in the army didn't allow for him to form a settled life. However coming from a relatively well-to-do family Gary was the only one of us who'd come back from our half term leave with an iron. We all said we'd buy one, but as I've already explained they were bloody expensive and neither one of us wanted to splash-the-cash. Gary had brought a steam iron back, bought for him by his parents, this meant that most of the time we had two operational irons in our room and when the issue iron wasn't in use it could be rented-out to another room for a couple of ciggies or a bar of chocolate.

We were now entering the time of full dress rehearsal for Regimental parade. Inspections of our No2s were stepped up and these took place in the evenings.

Firstly laid out on the bed would be hat, boots, belt and rifle sling; then in the second instance full dress - wearing everything but boots and hat.

At this point the shit hit the fan a few more times when a couple of lads weren't up to muster and we found ourselves fully occupied until 2100. But we were now able to take it in our stride.

We would be breaking up for our Christmas leave following Course 8 Pass-out parade on Saturday 18th December, both the 4th and the 11th would be full dress rehearsal. The Parade on the 11th would also follow the full inspection routine that would be carried out on the actual day. Although it was only Course 8 that came under the scrutiny of the inspecting Officer we all had to remain at attention while he wandered down the ranks stopping every so often to pass a comment with one of the lads moving on to adult service. It was December and bloody freezing.

Our one consolation was that as Intake troop we would not be parading with weapons. That would happen for the first time in April 1972 at the end of our second term.

We were informed that if we wished, we could have an end of Course 'Troop Jolly'. Two coaches would take us for an evening in London. We'd be dropped off around theatre land Regent Street and have some time to ourselves before meeting to see a show. As I recall, both the show and the transport would be paid for out of Squadron funds. We had to provide our own spending money.

We were all up for this, or at least the majority were. Many of us applied for a fiver from our banked funds, no-way would we have enough money from our meagre weekly allowance.

It was a great evening out. We were dropped by the coaches outside the London Palladium where at 1900 we were to return to see a variety of top 1971 performers star in... wait for it... 'Cinderella'... who's idea was that? A bunch of prospective finely tuned apprentice military warrior's queuing to get in to see Cinderella.

Anyway it had Clodagh Rodgers in it; a stunning female pop singer of the time so that may have been the reason... it certainly wasn't because of Ronnie Corbett or Ronnie Barker who also starred. A good time was had by us all, most of us found our way into pubs and if we didn't get served due to being under

age we went on till we found a pub who would serve us. I don't remember if anyone failed to turn up for the show, I'm sure a few preferred to stay in the pub rather than turn out for the top class entertainment on offer at the Pali; but we all made the coach home, there was no one left behind. Now anyone from my Intake reading this may ask, 'how do you remember all this shit Steve?' Well the answer is. I still have the show program. Along with my end of Course reports, B3, B2 Combat Engineering notes and all my notes from my B3 Signal operators

Course I have the 1971 London Palladium Christmas Panto program. Sad but true.

With a week to go Kevin Perry and our other JNCOs got us on the Landing to give us the low-down on what happens over the last couple of days leading up to Pass-out and Christmas leave...

'Well lads, a week to go and you'll no longer be Intake troop, how do you all feel about that?'

'Yeahhh!' We shouted.

Kevin was grinning.

'I would just like to say, and I know I'm talking for all your Room-jacks now - you've been a very good Course. It's not been easy for you guys, the number of you, which surprisingly hasn't dropped much, has made your training far more complicated and intense, it could have slowed you down or held you back but it hasn't. As we've told you before, most Courses are only half the size of this one. So you've done well. Before I give you the next news I'll warn you... anyone who shouts Hurray will spend the next week behind the guard - *pause for effect...* I will remove my red cravat and stripes next term as I'm in Course 8; I will not be your Troop Junior Sergeant. That miserable task will be taken over by Corporal Hill who comes back with his third stripe, well done Martin. *That didn't please me, he was a keen shit who didn't hesitate in handing out crap and for no particular reason I'd had more than my fair share of it.* Smudge and Mick will remain on the lines and I know you'll have another Junior Lance Jack, Gerry Chambers. Some of you may know him. He'll possibly be taking over your room Flanagan,' he said looking at Chris. There will be a couple of other new Room-jacks but which rooms they're allocated too as yet I don't know.

Next Saturday, we will act as we normally do for Regimental parade, we'll get up, eat, clean the lines, get changed and carry out the Parade. We'll return, get changed into our civi's, lock our gear away and providing our rooms are left tidy report to the Chiefs office to be given train warrant and money order. You will then mount the bus or truck to be taken to Dover Priory station. Any questions?'

There were no questions.

'Now I think a rousing three cheers is in order for the guys who've looked after you so kindly for the last thirteen weeks.' (Another big grin).

Mog Fawsett from Martin Hills room stepped forward.

'Three cheers for our JNCOs - Hip hip! HURRAY! Hip hip! HURRAY! Hip hip! HURRAY!'

All smiles we retreated to our rooms.

Over the next couple of days we were asked to which city we wanted our train warrants made out to and informed that we would receive our accumulated wages in the form of a crossed postal order, this meant it was only cashable by the person named on the order. I had my warrant made out for Bath Spa; I would stay with my gran until the Wednesday and head home buying a ticket from Liverpool Street to Great Yarmouth return from my own money. Here I made a mistake I should have done it the other way round as I found out, the price of a return from Paddington to Bath was £4.75 and the return from Liverpool Street to Great Yarmouth was £5.50... you could buy a great deal with 75p in 1971.

Saturday morning the 18th arrived very cold and crisp; Pass-out day. The whole Squadron was awake early; in civi's we were down to breakfast as soon as the doors opened. Then it was upstairs and into our cleaning chores, these had to be done regardless of the coming break, the block had to be left spotless.

Meanwhile for the other Courses they had the additional aggravation of having to go and draw a weapon.

We scrubbed and polished, all of us in a good humour. Then it was time to change into our gleaming and I really mean gleaming, No2s. We were called out on Parade; carefully we made our way with the rest of the Squadron into the quad; this would be the last time we would parade as Intake troop. We sized-off and waited for our next command.

Other troops were preparing around us and we could hear the scrape of metal studs on tarmac from those wearing personally purchased ammo boots. I knew that sometime during the next Course our Troop Sergeant would inform us that if we so wished we could buy our own ammo boots and 58 pattern webbing. I couldn't wait.

From 'A' Squadron quadrangle we would march behind Course 7 in descending order. Course 8 would bring up the rear.

On the road fronting the trade training wing we would line up in our three Squadrons. 'C' would march on first followed by 'B' and 'A'.

The last three troops would be the three Course 8s they would march on together; 'C' halting in front of 'C' Squadron, 'B' in front of 'B' and of course 'A' in front of 'A'.

They would be marched on together orders being given by the Junior Sergeants in charge of each troop. When in position, the Regiment as a whole would be brought to attention by the outstanding Junior Solider of the term; the Junior Regimental Sergeant Major.

Commands for this parade were given by either him or his Junior Squadron Sergeant Majors or the Troop Junior Sergeants. Permanent Staff played no part.

That morning it was bitterly cold. Although we were issued gloves we were not allowed to wear them and we shivered in our thin jackets with just a cotton shirt beneath. The sensible among us had added a bottom layer of clothing – vest cellular and johns long, yes long-johns white underwear that came down to the ankles, with buttons up the back so you can crap without pulling them down. These where the days before thermals and fleeces, but the 'LJs' really did keep you warm; in a couple of years' time on winter exercises in Germany I wouldn't have been without them.

Our instructors had given us a tip to avoid fainting while standing for any length of time at attention; lean forward gently taking the weight on the balls of your feet. Also tension and release the muscles in your calves; this action helps to prevent the blood from pooling in your lower limbs which of course is the reason for going into a faint.

There were too many of us to parade in open order in the quad, Courses 7 and 8 stood on the road as Troop Officers walked through their lines of men making sure all were presentable. Then we were off.

Course 7 leading the way; brought to attention first – right turn - quick march; around the perimeter road past the QM stores toward the trade wing.

Following 7 came 4,5,6, as one troop, then 3, 2, and bringing up the rear - our Intake troop. As we marched in troops passed the road leading behind our block down to 'B' Sqn, their troops were also filtering in, two thirds of the Regiment on the march, it looked pretty impressive.

Over to the left of us the West Square was being used as a visitor's car park, families and friends of the Course 8 lads who would be parading for the last time as boy soldiers. They would have two weeks leave and report to 3 Training Regiment Royal Engineers at Southwood Camp, Farnbourgh to finish off six weeks Combat Engineering on subjects that couldn't be taught at Dover.

Outside the trade wing on the expanse of tarmac we waited - three Squadrons freezing to death.

Eventually, we, Intake troop 'A' Squadron, were marched on, the last troop before the three Course 8's took up position.

We stood to attention, we stood at ease, we stood to attention again and again stood at ease; we marched past the saluting dais in extended line – 'Eyes Right', we done everything but jump through a hoop. I was glad when we were moving at least it got the blood flowing, God it was cold.

Eventually we marched off.

We got back in the block; we were literally blue with teeth chattering.

I made up my mind there and then that the only Pass-out I'd ever do again at Dover would be my own. There would probably another four or five Pass-out before my own but somehow I would wangle my way out of them. As Baldrick would say 'a cunning plan' was needed.

Smudge had gone straight to the armoury. His Course had been one of the first to leave the square and with luck he'd be near the front of the queue.

We started to get changed.

I was going to travel back to Bath with Smudge so I was in no rush. Eventually, changed and with bags packed we went to draw our warrant and pay.

The shuttle buses and trucks were going rapidly backwards and forwards to the station and the platform was full for every train; the ticket office swapped our warrant for a ticket and we mounted the half hourly train to Waterloo. On the busy London mainline station us Freds were soon swallowed in the crowd. Smudge and I took the underground to Paddington and walked across to platform two. The train to Bristol Temple Meads; stopping at Reading, Swindon, Chippenham and Bath Spa.

There were other junior soldiers on the platform they stood out a mile with short hair and army suitcases; but none we recognised – maybe from 'B' or 'C' Squadrons or other Regiments.

I couldn't see Taddy or Gerry; no doubt because I waited for Smudge they were a couple of trains ahead of us out of Dover.

Smudge and I went across to the station buffet for a drink while we waited for the next departure, we didn't need to wait long the trains to the West Country ran pretty regularly, almost two an hour.

The train came in, the carriages were open and we boarded. In no time at all we were both clambering out at Bath. It had been a good journey down; Smudge and I had sat and chatted about my first term and what we could expect after Christmas. This past term for him had been Course 7, his B3 Combat Engineering Course; it had been a full-on term for him and the gang of us had watched as he had studied in the evenings for his B3 exams and trained with others in seven for the annual British Legion March and Shoot competition a gruelling test of endurance and shooting skill; he would be returning for two six week half-Courses in trade; driver for six weeks and then signaller for six weeks a double dose of Course 5T before going into Course 8 after Easter.

'You'll find it very different next term Steve,' Smudge informed me.

'You'll drop a day of education, you'll only be going Tuesday and Thursday mornings; you'll also be doing SMG and LMG in the second half of the Course so you can expect a great deal of weapons training.'

'Well,' I said 'I'm glad you're remaining our Room-jack for another term. I suppose we're pretty lucky that most of our Junior NCOs are staying.'

'You're in the swing of it now mate, unless you're foolish, life should be settled, you've all got the measure of your kit and what's expected on a daily basis. If you like it now you'll continue to like it, it only gets more interesting and more fun. Also you'll find responsibility comes your way.'

Our room had been extremely lucky to have had Smudge as our Room-jack, he'd been fair with us and a great mentor, he'd been patient and very helpful and even now on the train down to Bath he was telling me about Course 7 and what his troop had done over the last thirteen weeks, mine-warfare, demolitions, bridging. He'd kept our room entertained throughout the last term on his daily routine but not in depth, now with just the two of us together he gave me a far bigger picture. This kind of conversation and what we were going to get up to on leave occupied us and in no time we were getting off the train in Bath, me to board the 264 across the road in the bus station, where a sign of the times told me to 'tender exact fare and state destination' for the short trip to my old home, Winsley; while Smudge waited for his connecting train to Westbury. We shook hands and I left him on the platform.

I spent a great few days in my old village catching up with my mates, sitting talking to Gran, my auntie Dot and uncle Bert Blackmore. I visited my auntie Dart and uncle Bert Smith in Farleigh Wick who was delighted to hear my Sapper stories and choice of trade; he'd been a Royal Engineer plant-op during WW2 and fought in the campaigns across North Africa and up through Italy.

I took a trip to North Bradley to see more old friends in the village where we had lived for the final year prior to our family departure to Norfolk. Also I met with my old flame Clare a couple times in Trowbridge.

I hoped I may get a shag but we had nowhere to go. We gave it a go in the bandstand in Trowbridge Park but after being disturbed by numerous others and Clare telling me her last bus was at 9.50 (that's at night not morning) I felt like I was qualifying for some event and with the cold it all went to pot. Oh and I remember her tights were a problem... Let's move on...

But time was short and the weather was very cold. Our normal pastime of sitting in the bus shelter drinking coke and eating crisps was a summer occupation not something to do in the winter. We weren't old enough just yet to pass scrutiny in the pub; so I sat round at Jeff's with him and his brother Bernard or over the road with Kevin and Angela Holt. Angela had been my girlfriend right through junior school, we'd gone to different secondary schools but were still close friends; she'd written to me a few times during my three months at Dover and it was nice to be able to recite my escapades in person.

I was also proud of what I'd achieved and felt chuffed with the interest shown by my friends as well as their parents. I'd had a bit of a reputation in Winsley as being unruly and been in trouble with the local Copper on quite a few occasions; I'm sure there were more than a few ex-neighbours in both villages who were waiting to see if I could go the distance with the army, would I sink or swim? To-date I'd proved I could swim.

However by the time I left I'd got pretty fed up with reciting the same story, 'my life to date at Dover'.

On the Wednesday I gave Gran a Christmas present and card and departed to Norfolk. I was sad to leave her on her own and had tried to persuade her to come up to Norfolk and have Christmas with the family. I could have brought her back down as far as London and put her on the train at Paddington before returning to Dover. It would have been easy and stress free for her to just get off at Bath. She'd been on the train to Swindon many times. But it wasn't the journey.

She told me that mum and dad had already suggested Christmas in Norfolk but she would not put her vicious little Jack-Russel 'Trixie' in the kennel. It would be another three or four years before the dog died and gran made the journey to East Anglia.

Alone I boarded the Intercity 125 for Paddington.

Dad picked me up at Yarmouth station and twenty minutes later we were home. This leave I'd be in Norfolk for another 17 days; we had to be back for parade on Tuesday January 11th 1972.

The following day I went into Yarmouth with my parents in the car, I'd given mum some money for 'My keep' during my time at home, around ten pounds; this believe it or not was money for food and lodgings. I doubt very much if parents do this anymore – take lodging money from their kids, but it was quite the expected way to act in the decades leading up to the eighties.

After settling up with mum I still had quite a large pot left over from my savings during the term. I'd spent some in Wiltshire; I bought Christmas presents for my brother and parents but had no intention of splashing out with my left-over cash. I wanted to take money back to Dover; I knew this term we'd be given the go-ahead to buy our own 58 pattern webbing and ammo-boots. I wanted to have that money to hand for when the time came.

Anyway there really wasn't much to spend my money on. We lived in the middle of nowhere. I had no mates in Norfolk and so the only way to occupy my time was either helping mum and dad in the chicken sheds or going boat fishing on Ormesby Broad; a pretty inexpensive pass time.

We had a lovely Christmas and Boxing Day and the time drifted through to New Year. Things had changed in our house. The constant bickering between my father and me and the major arguments had stopped; the feeling of conflict that had surrounded us during the last eighteen months or two years before my departure was no longer hanging in the air and disrupting the family home. I'd changed and possibly my dad had also changed. I was no longer the disgruntled teenager. The army had given me direction and purpose. I had also learnt how to compromise; sharing a room with five others was a lesson in being a more rounded person, sharing, working together and being more tolerant of others.

Mum and dad gave me a Ronson comet Vari-flame cigarette lighter for Christmas; gas refillable, in blue with... get this – a guarantee it would light in storm force winds. Wow! My smoking at home had been accepted.

Before I knew it, it was Monday and time to return to Dover.

Course 2 January 1972

This was the year that President Idi Amin expelled 80,000 Asians from Uganda, Margaret the Second became Queen of Denmark and Richard Nixon was re-elected as President of the United States. In the world of music, it was a good year for the Osmond brothers with Donny spending 5 weeks at number one with 'Puppy Love' and Jimmy also topping the chart for 5 weeks with the Christmas hit 'Long Haired Lover from Liverpool'. Quality music year then...

Once again trucks and buses were waiting to greet the trains into Dover Priory.

A group of us clambered aboard. Some lads knew each other and were chattering away while I sat in reflective silence as the bus made its way up London Road and Whitfield Hill; I knew none of the lads with me on the bus.

Looking out the window to the right I could see the line of the footpath running round the steep slope that was our cross-country track. Such hard work four months ago, most of us could now take it in our stride. Our fitness levels had gone through the roof.

We got off the bus at the Guard-room; and in no time I'd dumped my gear in my bed space and headed downstairs to tea. (Tea being dinner as it is now commonly referred to). Looking around the room it seemed both Ray and Gary had returned. Those two would be downstairs; the others had not yet got in.

With my food from the hot plate I joined my mates at the table. They looked very sober.

'Fuck sake, who's died'? I said sitting down.

'No one – it's mum', said Gary. 'She's bloody worse than ever; I thought she'd have got over me being down here by now but no.

She was a nightmare this morning when I left. She was ok until after New Year then she started the 'oh why must you go back, I don't want my son being a soldier, carry-on; and I've had that for the last week. To be honest I'm bloody glad to be back.'

'Well I'm glad you're back,' I said. 'Did you bring your Crombie?'

Gary looked at me. 'Thanks mate – all you're worried about is borrowing my bloody coat. Not a care for my personnel trauma.'

'Cheor up hinny it ma nivvor happen,' consoled Ray. (Translated from Geordie this means cheer up mate it may never happen).

'Ray, I've lived in the same bloody room as you for nearly four months and there are still times I can't understand a word you're on about,' this from Gary. We both burst out laughing. Which put Ray into a mumbling sulk causing us to laugh even harder.

At this point Doddy and Les turned up and joined us.

'What's up with you two then?' Enquired Les...

'It's Ray, he's still struggling with his English,' I said.

'Bloody hell weor deeyuhn alreet till yee coined up Burtie, it wes aal peaceful leek.' (Bloody hell we were doing alright till you turned up Burtie, it was all peaceful like).

Ray was getting his own back; he knew I hated being called Burtie.

'It's my mum again,' said Gary despondently; he was now looking for mass sympathy.

'She still carrying on? God surely she can't still be having that breakdown, it's been four bloody months.'

This was a typical foot-in-the-mouth statement from Les.

'You're back in Dover now mate, room ninety six, among ur muckers, put mummy out of your head, press on into Course two, it'll all be ok in the end. She'll come round you'll see.'

The indefatigable Dixon... But Les would be wildly wrong in this positive prediction.

The subject was changed and we sat for ages discussing what we'd done on leave, who'd got a shag and as in my case who hadn't.

Back upstairs the chatter continued, other than Smudge and Steve it was full house. The lines were filling up; the shouting and exchange of stories vibrated around lines while lads unpacked and others prepared for the following mornings parade.

'Orders... anyone read orders?' I enquired.

No one had. Once again we traipsed downstairs to the office area to read Regimental and Squadron orders. They were brief; parade 0830 in works dress.

New intake would be joining the Squadron on Thursday. They would be going through the same thirteen weeks of shite we'd been through. They would occupy the line on the second floor below our room. Our Course due to its size would remain in the same lines until the end of Course 3. We needed all the space available on the upper floor and the bridge lines.

We returned upstairs put some music on in the room and started preparing our kit for the following morning. Smudge and Steve returned and once again we were a full complement.

The following morning we picked up where we left-off. The chores we'd been allocated before Christmas break were the chores we carried out that first morning back.

Our J/Sgt from the previous term, Kev Perry was now in Course 8 and he had been replaced on our side of the lines by the newly promoted J/Sgt Martin Hill. Hill had been an ultra-keen room NCO, we expected him to be a bit of a pain this coming term. However we were now Course 2, surely we'd get it a little easier. We were wrong.

On parade Tuesday morning we were greeted by our Permanent Staff NCOs and our Troop Officer; who continued on with us from the previous term. They would remain with us until we finished Course 3; in short they would be with us for a year. I'm pretty certain we were all glad of that, we had come to know our NCOs and our Troopy; we knew what they expected of us, their idiosyncrasy's, what they looked for on inspections, and how far we could go with them having a laugh and a joke. They were in truth a decent bunch and we had a great deal to thank them for.

Our time table had been arranged. Apart from education Tuesday and Thursday morning we would be learning, and continually practicing – parade drills, patrol, field craft and section weapons. Many hours would be spent on the ranges and in the countryside surrounding Dover; Mereworth Woods and what was called the East Kent dry training area. Why 'dry' heaven only knows I can remember plenty of times both night and day when it was pissing-down with rain.

Our first day back there was no education, the day was spent bringing us back up to speed on the parade ground and a couple of times round the cross country track.

We never had a long working day; it was around seven hours when in the barracks. However we done plenty of out-of-hours stuff; if we were out doing night patrols or night shooting and got to bed at 2am we would still be up at the same time in the morning going through our set routines; so I suppose it balanced out in the end.

Also we never had the Easter or Whitsun bank holiday break. It wouldn't fit with our training routine. It was no good going home for Easter only to return for two weeks prior to our two week leave.

We had set terms and a certain schedule had to be fitted into those weeks. For instance the Easter of 1972 fell on the 31st March - 3rd April; this was only just twelve weeks into the term, eleven for the new intake who only joined us on January 13th. The full term schedule would not be fitted into a reduced time span and of course the training that was required during those weeks of term depended on what Course and subjects you were taking. Combat Engineering time allocation was set more or less in stone.

This term we would break up following Course 8 passing out parade on the 16th April returning on the 8th for work on the Tuesday 9th May.

That evening we were called onto the Landing to have a pep-talk from our new Junior Sergeant. You would think that having been with us the previous term and knowing us all by name he would be at least a little bit friendly within the confines of his rank; but no he was sharp and ruthless. Reading the riot act and warning us of what we could expect if we didn't measure up to his expectations, which he told us would be higher than Kev Perry's.

'Right, the lot of you on the floor – twenty press-ups. GO!'

This was going to set the scene for the next fourteen weeks... a long term! Come back Kev, all is forgiven.

We prepared our works kit for the following morning; at least we weren't starting education until Thursday.

The previous term we'd tackled foot drill and briefly, stationary rifle drill; this coming term we would continue with more advanced rifle drill movements, both standing in rank and on the march.

We would also start to drill with the SMG the small submachine gun with the metal folding Butt. This weapon and the LMG, the bipod mounted section light machine gun, would occupy a great deal of our time this coming Course.

It was within the first few days of our return we drew from the armoury an SMG with a magazine.

We were keen to get our hands on another piece of lethal hardware and this weapon fired on automatic with thirty round magazine. This would be great fun.

This was not an allocated weapon in the same way as our SLR. We never had a specific weapon number and zeroing never took place as with our personal rifle. This weapon was for close quarter - more of a point, pull the trigger and hose-em-down, rather than aim weapon.

However the routine with the SMG was similar to that of the SLR; we had to learn how to handle it, it's safety features – which I might add were pretty rudimentary with this weapon as I'll explain. We had to go through the stripping cleaning and re-assembly process over and over again just as we'd done with the SLR.

The weapon was lethal… well I can hear you say, it probably is… it's a gun that fires on automatic with thirty rounds in the magazine - of course its lethal.

Well I don't necessarily mean against 'foe'; it was a lethal bit of kit even for the squaddie clutching it in his grubby paw… Let me explain.

This gun is basic in the extreme. You could probably make one in your garden shed; it consists of about five main parts all held in place by an end cap. Press down and twist the end cap and the whole bloody thing flies apart. The cap, a long spring, the breach mechanism and the cocking lever and that's pretty much it. It has a thirty round curved magazine and a metal butt that folds closed onto the stock. When collapsed the weapon measures a meagre 18" at the most. It has a killing range of less than 100 yards and a yard or so over this range you could probably catch the bullet in your hand and throw it back. It was designed for close combat, city or street fighting and house clearance, and used in this capacity it was perfect.

Spatts, our illustrious weapons instructor took great pleasure in explaining how he'd cleared houses full of terrorists in far-flung corners of the Empire; with butt collapsed and the weapon's body pressed against his belt buckle; he explained how he'd go from room to room jumping through the door frame, legs spread, crouched forward, blasting five round bursts into anything or anybody getting in the way. 'Yeah'! We said, 'bring it on'!

So, what's dangerous about the weapon then?

It's the way the weapon is armed. Unlike the SLR where the working parts are forward, the SMG has to have the working parts held to the back of the breach chamber when in the 'Ready' mode.

In the load position the magazine is taken from your pouch and pushed into the recess on the left side of the gun - after first checking the safety is on.

When you get the ready command you pull back on the cocking lever on the right hand side, the breach is dragged back until it clicks in place and there it's supposed to stay.

If the weapon mechanism is in good condition this is where the working parts remain until you want to shoot, whereupon you flick off the safety with your thumb to either auto or single shot, pull the trigger and the working parts are released, flying forward and collecting the round from the magazine on the way. Round goes into the barrel and firing pin strikes the percussion cap, BANG! - Hey-presto it's a hit or miss. Breach block comes back and if you've released the trigger that's where it stays – if you haven't well it just keeps on firing.

However that is best case scenario, there are a few other factors that can upset the apple cart with this little beast.

Wet hands – you lose grip on the cocking lever before its clicked home, breach flies' forward and BANG. Round is discharged.

Worn safety mechanism – block is retained and safety is on but a reflex pull on the trigger the safety malfunctions and BANG again. Also, and finally, if the weapon is either dropped or banged against something in the 'cocked' position; this is also likely to send the working parts forward.

So you can see why I call it a vicious little beast and one that has to be handled with a bit of care. They were also prone to trigger malfunction which happened to Steve Cottle one day while on the range at Lydd.

We were moving down the range in extended line while the targets were spun for a few seconds toward us and then turned back, thin-edge on.

Each time the target was face-on we had to fire a 3-5 round burst. We had to do this in a number of way's – aiming with the butt in the shoulder while walking; stopping going into the kneel and aiming, then standing and continuing forward and also walking forward with the butt folded and the body of the weapon against the stomach or belt as I've already explained, in effect aiming by eye – line of sight. We would advance from around sixty yards right up to within ten yards of the target, clear the weapon, go back and do it all again.

Firing on automatic required concentration because as you pull the trigger the weapon will creep upward, it needs a conscious effort to hold the barrel down and a 3-5 round burst is a good way of controlling this.

Steve pulled the trigger for a three round burst, released his finger but the weapon just kept firing; the trigger mechanism had failed, snapped or jammed. He loosed off a complete magazine of thirty rounds and in the heat of the moment, in shock, turned round to look at either Spatts or Spriggsy and in so doing sprayed the air and trees above our heads. It was a bloody good job he wasn't holding the barrel tightly, the rounds went upward on their own accord. We all hit the deck and Steve got a week behind the guard. Good job he didn't kill one or more of us he'd have got two weeks.

What a gas though eh!? I'm still three months off my sixteenth birthday and this is the stuff I'm doing on a daily basis!

We were a few weeks into the term when Gary was called to the office. He returned absolutely gutted.

His mother's GP (doctor) had written to the army explaining that her son being in the military was having a severe impact on her health. That the four plus months he had been away serving had not changed whatever problem she was suffering with. That it was strongly recommended that the army release Gary regardless of his own wishes. This had been brewing for some time – well almost since day one. Gary had desperately hoped that his being home at Christmas and his mum seeing how well and happy he was would change her opinion and get her out of the depression or whatever it was she was in.

But it hadn't, and following the completion of some formalities, paperwork etc. he would be discharged.

We were all thunderstruck and as sad about it as he was. We were a very close-nit room. Since Gerald's departure the following term we had worked together well as a team and we were all great mates. We would be sorry to see Gary go.

We all had an evening out in Dover, walked into town, went to the flix and then for a coffee in our regular coffee bar, we all had a bit more money; the previous term we'd been on a shoestring with our one or two pound per-week. Wisely we'd all saved some of our bulk payment from the previous term and used that to subsidise our weekly income.

As we sat chatting around the table in the coffee bar a bunch of girls came in. They were the usual crowd we'd see hanging out around town. They'd cat-call and whistle but weren't really interested in us Junior

Leaders. Normally they just sat at a table and kept themselves to themselves.

However this particular evening I couldn't help noticing the one blonde lass that I'd seen a few times the previous term, the girl that not only had the foreign features but stood out from the others with her looks; she looked very much like (for those who remember her) a very young Diana Dors. I kept meeting her eye and even got a smile which prompted a few elbows-in-ribs at both their table and mine.

'She giving you the eye mate, you're in there,' said Les.

'Rubbish,' I replied...

'Hey Pet do yee fancy me mate? He buy yee a cup of coffee frea shag.' Ray called across the Café.

'Ray for fuck sake! What are up to'...?

Fortunately his enthusiastically shouted offer came out in Geordie and no one could understand a word.

The girls burst out laughing.

'Are you English,' one called across.

'We are,' Les replied. 'We're not sure about him though', he said pointing at Ray. 'However we apologise for his lack of manners.'

This was said with tongue-in-cheek; they don't do apologies in Manchester's Moss Side.

'Should think so - they might call their women 'Pet' up north but down here we keep that for the cat or dog, he needs some training your mate. *(Pause)*Are you JLs?'

'No.' This came from Gary and I suppose in his case it was true.

'What are you then? Only Junior Leaders look like that.'

They were all in stitches at this remark.

'What'd ya mean – look like that?' Said Les indignantly. 'What 'look' do we have exactly?'

'Where'd you want us to start - thin, starved, miserable, odd... Oh! an broke... take ur pick love, all you JLs look the same.'

'Odd? Odd? Cheeky cow.' Les was getting on his high horse, but the rest of were laughing now.

'We were gunna offer you all a coffee, but...' Les never got time to finish before he was interrupted.

'But that would have used all your spending money for a week,' this from another one of the girls, 'you best keep the money for yur boot polish boys!'

We were all laughing together... as we got up to go the girls got up at the same time and we walked out together.

'You're right,' I said on the pavement, 'we are JLs, odd and broke; seeya.'

'Take care boys, sure you'll get home all right?' They shouted laughing as they headed left for the prom and we turned right up the London road.

In a group we made our way back to Old Park.

'God,' said Doddy, we'll never get a girl in this God-forsaken town. We're odd – odd; I've never been called odd in my life, is this what the bloody army does for you? Makes you celibate and odd.'

'Well you should be bloody celibate ur only fifteen years old,' said Steve.

'Well mate you may be a virgin but I'm not; I was getting my rocks off before I came to Dover. If you ain't had a shag yet you wanna get going.' Came from Les.

'Well what of fifteen... shagging at fifteen is legal isn't it?'

'No it's bloody not, it's sixteen in this country,' I stated.

'Fifteen for boys then?'

'No of course not, it's sixteen for boys and girls. I'll tell you, that's a fact, I'm well aware of what the age is.'

'Oh yeah of course, Sam told him thirty seconds before she shagged him,' said Steve looking round at the others.

'Oh yes the voluptuous Sam – of course, you would know wouldn't you mate. The oracle on all things about sex...'

They were of course referring to Sam the farmer's wife in North Bradley who regularly had her wicked (but very nice) way with me while I delivered the early morning papers through the village a year before. I was only fourteen at the time. But it didn't bother her and it certainly didn't bother me... It might of course have bothered her husband if he'd known. But there you go; what the eye doesn't see as they say.

This was how the banter went on as we walked up the hill. Collectively we wondered if we'd ever get a girlfriend.

We booked in and went to our room.

The last thing that was said before we went to sleep came from Ray. 'Tha blonde lass fancies yee, yeenaa Steve, yee want te try ya luck there ye knaa.'

I went to sleep wondering if he was right.

Gary's Parents picked him up on the Saturday. We all said goodbye before we went off on Regimental parade.

We swapped address and promised to keep in touch. We did for a while but no kid of fifteen wants to write letters and for Gary a new life outside of the army was about to begin. We heard he had got himself an apprenticeship and his mum had made a miraculous recovery.

When we returned from parade we found his bed space was empty, kit handed in and gone; on my bed I found Gary's Crombie with a note.

I'm leaving this for you Steve, I know how much you like it. If anyone else wants to borrow it from the room lend it to them. All the best Gaz. P.S my parents will go ape-shit when they find out.

What a great gesture, I was chuffed to rocks. No one from the room would borrow it they were all much shorter than me or Gary, except perhaps Doddy, but he was your hippy Afghan coat type of guy, you wouldn't see Doddy in a Crombie. He also left his iron – good on him!

We started drilling with the SMG. This is an odd little weapon to drill with but it goes without saying that some minor drill movements were needed for when we were required to parade and march with the weapon. It wasn't used for ceremonial parades but for standard everyday uniformity... Standing to attention, at ease or how and where to hold the weapon when marching as a squad.

January and February, even March are bloody cold months even in the garden county of Kent. Our green army jumpers, wool for the use of, were no match for the biting winds coming in off the Channel and hurling their freezing way north across the middle of the West Square in Old Park Barracks.

We stood and shivered, in some cases so violently that we almost dropped the weapon. Our Drill Sergeant seemed impervious to the cold. Dressed the same as us, no coat, just a woolly-pulley, wearing his peaked No2 dress hat; he would take us through our drills completely oblivious of the rain or snow latching down.

On occasion we would retire to the drill shed at the end of the square where it was at least a quarter of a degree warmer and out of the wind and rain.

This was the time I caught the flu and caught it big time.

I awoke one morning feeling rough; I got up and went through the normal routine but I was poorly and by the time we were ready to parade I was really ill.

'Blimey,' said Smudge. 'You need to grab your small kit and join sick parade mate you really are in no fit state to work.'

And I wasn't, I was very poorly.

I packed my small-pack; PJs, book, slippers, washing kit and went downstairs; I could barely stand.

I joined the line of SLLs (sick, lame and lazy) and waited for the most senior of the group to be authorised to march us, yes march us to the M.R.S.

I remember only just getting there; on arrival I almost collapsed into the waiting area.

I saw the Quack as we called the doctor; he took my temperature which was sky high and I was admitted. I was in the M.R.S for almost ten days, the first three days I was barely conscious; I was running a hell of a fever. Slowly I got better and took advantage of the time to relax, I suppose to some extent I played it up a bit and gained a couple of extra days.

As I recall there were two wards on the upper level of the building. One ward held four or five beds; this was the isolation ward, the ward to put lads who were contagious.

The other ward held around sixteen beds and they were occupied by ailments or injuries that were not catching.

I spent four days in the small ward before moving across. I don't remember there being any TV or radio on the wards.

As we recovered we were expected to help out with chores such as dishing out the meals and collecting the plates following meals to be returned to the main cookhouse.

The M.R.S was a leveller with regard to rank and status.

Within the Squadrons the Junior NCOs stuck together and each Course would mix and socialise within their own Course. It was rare to talk to or mix with any lads in a higher and lower Course. In the M.R.S however we were all in it together so to speak and we all chatted played draughts or other board games without any hierarchy and talking to the more experienced lads I picked up some good do's and don'ts.

On Saturday morning we all watched out of the end window as the three Squadrons marched round to the East Square for Regimental parade; as we stood watching a Course 8 lad in the bed next to me told me he was passing out this coming end of term. He said he this was only the second passing out parade he'd done while at Dover; he'd missed all the rest.

'How did you pull that one off,' I asked, and he told me.

'This is a tip you wanna keep to yourself Steve,' he whispered while checking there was no one in ear-shot.

'Achilles heel, strained Achilles. As long as you go sick knowing the right symptoms they'll have no option other than to give you light duties for a week. Ok so you'll have to do the parades leading up to the last week of term but you'll get off the last dress rehearsal and instead of doing the Pass-out on the last morning you'll be in your room packing yur kit to go home.

We'd heard very early on during Intake how different methods were employed to get a few days or longer on light duties. Tapping your wrist with a spoon for twenty minutes will cause your wrist to swell up for a short period – long enough to pass-off a wrist injury in front of the Quack.

Soaking pieces of cotton wool in TCP, (trichlorophenylmethyliodosalicyl – try saying that after a couple of pints! No wonder it's abbreviated to TCP) and binding them tightly to the soft skin of your inner arm will cause a burn like blotch to the skin. A couple of blobs and it looks like any number of skin problems. Probably the harshest and most painful stunt to pull for light-duties was breaking your own finger, or getting your mate to do it, and believe it or not this was quite a common event. A lad would lay his finger over the bed-end and a mate would then whack it with a broom handle. Bingo! One broken finger, two weeks light duties. Everyone had something they wanted to avoid and these numerous self-inflicted injuries were the way to do it.

Anyway the secret of the Achilles heel was passed down to me and at the end of term I limbed my way to the M.R.S complaining of excruciating pain running up the back of my leg. Every time the Doc flexed my foot I would scream in agony.

'Well Burt, this looks very much like a strained Achilles. I'm afraid you'll not be able to march for at least a week. As its end of term next week I'll sign you off for the rest of this Course. Take it easy, no marching or running activities is that understood?

'Gosh Sir, is it really that bad? I so desperately wanted to take part in the Passing-out parade, oh, shucks my disappointment is overwhelming.'

I took part in two passing out parades at Dover, Course 1 and my own in Course 8. I seemed to have this reoccurring Achilles problem that manifested itself a week before the end of every term.

However I would like to say in my defence that I never used this excuse at any other time and never again after leaving Dover.

My flu cured I was discharged back to my Squadron and life resumed.

Gary had departed and our room was somewhat bare. We were now five in number and we had plenty of room to spread out. However other rooms, the big-end room especially was pretty full; they hadn't lost anyone and remained in the same numbers as from day one.

Smudge told us Martin Hill wanted to move someone out of the big-end room into our room.

This was brought up at one of our Landing meetings.

'I want someone to leave the big-end room and go into room ninety-six.' Sgt Hill announced one evening.

We five kept our fingers tightly crossed that there would be no volunteer.

There was silence...

'So, no one is prepared to volunteer eh? Well I'll just go on and pick someone then.'

He looked over to the left side of the Landing; this was where the big-end group tended to stand.

'Anderson, you'll do. Move your kit into Cpl Smiths room for room inspection tomorrow morning. Terry Anderson looked well pissed-off and we weren't that chuffed either.

Not that Terry was a bad bloke, he was ok; he smoked, didn't scrounge and kept himself together. We all hated scroungers of which there were quite a few and a couple who drove you mad begging everything from everyone; Jago and Jackson the two dog-end vultures. They hung round together and were a right fucking pain, the pair of them. I even ended up in Course 7 with them but fortunately not in the same room.

In the end the move never happened. Terry moaned to Mick Foster his Room-jack; Mick moaned at Martin Hill. Smudge was asked for his opinion and things remained unchanged. We'd all got used to living in our respective rooms with our respective routines. If it isn't broke don't fix it. I suspect that's what Mick and Smudge said to Martin Hill.

One evening however we were given great news. Restrictions that had been imposed on us as sprogs were going to be lifted. We were going to be allowed to modify our kit.

These modifications were not openly allowed but they went on and a blind-eye was turned by our Permanent Staff and JNCOs.

Our KF shirts could be tapered, meaning taken in at the sides. These shirts were like tents; do up the buttons and put a pole under the collar and you had a pretty serviceable replacement Bivi. Trying to look smart in shirt sleeve order was almost impossible unless you were BIG in girth. We ironed in pleats, pinned down the crease and hand-sowed in the taper, job-done – perfect – should have been a seamstress. As well as tapering our shirts some sewed creases down the front of their denim work trousers, this had to be a really neat job, not a task that could be done by hand, guys either got the sewing done at home, or had the Regimental tailor do it.

The linings could disappear out of our Beret's. This would allow us to shrink the Beret and get a better shape to the head-wear.

We could cut the sleeves off one of our No2 dress shirts. This allowed them to hang better under the jacket and not pull as you marched; you could also swing your arms without restriction.

The one thing we were not allowed to do but went ahead and done it anyway was to slash the peak of our No2 dress hat. This I'll come back to and explain later on.

We were also told that if we so wished we could buy our own pair of ammo-boots and 58 pattern webbing. This was the best news ever!

Half term was fast approaching. I'd kept back twenty five pounds from my Christmas payment to buy the boots and webbing; very little of this I'd spent, I'd been given some idea by Smudge as to how much I'd pay for the kit and until I'd bought it I was reluctant to spend and leave myself short, remember there were no cards, no service tills or holes-in-the-wall. If you wanted money you went to the bank and cashed a cheque or took cash from the tin on the kitchen shelf.

We would not have a bank account until we were in Course 8.

Our little world was the world of the cash payment on a Wednesday and a military money order at the end of term.

If I turned up at the surplus store in the Strand short of cash for my kit; that was it – no kit; come back later sonny, and later meant another month and a half or two month wait.

Half term came and we headed home, it was Friday 26th February, we'd parade again Tuesday 29th; it was a leap year.

I told Smudge I was going home to Norfolk, but asked if he'd come with me to the army surplus store in London's Strand. It's hard to believe it now but just opposite Charing Cross station, near Bedford Street was an army surplus store and a very big one at that. I believe I'm correct in saying it was 'Silvermans' which today has relocated and is still going strong in the East End, the Mile End Road near the tube station.

We went in the door; there was stuff everywhere – on shelfs, hanging on hooks and in piles on the floor. I was captivated. Just as I was as a small child going with my dad to Tommy Bests the big army surplus store in Bath; I loved looking at all the different and available surplus army gear.

A chap came from the back.

'Hello lads, and what can I do for you?'

I looked at Smudge…

'Well, go on ask him,' he said. 'Don't expect me to do the talking for you; I'm just here to make sure you get the right stuff… Ok ok… first off he wants a pair of size nine ammo boots, no gashes or scratches in the heel or toe caps, full complement of studs, mate.' 'Junior Soldiers eh?'

'Yeah,' both Smudge and I replied together.

'What breed?'

'Royal Engineers, Dover,' replied Smudge again.

'Sappers eh, good lads the Sappers my old man was a Sapper in the war. Lost a leg crossing the Rhine, hates the Krauts, me mum wanted to go to the Christmas market in Cologne, had to go with me aunt, he wouldn't go, refused point bloody blank,

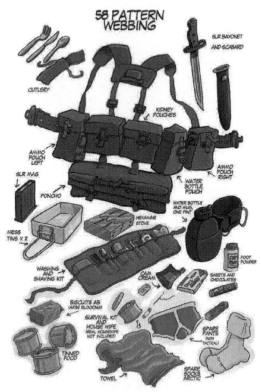

wouldn't pull one out the river if he was drowning, probably put a foot on his head and help him under. I tell him – move on dad it was twenty five years ago, but no; it's the leg you see, they still got it, he thinks it's still at the bottom of the Rhine.

He ran on for another five minutes. Neither of us wanted to interrupt him, but we had to; we both had trains to catch.

Smudge butted in.

'We need a full set of 58 pattern as well; everything; have you got a full set?

'Got the lot mate – hang on let me sort some good boots first.'

He came back a few minutes later – 'Here try these on.'

I looked them over; they were in good 'Nick' no scratches in the leather and the sole in tip-top condition.

'Just worn in son, they'll do you just fine, nice and comfortable and ready for bulling. Try em on while I get the webbing.'

Of he went again and started loading up the large counter work service.

Belt, kidney pouches, yoke, bum-role, ammo pouches, water bottle with the plastic mug, large pack. Each item he showed us was in perfect condition. All the time he was rabbitin-on.

'I'll chuck in a third ammo pouch and I strongly recommend a second bum-roll, and look lads I got the new army poncho, I bet you haven't even seen one of these.'

He unwrapped this lightweight green rectangular poncho; it was about six foot square with poppers down both sides.

'Feel the weight, light as a feather, better than those bloody ole ground sheets. They pop together to make a good sized basher. Want one?'

We were sold; mine was added to the growing pile of gear and Smudge took one as well.

'So, anything else lads?' He asked.

'Pea-green denims and Puttees if you got any? Asked Smudge.

'Two pairs of both? He said looking from one to the other of us.

Smudge looked at me. 'Not worth you getting Pea-greens Steve, you can't wear them till you've finished Course three, you can have mine when I leave Dover. May as well get a pair of Puttees you can't wear them till course 8 but at least you've got them and I'll be taking mine with me.

Eventually we were kitted out; I parted with, for all that kit a grand total of £15.00. It seems looking back, an unbelievable small price for all that stuff and yet a pound in 1971 is around thirteen pounds in 2016. That makes my purchase approximately £200.00.

Every item I'd bought was crammed into the 58 large pack, we paid up and left heading back to the tube.

'Thanks Smudge, I really appreciated your help, I'd have been a bit lost on my own.'

'That's ok mate, buy me a coffee.' You can spend all weekend working out how it goes together and don't forget when you leave Old

Park you'll be able to sell it on to some other Sprog, so you won't have lost out on anything.'

That was a fact I'd already considered; getting my money back.

We drunk a coffee in the station buffet and talked about buying our own kit. Pea-greens were a much coveted item; why, looking back on it I don't know, and why we were allowed to wear them I don't know either. Unlike the normal Khaki green uniform colour - 'Pea's' as we called them were lime green in colour – staggeringly bright on the eye and you could hardly call them military in appearance. However we considered ourselves well-cool if we owned a pair. They were hard to get hold of, much in demand and only a few lads in any Squadron had them. Puttees, a relic of the first war were in total about three foot long. We'd cut them to a third of that length so they turned around the ankle and over the top of the boot only three or four times. Smudge would help me with this when we got back to Old Park.

Coffee finished we went down to the Circle Line platforms. Here we went our separate ways Smudge west bound for Paddington and me east bound for Liverpool Street.

Arriving in Gt Yarmouth I phoned dad and waited half an hour till they came to pick me up. It was good to be home, to relax and tell my brother and parents what we'd been up to the last six weeks.

It was cold and wet, not even fishing weather so I sat indoors and burnt the pimples off my new second hand boots. I even started bulling them; it began with me showing my brother how it was done and as I saw the base layer growing I just carried on, I was quite content to sit quietly at home and do this.

I spread the webbing on the floor and put it all together. I found I also had two belts, the second rolled up and pushed in the bottom of an ammo pouch; not that a second belt was necessary, but still you never know. All said and done I was well chuffed with my acquisitions.

The weekend over and back in Dover I was the only lad from our room to have splashed out on private kit, but I could sense the jealousy among my comrades. In fact, as it turned out only a couple of us had bought our own gear, others were waiting till the end of term.

'You all have the same money as me,' I told my mates while parading around the room in my 'Rambo' attire.

'What else are you gunna spend it on, you may as well buy the webbing use it and flog it when you leave here; you'll get the money back and maybe a bit more besides.'

I got the feeling they were waiting to see how successful I'd be with my purchase and come the end of term they'd be asking me to accompany them back to the shop.

Les echoed my thoughts.

'You can take me when we break up can't you Steve?'

'Sure but you'll need to draw twenty quid in cash before you leave here then, won't you.' I told him.

'You told me that lot cost you fifteen?'

'It did Les, but it might not be fifteen the next time we go in might it? It might be sixteen or seventeen and then what'll you do? Leave a fucking ammo pouch behind or only take one bloody boot? You'd be well pissed-off if you arrived without enough money.'

'That's all right – I'll see the AO near the end of term, he'll be ok.'

'You draw the money Les and I'll come with you.'

I knew he would – Les was that kind of kid, he wanted the modern easy to use kit whereas my other room mates were contented to carry-on with the old 37 pattern webbing and their issue DMS for best boots.

58 with second bum-roll and gas mask holder on the left side.

During this second half of this term a great deal of time would be spent wearing combats and webbing, our trips to Lydd and Hythe were becoming more frequent. There seemed to be no restriction on the amount of ammunition we expended in our training routine. It was set to increase even further when we were presented with the section Light Machine Gun, the LMG.

This weapon was not belt fed it had a curved thirty round 7.62 magazine or it could be used with the twenty round mag from the SLR. It was a mean bit of kit. Where the SMG looked like something knocked together in the local blacksmith shop the LMG was a complicated, intricate and heavy piece of hardware.

We didn't need to worry about drilling or parading with this weapon, this was carried over your shoulder or slung around the neck in a 'Rambo' style; no way would you present arms with this beastie.

Again we went through the routines of stripping and cleaning and reassembly. A great deal more complex than the previous two weapons; also a great deal heavier at ten kilo's loaded, to lug around the woods and fields of Kent while practicing our section patrols.

One member of the section had to carry it and generally that job went to the biggest person in the section, he would share the chore with the guy who proved to be the best at handling the weapon on the range, Number one and number two would work together; number two providing cover during a fire-fight while mags and red-hot barrels are changed over.

The other weighty item that went with this weapon was the ammo; at 500 rounds a minute it could burn through a magazine of thirty rounds in seconds. The section LMG ammo had to be shared out within the patrol; everyone except the radio operator carried his own ammo as well as the LMG ammo. A bandolier of a hundred 7.62 rounds weighed approx three kilos; as a fighting soldier in a patrol you could find yourself carrying three or four of these as well your own two magazines, forty rounds for the SLR.

When we were completely geared up we could be carrying as much as thirty five kilos plus, so fitness was absolutely imperative.

Fitness was an everyday event; we would road-run in the mornings and cross-country run in the afternoon, we would throw ourselves at the assault course at least once a week which was a killer yet held some macabre satisfaction as over the terms we'd got quicker and more agile at manoeuvring through and over the obstacles; but the one thing we all unanimously hated was running with the pole. Where the assault course was just a killer that you adjusted to and got better at, the section pole run was death by a thousand knifes. It consisted of six or eight of us running with a section of wooden telephone pole. We'd run round and round the barrack circle road. Some circuits would be with the pole on the shoulder other times with a rope wrapped round your wrist and held in the hand.

The important thing when running with the pole was to make sure you ran with guys almost exactly your height. If you were taller than the others the weight fell more firmly on your shoulders and of course those slightly shorter in stature wouldn't carry quite so much. Our arms would almost drop off after these runs and our shoulders would be bruised and rubbed raw.

Until September 1972 Course 8 had been billeted with their respective Squadron's and they would represent the Squadron by completing in the Inter-Squadron assault course competition. Following September 1972 all Course 8 were billeted above the education block together as one single large troop. The assault course competition was handed down to the three Squadron Course 7s. Course 8 personnel then concentrated solely on passing B2 Combat Engineering.

My Course 7 would prove to be a gruelling Course, as this Course would also fall at a time when the British Legion March and shoot took place.

This was an Inter Junior Regimental competition where we would be up against not only the extremely fit Junior Para's and Marines but the two other Royal Engineer Junior Regiments, the RE Junior Apprentice Collage Chepstow and the Junior Tradesmen Collage at Rhyl. Seven miles in forty minutes on roads and over rough terrain wearing full belt kit, carrying rifle and ammunition. Prior to the competition kicking-off belt kit would be inspected, everything – spare socks, pants, washing kit, cleaning kit for boots and rifle, spare KF shirt had to be folded and packed everything had to be uniform; presented in the same way. Water bottles had to be full. Dress would be inspected and points awarded.

The training for this competition would literally draw blood.

Many of us were pretty fit on arrival at Dover – many were not; but as the months had gone by our fitness levels had gone up dramatically.

Runs in battle order, route marches and other everyday events that required high fitness levels such as getting geared up for section field training, donning our webbing and ammo for patrol practice just became normal routine. Throwing 10 to 15 kilos of webbing on our back, collecting weapon and ammo and climbing in the back of a truck or marching for five miles just became second nature.

I had my 58 webbing and I was well happy. This made life so much more comfortable and it was very user friendly.

The addition of the LMG into our training routine once more increased our trips to the ranges.

For LMG live firing practice it was mainly Lydd ranges. Rain or shine we'd pile onto the trucks for the journey through Dover and Folkestone to the bleak coastline of Lydd.

Firing this weapon was awesome for us; later in our careers and at our different postings we'd get to use weapons with even greater stopping power such as the belt fed GPMG, the Browning 30 or the Carl Gustav anti-tank missile launcher. But at this moment the LMG was the biggest we'd handled and was great fun.

We fired from the prone position, the bi-pod supporting the weapon below the barrel and the butt pulled and held tightly into the shoulder. As you control the trigger with your right hand, or in my case the left hand the other hand held the butt hard into the shoulder; if you didn't hold it in this manner the weapon would literally run away from you.

The LMG was introduced into our patrols. More of our time this term was spent outside the barracks practicing the various section tactics.

There are around half a dozen patrols of different types, fighting patrols – those deliberately sent out to engage the enemy, kill and capture a prisoner. Ambush patrols where we would lay-up and wait for the enemy to stumble into a pre-laid and organised trap. Reconnaissance patrols where information is gathered and enemy contact avoided. A lot of planning goes into patrols and during our patrol training we took turns in being the patrol commander or the patrol 2i/c (second in command).

Patrol formations are used for safe movement in hostile terrain.

The mission of the patrol heavily influences how it is organized and how it will react to enemy contact. Not all patrols will stand and fight, even if they are superior to the enemy. For those readers who are not from a military background I'll explain the purpose and practice of patrolling...

All patrols have several things in common. They must go into the operational area, avoid getting lost while in it, and get out of the area without getting caught, ambushed or engaged by enemy forces.

You leave from your secure area, a position protected by mines, booby traps, barbed wire and machine guns or you could be dropped off by vehicle.

The perfect plan would be for the patrol to come back via a different route to avoid getting ambushed by an enemy that may have seen them leave. This requires coordinating with the front line friendly units so the patrol is guided out safely and back in safely. Usually, when a patrol comes back in they'll radio ahead so the guard is expecting the patrol. Due to the possible presence of enemy forces this is an operation that requires great care, especially when it is done at night. You never know if those people you are approaching, or approaching you, are friend or enemy. Passwords, locations and other relevant data are important.

Once a patrol has safely left friendly lines it must move quietly and avoid getting ambushed; the patrol leader will frequently stop the patrol so they can listen to their surroundings.

On patrol training we would wear fighting order – ammo pouches water bottle and kidney pouches if you had a set of 58. Our faces and hands would be blacken by burned cork or cam cream, cam nets would be worn round the neck or over the face, our trouser legs would be taped tightly to the legs to stop material rustling. On our heads would be the cap comforter and we'd wear or carry nothing that rattled or glinted in the sunshine or moon light. Prior to leaving we would stand in a line and the section commander would inspect us; at the same time we'd jump up and down to ensure nothing clanked, rattled or squeaked on our person. Believe it or not this is harder than it seems, even a half empty water bottle can make what seems a small barely audible sloshing noise in daylight but sounds like Niagara Falls at night.

Every so often the patrol leader will stop and designate that point as a rallying point, an RV, which is usually an easily recognizable land feature. When the patrol is near the operation point a final RV will be established. At this point the patrol will form a perimeter while the leader does a recce (reconnaissance) of the site.

When the patrol has accomplished its mission it will have to return to friendly lines.

A Recce patrol is usually small, a few men. Recce patrols make every effort to avoid getting in a fight, or being detected by the enemy. The main weapon of a Recce patrol is stealth. The mission of a Sapper Recce patrol is to gather more detailed information about an engineering obstacle like a ravine that may need bridging a road that may need blowing, or a field that may need mining. The Recce patrol will gather any and every bit of information about its objective that it can.

With an ambush patrol good planning and a large amount of firepower are the key to success. If done correctly a small unit can inflict casualties far out of proportion to their size.

One method of setting up a good ambush is for the leader to do a Recce of the site on his own from the final RV. If the ambush is on a trail or road, at least one person will be placed at either end of the ambush site to warn the patrol of the enemy's approach. Whatever means they use to inform the patrol leader of an impending enemy arrival, it must be done quietly or the whole surprise element of the ambush is gone and there's a high likelihood of getting killed!

Any gear the patrol doesn't need at the ambush point, like packs should be left in at the last RV.

Fighting patrols as we called them back in 1972 are the most aggressive use of patrols. Heavily armed patrols are assigned areas in which they actively search for enemy forces. Once the enemy forces are found the patrol attacks and attempts to destroy them. The size of a fighting patrol can range anywhere from a section of eight men to a Squadron or Company as the Infantry call it.

Patrols are usually very highly organized with everyone having a specific job, field of fire and location within the patrol. Before the patrol even leaves friendly lines there is a great deal of planning that takes place.

Usually, the first thing a patrol leader does when he finds out he is going on a patrol is issue a warning order. The Warning Order lets people know who is going on patrol, what their position is, and other similar information. It warns them so they can get ready. The patrol leader obtains maps of the area.

Any special weapons or gear can be drawn from stores, radio frequencies and call signs confirmed, fire support can be arranged, transportation can be arranged, headquarters can be notified of code words and routes. The patrol has to plot a route; someone has to talk with the front line units so a guide is available to let them in and out of the defensive perimeter. The locations and types of other friendly patrols in the area should be determined. If another patrol has been through the area, they should be contacted for any knowledge and suggestions. The availability of food and water must be considered. Possible landing zones should be noted in case someone is injured and needs to be extracted. An excellent aid to the op is a terrain model for the briefing; holding up a map for twenty men to view just doesn't work. It is much better if they can gather around a model of the terrain that has markers, string for gridlines, tags, etc.

It is virtually impossible for one man to do all this in a decent amount of time so the wise squad leader assigns patrol members to do different tasks. When all this information is gathered, the patrol leader writes his order which will detail all important information.

Finally, when everything has been figured out, the patrol leader gets the patrol together, checks their work and issues his order. Final preparations are done and then the Patrol Leader inspects the patrol. If possible rehearsals are conducted and then final preparations. When the patrol is ready to leave, the patrol leader does a final inspection to make sure everyone is silenced (done by making them jump up and down, noisy items are taped down) and has the required equipment.

The planning will pay-off in a big way. If everyone knows what is going on and what is expected of them the entire patrol will go much more smoothly and safely for everyone.

So – that was an extended insight into the art of patrolling.

The handling of weapons became second nature to us, they were like an extra appendage that we carried, cleaned and used without a second thought. However the safety of the weapon was of paramount importance and whether we used live rounds on a range or blank rounds on a patrol exercise the clearing of a weapon was equally as rigorous and important.

If a weapon was discharged by accident and I say accident loosely, because it was never referred to as an accidental discharge but a negligent discharge.

As Spatts informed us an accident is the way things happen without any planning, apparent cause, or deliberate intent. If your weapon is discharged when it shouldn't be it's because you weren't following your training, weren't concentrating on what you were doing, or just being plain stupid. Therefore it's not an accident it's negligence on the part of the person concerned. Negligence in the dictionary is defined as careless or irresponsible. Anyone therefore having a negligent discharge is careless and irresponsible if you're either of those as a soldier you're up before the OC; loss of pay, behind the guard, or 14 days detention. Harsh? Yes; but it could very easily be a matter of life and death. Apart from Steve spraying us with 9mm rounds from his SMG that day at Hythe I was never in the presence of a soldier having a negligent discharge and never had one myself. Although another Smudge Smith, a lad in our

Course did shoot me in the back during a night patrol in Course 7. This I'm relieved to say was with a blank round fired from an SLR with no black adaptor. I'll return to this further on...

Where my Military skills were completely on track and I enjoyed what we were learning, my academic education was still a struggle. I was as hopeless at Dover as I'd been at school.

I needed to achieve certain modules for my proposed trade as a plant operator; a digger, dozer or grader driver, but I was not getting there.

As well as modules one to seven, the minimum required by all of us, I needed ten and fourteen. I can't remember now what these extra modules consisted of but I'm guessing because my planned trade was mechanical engineering orientated that they were maths modules. The likelihood of me getting these was slim to put it mildly and I was called in by the head of the education wing Major Millsop - Royal Army Education Corps and told I had to focus...

I said 'Yes sir' Saluted and marched out. I had no intention of doing any such thing.

We were now a few weeks away from the term's end and a week away from the Easter weekend. We'd been told that we could have Good Friday free to do as we wished; Saturday would be a normal working day with a full dress Regimental parade. Sunday would be a Regimental church parade, attendees to be announced. Monday the Course 7 assault course competition would take place as well as other Inter-Squadron events. Those not completing would be giving support from the side-lines.

The 4th April was my Birthday, It would be my sixteenth. Unfortunately it would fall on the Tuesday the day following our Inter-Squadron sports-day; it would be the first Birthday I'd spent away from home. This didn't bother me in the slightest, we'd had other birthdays in our room since September, the person concerned would get the bumps, maybe a French-bed or some other trick played on them, it was par for the course; but usually a Birthday meant a food parcel containing cake or chocolate that we shared around the room. I had no doubt that I'd get a parcel from home and no doubt a card with a fiver from Gran. A French-bed for those not familiar with the term is when the bottom sheet is untucked from the foot of the bed and folded back to the top and made off like the top sheet would be. On climbing into bed your feet could only get a third of the way down the bed. Another trick was to sprinkle a few sugar granules in someone's bed. Once you get into bed and the body warms up the sugar melts, its horrible sticky and the only thing to do is wash the sheet. This was one of the milder pranks we played on each other! Others were so extreme it's a wonder the person concerned wasn't killed. Like hanging someone out of the top floor windows by their ankles or wrapping them in blankets and leaving them in the drying room at forty degrees centigrade until they almost boiled to death. If you just got sugar in the bed you were getting off lightly!

It was Thursday evening 30th March and the room was quiet.

The following day we were free and a conversation was flowing backwards and forwards across the room... what would we do the next day?

'Why don wi gan te tha castle' said Ray.

'What, Lindisfarne,' replied Les sarcastically.

'Ne man Les, yee knaa well what castle ah mean, this one heor in toon man.' (I'm trying here to mimic in writing Ray's very strong Geordie accent; if I'm not doing such a good job I do apologise).

'Why the fuck do we want to look round a bloody old castle for, I'd rather go to Margate fair,' countered Les.

'Have you got money to go to Margate then?' said Doddy? 'I know I haven't.'

'No, neither have I,' came from both me and Steve simultaneously.

'So whose fre the castle then?' Said Ray.

We were all in; I didn't know it but this trip to the castle would lead to a dinner in Dover on the Sunday and a shag! Best birthday present this year by a mile.

There was no inspection the following morning, also no cleaning duties. Good Friday was treated as a Sunday and a brunch style breakfast was served in the cookhouse.

Finally we were all ready and departed for the good three mile hike through town and up Castle Hill to the gates of what was and still is a very imposing castle. Even Les had to admit it was a pretty impressive structure.

A short distance up the hill and the other side of the road was Connaught Barracks home of the 1st Battalion The Queens Lancashire Regiment; this Infantry Regiment had recently been formed from two other Regiments, The Loyals and the 1st Battalion of the Lancs. Unlike us of course they were adult soldiers and gave us a hard time when we met in town.

We spent around an hour walking around the walls and the outside of the Great Tower; in 1972 you didn't have to pay to get into the grounds, only into the tower proper. Les by now had had enough.

'Are we through?' He asked. 'I've had enough.'

'Aren't you going inside the tower then?' This from Ray.

'No I'm bloody well not, I've better things to spend my money on. Who's coming back to town for a coffee?'

I never visualized Ray as being a culture junky but there you go, you learn something new about someone every day when you live and work in such close proximity. I could see the disappointment on his face as he looked for support.

'I'll come with you Ray,' I said.

The other three decided to go back to town; they turned and made their way back down the hill toward the arched gate.

'We'll wait for you in the Wimpy,' shouted Les as they disappeared out of sight.

Ray and I paid what was only the price of a coffee to get into the tower and wandered round the different levels.

I was interested in history and I found that Ray was as well; he told me he'd visited Lindisfarne Castle in the north east, one of England's most famous castles.

'Tha castles what the bands named affta ya kna,' he told me referring to the Newcastle band who's record 'Fog on the Tyne' was big at the time and all the lads from the north east were walking round singing.

I acted impressed but for one-upmanship I told him I'd been to Conway Castle where the Prince of Wales investiture had taken place.

His reply to this was all the Royals belong in the south; they never visit Sunderland, Durham, or Newcastle. They don't know what life's like where we live.

I left it at that; Ray tended to get a bit deep and melancholy if you set him off on a subject he wasn't enthusiastic about.

Finally everything seen that could be seen we headed back to the town centre.

We were hungry, a Wimpy and a cup of tea would go down well. We entered the café and looked around for our three mates... there was no sign of them...

'Hey soldier boy, your three mates have gone,' a voice came from the corner.

162

I looked over and there sat the blonde lass, the one that seemed to be everywhere.

'Oh... hiya,' I said.

'You're looking for them three lads you were with last time aren't you? They left about twenty minutes ago.'

'Thanks,' I said.

I'm starving Ray, I'm staying for a burger and a coke, what about you?'

'This is your chance Steve, get in there mate.' Ray whispered nudging me in the ribs.

'Ray, leave it out, are you having something or not?'

'Yeah ok,' he said.

We went up to the counter and ordered our burger; unlike today where burger franchises have the food waiting in racks the Wimpy bars of the seventies had to cook to order; we were told we'd be called when it was ready. I moved away to find a seat...

'You can sit with us if you like'. This was from blondie sitting at the table in the window. 'And ur mate as long as doesn't call me 'Pet' again.'

'Thanks - don't worry I'll keep him under control.' I said sitting down. 'He can't help it he's from the untamed north-east.'

'Oy! I heard that,' came from Ray.'

'As we seem honoured to be invited to your table would you girls like a drink?' I asked. There were only the two of them today, although I wasn't that flush with money I knew I'd be having a fiver coming from gran on Tuesday for my Birthday. They both said yes and I called across to Ray 'plus two coffee's mate, I'll give you the money.'

'Sure you can afford it,' she said sarcastically.

'Look,' I said. 'You know we're hard up, we know we're hard up, but I asked you if you wanted a coffee, if however you're going to continue the piss-take we'll just move to another table.'

She looked at me in surprise - 'Ok, I'm sorry, sit down, thanks for the offer.'

We seemed to have arrived at a point where normal conversation could resume, without the constant needle. Ray came over with the coffee and introductions were made.

Then we hesitantly began the getting-to-know-you conversation.

Blondie's name was Myleene, I can't remember her mate's name (I'll call her Sue) but she wasn't a patch on Myleene when it came to looks.

'I've not seen you at the Old Park disco's,' said Ray.

163

I looked at Ray not quite believing what I was hearing, I think he'd been to the NAAFI disco once since we'd been allowed to go following mid-term leave during our Intake Course.

'That's because we don't go - for one thing it's too far to go, right up there in Whitfield and for another there's no drink. We go to Connaught; the lads up there have dances and discos and they have a proper bar. They can also afford to buy us a Port & Lemon or Babycham... what would we get at your place – a Coke or a Tizer and probably have to pay for it ourselves.'

'How do you get in there? You aren't old enough to drink are you?' Ray interrupted.

'No, course I'm not silly, but when I've got my heels on and make up, I easily pass for eighteen and they don't ask for any proof of age do they Sue?'

Before Sue could answer she was off again.

'Anyway I'm sixteen next week, so I'm not too far off drinking age and it's a stupid rule, I can get married, have kids, smoke, but can't drink and while on the subject which of you two's going give me a ciggie?'

I got my packet out and offered her one.

'You say your birthday's next week? What day?' I asked.

'Tenth, I'm Aries I am - what about you, when's yours?'

'It's my birthday on Tuesday, the forth, I'm Aries too; I'm not only spending Easter in Dover but my bloody birthday as well,' I said morosely.

'Cheer up and give me a light, it could be worse, if you were down in Zummerset you wouldn't be here talking to me would you.' She said with a laugh.

'It's not Somerset but you're close – I come from Wiltshire, West Wiltshire on the Somerset border near Bath.'

Then I went through the explanation that I now lived in Norfolk and how we got there.

Ray had given up adding bits to Myleene and my conversation and he and Sue were talking to each other.

I was looking at Myleene closely, she was very pretty but I was certain she wasn't English.

'Are you English,' I asked.

'Why do you ask that?' She said, but it came out quite defensively.

'I just wondered – you're very pretty but not in an English way, that's all.'

'And how would you know – travelled the world have you?'

'Well not the world, but I've travelled most of Europe since I was a kid and you just don't look English; sorry I didn't mean anything by it... anyway there's nothing wrong with not being English, my mum's German and it doesn't bother me. I'm having a cup of tea, anyone else want a drink?' I got up and went to the counter; Myleene followed me up.

She stood next to me quiet for moment, then said - 'Polish, my Dad's Polish, I'll have a coffee, he and his brother escaped the Nazi's at the beginning of the war, they both ended up here and joined the Navy. Their parents, my grandparents I suppose, were killed by the Germans; dad hate's the Germans, he'll never forgive them as long as there's breath in his body. I couldn't go out with a German – he'd murder me.'

'I think there's a lot of people like that,' I said remembering the guy in 'Silverman' in the Strand.

'But we're not going out so it doesn't matter does it.'

'No but you'd like to wouldn't you,' she said with a grin.

'God, you're pretty sure of yourself aren't you,' I laughed. 'Yeah maybe I would like to go out with you... but what about my girlfriend at home?'

I was digging out my money as she put the two coffees and two teas on a tray.

'Ur out in the big world now soldier boy, remember what they say 'what the eye doesn't see, the heart doesn't grieve over'.'

'Are you prompting me to ask you out then?' I really thought my luck had changed.

'Nah – I told you, I don't go out with juniors, there's no future in it, we're just having a chat, but don't be disappointed I do like you a lot.'

I came to the conclusion this girl was a serial heart breaker and best left alone.

'Yeah you're right, I'll bin that idea then,' I said with a grin, hoping the grin masked my disappointment.

We sat back down and continued talking amongst ourselves, general chit chat without the banter.

Time was getting on and I noticed the staff were looking over at our now empty cups. They weren't in the business of providing a warm chat venue for teenagers and any moment we'd be asked to leave. I looked at my watch it was gone four, Ray and I needed to get back for our evening meal.

'We going Ray?' I asked him.

'Yeah lets go, I've been waiting for you this last two hours.' He replied.

'We've got to go as well,' said Myleene. 'But hang-on, before you go, you say your birthday's on Tuesday? What are you doing Sunday?'

We were all heading for the door...

'What this Sunday?'

'Yes this Easter Sunday - in the afternoon, we're Catholic in our house, I've got to go to Church in the morning. Would you like to come to dinner Sunday evening? We'll eat late, dads on shift in the docks and he won't finish till four. When he's on a Sunday shift we eat about five; would you like to come? It'll be a birthday meal for you; you're not at home so join us.'

I must've looked stunned. It was a generous offer from someone who didn't even know me and took me slightly aback but before I could say anything...

'It's not a big deal, it's not a marriage proposal, just a meal.' She said.

'Go on man,' said Ray. 'Of course he'll go, won't you Steve.' Ray was making sure I didn't refuse.

'Hadn't you better ask your mum and dad first? You go home and tell them I'm coming and they don't agree how will I know?' I wasn't at all sure about this...

'Ok - I know they won't mind but if it makes you happy here's my number.'

She rummaged in her bag, brought out a pen and getting hold of my wrist wrote the number on it. This girl was to bloody quick for me...

'Better not wash tonight soldier boy,' she said laughing.

'Phone me tomorrow after one-o-clock and I'll meet you Sunday by the old Town Hall. I don't want you wandering around town on your own... you can use the phone can't you?'

I opened my mouth to reply but she beat me to it... 'Ok, ok, I'm only joking.'

Both of them were walking away and with a laugh and as a parting shot she shouted – 'And don't mention you're a German!'

Ray and I turned making our way up the high street.

'God, what a girl,' I said to Ray.

'Told ya didn't I, told ya the first time we saw em, she had her eye on you mate – not a marriage proposal – na maybe not but she fancies ye, ya lucky bugger. Sunday lunch at her house, bloody hell that's called getting yur feet under the bloody table early that is.'

God wouldn't he shut up – 'Ray fur fuck-sake give it a rest, yur either saying fuck all or running on like a fuckin record.'

166

'Ah well, you can say what you like you know I'm right – wait till the lads hear about this.'

I glowered at him; I knew this would be round the lines in no time. But in a way I was pretty chuffed; she must be the most attractive lass in Dover... well sixteen year old anyway.

We got back, the others had eaten and were laying on beds.

'Where the fuck have you two been,' said Les. 'Don't tell me you been in the bloody castle all this time?'

'Nah man, you won't believe this...' Ray was off... he couldn't bloody wait. I took my nosh rods from my locker and went for my tea.

Ray eventually came down and joined me at the table.

'Guess what.'

'What Ray? Tell me...'

'We're all ganna come wi ya ta toown Sunday.'

'WHAT! No you're bloody well not, that's the last thing that's going to happen... what's the idea of that? You want me to look a prize twat or what.'

'No man, calm down, course we don't; but the lads don't think it a great idea yee wandering around Dover centre on ya own. It might be a set-up yee'na, yee might bump into one of those Dover gangs and get done over. We're not wrong yee'na.'

'It's not a set-up Ray, you were there this afternoon, you heard her ask me, you don't think for one moment she's going to go running to some gang and have them ambush me in the High Street on a Sunday, are you mad or what?'

'Nah man, but yee still might bump into a crowd of them and then what?'

'And getting back,' I countered... 'are you lot gunna wait four hours in the Wimpy to walk me home?... yeah right; jeez; let's go upstairs.'

We scrapped our plates and went back to the room where a further debate started that ended up spilling over into other rooms. In no time my dinner date was broadcast round the lines and what was supposed to have been a nice family orientated afternoon in a normal family setting had turned into a battle with the locals.

I put a stop to it by saying I would go and come back by taxi. Of course I had no intention of doing that, I was not likely to part with my limited financial resources on a private bloody chauffeur.

We let the topic of my date die down and set about sorting out No2 kit for the morning; after all we still had the Saturday Regimental parade to get through yet and this was the first of two full dress rehearsals prior to the big one on the fifteenth; if our kit wasn't perfect for inspection the following day the shit would really hit the fan and we'd probably be going nowhere for the rest of Saturday and Sunday.

And that in essence is exactly what happened.

Our beloved Junior Sergeant Hill was not pleased with our turn out on the Saturday morning and as a punishment we had to work on our kit all Saturday afternoon with a further parade in the evening, however it was again only our side of the lines. Not only were we deprived of our Saturday afternoon and evening by Hill, he also put our side of the lines forward for the following mornings Easter Sunday church parade. I prayed nothing would crop up to spoil my planned Sunday evening at Myleene's.

However one ray of sunshine did come our way during the Saturday evening inspection. Sgt Hill informed us on the Landing that following term he would no longer be our Course Sergeant. He was promoted to Junior Squadron Sergeant Major.

Of course we went through the rigmarole of congratulation, but in truth each and every one of us thought 'thank fuck for that'. Now the whole Squadron will suffer him not just us.

Our replacement Troop Junior Sergeant for Course 3 would be Abe Bateman; Smudge our long serving (and suffering) Room-jack would move on to Course 8 as would Mick Foster another of our junior line NCOs. We'd miss both of them, they'd both been good mentors during our Intake Course, hard but fair and during this Course they'd treated us far more as equals and friends. Now we had to wait and see who the replacements would be.

On Sunday morning at 0900 we paraded for the ten-o-clock church service. This was a real shitty trick for Hill to pull especially as it was only half our troop; his side of the lines.

Easter Sunday Service with all the vocal trimmings; *'There is a green hill far away without a city wall'* and all the other hymns of that particular religious festival.

The Officers and families all turned out in their best, plus 'B' & 'C' Squadron minor offenders.

The collection box came round and as usual everything went in except for money; pebbles, washers, compressed silver paper and even the occasional condom from lads who'd desperately kept them in their wallet unused for so long the wrapper had worn through. The service ended; we marched back and I sat on my bed clock watching – waiting for one-o-clock to phone Myleene.

1300 came and I hung on another ten minutes, I wanted her to be in when I got there; what I didn't want was to get to the guard room phone and find she wasn't in, then hang around trying and trying again.

As it happened she was in and we agreed to meet at 1530 at the town hall.

When I told the lads Les informed me they'd all decided to go into town that afternoon and they'd walk with me. It was no good, I couldn't win so I shrugged and agreed. In a way it was a solid thing to do for your mate and I appreciated the concern.

However I was emphatic – no piss-take or ribbing when we got there. All I got in reply to that statement was a bunch of grins. Bastards.

At 1430 with me dressed smartly in my inherited Crombie coat, a pair of silver-blue Levi Sta-Prest trousers and black Loafers with a tassel on the tongue; the fashion of the time; we all made our way down to the duty office. Les had made me a present of a very tatty looking packet containing a Durex Featherlite on a promise that if I got the chance to use it I'd buy him twenty fags; he'd given up hope that he'd use it himself. I thought this a gesture of pure generosity from my friend but doubted he'd keep his mouth shut about it when in a short while we met up with Myleene.

The conversation on the way into town covered a range of topics; our up and coming move up the ladder to Course 3, buying our own gear, lack of an end of Course 'Jolly' and of course girls.

As we walked down London Street I could see the town hall clock high on the wall in the distance; we were on time and there leaning against the steps leading up to the medieval doorway was Myleene looking very lovely in her Sunday best.

'God you brought your entourage with you,' was her opening shot.

'I hope they're not all expecting lunch?'

'My bodyguard,' I replied. 'They decided I needed an escort in case I was jumped by a gang of locals, or you set me up to be mugged. That's the mentality of those in the North.'

'You needn't worry boys he's safe with me,' said Myleene looking around at my motley gang of minders. 'To be honest the bunch of you don't look that frightening to me – ok let's go, you lot clear off in whatever direction you fancy – I hope you're not expecting to walk him all the way to my front door?'

'No pet, we'll git ganin, he looks leek he's in safe hands.' Said Ray.

169

'He is and it's not 'Pet' for the last time.'

We were crossing the road into Effingham Crescent and Myleene had her arm looped through mine; wow I thought this is great. The lads carried on down toward the Wimpy in Market Square with the final shout coming from Les 'don't forget that's twenty fags you owe me!' At least that was all he shouted.

We walked around Effingham Crescent until we met the Folkestone road, crossed over and carried on for a short distance before taking one of the roads off to the left. Myleene's family lived in a house backing onto the old military road and the Redoubt fort; Myleene point this out as being a kind of park with footpaths leading through.

'I'll walk with you back as far as the town hall later and we'll go through the park and along the road, you've never been up this part of town have you?'

I told her I hadn't.

We arrived at her house and I was reminded again by Myleene not to mention the Germans. 'Are you really serious,' I asked. She assured me she was.

We went in and I was made very welcome by her parents, I thanked them for agreeing the invitation made by their daughter. I got the feeling I wasn't the first waif that had been brought home for food by Myleene. We talked about my home and family; I managed to steer the conversation around my mum's country of birth; leaving home, being a Junior Leader in Old Park and loads of other trivia. It was very pleasant evening and my time to leave came round far too soon. I had to be back for 9pm.

I said my goodbyes around seven thirty in the polite manner in which I'd been brought up and said I hoped to see both Myleene's parents again.

'Well son you may need to catch a train for your next meal,' came from Myleene's dad. I wondered what he meant and looked at Myleene expecting her to enlarge on the statement; but she didn't and just looked daggers at her dad. I got the feeling I should say nothing at this point.

We walked out into the dusk, but instead of turning up to the Folkestone Road Myleene headed for a footpath through the houses, and the next thing I knew we were on a kind of common with footpaths criss-crossing and a big brick building over to the right of us. 'Where are we?' I asked.

'We're on the Western Heights,' she said. 'I told you we'd take a different route back, its lovely up here. I'll take you over by the old redoubt, that's just one of the old clifftop forts; they were built to defend against Napoleon you know?'

She had hold of my hand now and was almost pulling me along while giving me this history lesson; after a couple of hundred yards we crossed a small road and again we were on the common.

'I know this place like the back of my hand,' she said, 'I've played out here since I was five years old, it's really lovely in the summer, you get crowds of people up here having picnic's.' She was now dragging me off the footpath over to the side of the high wall of the fort and in a moment we were out of sight of anyone.

Leaning against the wall she pulled me toward her and smacked her lips onto mine.

'You've wanted to do that since you first saw me haven't you,' she said when we eventually came up for air.

'Yes,' I gasped.

'Have you ever shagged a girl?' She then asked.

'What? Why are you asking me that?'

'Oh, just curious – you're a good kisser, I don't think you're as innocent as you look… would you like to shag me?'

I was thunderstruck and stuttered a lame excuse. 'I can't, not now, we haven't got time and I haven't got anything. *Liar! – it was nerves, short and sweet; Les's condom was burning a hole in my pocket.*

'Rubbish – you've got time and I've got a condom (*why didn't that shock me*) come on let's do it, this may be your only opportunity.'

Really? This wasn't the time for questions…

We walked hand in hand back to the Military Road and down to Worthington Street (this was before the A256 cut the town in half). Along the way I asked her what she meant by 'my only opportunity' and also about her dads comment on the train ride.

'We're moving,' she said. 'My dad and his brother both married sisters. My uncle lives in Chatham and works in Chatham Naval dockyard, my aunt is suffering with some illness which is getting worse, my uncle's found dad a job in the Navy docks and we're moving to Chatham so mum can help look after her sister. He starts at the beginning of May.'

She could see the look of disappointment on my face.

'Cheer up soldier boy, you've had a lovely day and shagged the prettiest girl in Dover. You wouldn't want to go out with me anyway – I'm young and a flirt, I don't want a steady boyfriend yet, I'd only end up breaking your heart.' (*She obviously didn't realize she was in the process of doing that right there and then*). This was the Myleene from the café talking.

'With luck we'll get to see each other a couple more times yet and then – well – we'll go our separate ways. What are you doing tomorrow?'

'Sport,' I replied. 'All day.'

'Well come down in the evening we'll go for a movie or if you can't afford it we'll just go for a walk.'

'Ok but if I don't get a move on I'll be going nowhere tomorrow other than parading behind the guard, we get five minutes lee-way max, if we're later we're in the shit – I'd better run.'

By now we were at the corner of what was Priory Place now under a bloody great roundabout.

I quickly slowly kissed her goodbye, promising to phone as soon as our sports day had finished and headed off at a brisk march up Priory Road, a big smile on my face.

From behind me came Myleene's, now standard parting shot of 'Get home safely solider boy, don't let the bogey men get you!' I wished she wouldn't do that. Without turning I waved my hand in the air and upped the tempo I had twenty five minutes to get back and that included a five minute grace.

I just made it, signed in and ran upstairs into the room with a - 'not now I'm getting a brew,' before the inevitable questions came pouring in my direction I grabbed my mug and shot back down to the cookhouse foyer for a cup of tea and a bun.

If the canteen door had been open I've sat quietly inside and drunk my tea in peace but it wasn't, so I returned upstairs to tackle the onslaught.

'Before you start,' I said on entry, 'no I didn't and Les here's your unused 'Johnny' back, thank you very much, I do not owe you twenty fags.' I wasn't going to brag about my shag. As far as my mates were concerned I didn't get one.

I told them about my evening, the meal, the walk over the heights and the fact that Myleene was moving to Chatham, went for a wash and turned in. The following day I was representing the Squadron in Course 2 events - 100 yards and 800 yards. Les was 'Fencing', a sport he'd become very good at. The rest of our room were set to support field and gym events as well as Course 7 in the assault course competition.

It was a great day, I got a second and a third, Les got a second in the 'Epee' and 'A' Squadron won the gruelling assault course which wasn't just the assault course itself, but a circuit of the road with the section of telegraph pole before being confronted with the assault obstacle course proper. The log went with them. We all knew we had this purgatory to look forward to in the future.

By 4pm it had started raining, what started as a drizzle became one of those rain storms that blow in off the channel and you know will continue on through the night. I was knackered and as much as I wanted to see Myleene I really didn't fancy trekking down the back hill and along the London road into town. The pictures would be good, the town cinema was showing 'The Cowboys' with John Wayne but we wouldn't get the early show and the 7pm showing didn't give me time to get back before curfew at nine. It wasn't a night to be walking along the seafront or trying to get into her knickers on the Western Heights; I'd stay at home, if home is what you can call a barrack room.

I went to the phone box and telephoned Myleene, her mum answered the phone; she wasn't in. I asked her mum to pass the message I couldn't make it and despondently mooched back to the block to get my kit ready for the next day.

Tuesday 4th April 1972, my sixteenth birthday. I got tipped out of bed and then given the bumps. At mail call I got a parcel from mum and a card from my gran with a fiver in it; a lot of money. The parcel contained a coconut and cherry cake, chocolate and other goodies; all but a box of 'After Eights' would be shared with my roommates.

I had a plan for the 'After Eights'.

That evening again I phoned Myleene and made a plan for the coming weekend. She said she'd see me Sunday afternoon, we'd go to the 3pm movie, she couldn't see me Saturday as she was going to a dance up at Connaught Barracks. I walked back to the block thinking how lucky I'd been to get the shag and also seeing the personality behind the girl. Maybe it was a good thing she was moving to Chatham.

We were into the last two weeks of term; Saturday we had another full dress Regimental parade and Sunday I went again to town carrying the box of 'After Eights' wrapped in the same paper that they'd been sent to me by my mum with an accompanying card to Myleene; her Birthday was the following day and I hadn't forgotten.

I'd received a mega ribbing from everyone while trying to smuggle these out of the lines; such is life in the army.

I met Myleene outside The ABC cinema in Castle Street, this was a lovely cinema formally the Granada and still called that name by locals it had originally sat around sixteen hundred people in the circle and stalls. It had been refurbished in the late sixties and opened with only the downstairs seating being used; seating for around six hundred.

They called it a 'Luxury Lounge' cinema. What was luxury about it I can't remember but you could smoke and buy a vanilla tub in the intermission while listening to 'Pearl & Dean' adverts. We saw 'The Godfather' with Marlon Brando; everyone was raving about it. It seemed to go on for ever and I couldn't remember much about it at all... possibly because I spent most of the film snogging and trying to get my hand inside of Myleene's knickers.

When we came out we walked back to her house – up the Folkestone road, not over the common much to my disappointment.

We had a birthday tea, sandwiches and cake, her dad was on earlies and the family had Sunday lunch proper at midday. We talked and watched TV.

ABC cinema Dover 1971

At 8pm I got up to leave and it was lashing down. I decided to stay another half hour and if the rain hadn't stopped I'd get a taxi. As it happened Myleene's dad ran me back to Old Park in his car. This of course prevented any hanky-panky; I gave her a peck on the cheek as I got out of the car, thanked her dad for the lift and said I'd ring the next evening.

Monday morning I woke up with a very dull yet excruciating pain in my right ankle tendon, I told Smudge I'd need to go and see the quack I could barely make it down to the cook house.

Following sick parade I wasn't able to join in the march to the M.R.S, I had to hobble my way over on my own.

When I got in to see the Doc I explained my problem and while he bent and twisted my ankle I sat and done all the och and ahhs! 'Yes there! Very sore, yes sir that's right; right up the back of the leg.'

'Well Burt without doubt you've damaged your Achilles tendon. No marching for at least a week and no boots, I'll give you a light duties chit, take it to your Chief Clerks office on your return to the Squadron.'

The down side to this master stroke in skiving was the need to remember to limp for at least the next three days as my supposed tendon rupture repaired itself.

My room mates were flabbergasted.

'You jammy git! When the fuck did that happen?' Came from Doddy.

Whereas from Les I got the expected reference to sex... 'Knee trembler', that's what done it, last night against the wall, up and down on your tip-toes with blondie - recipe for calf and Achilles strain that is...'

'Yes Les, of course, and you would know wouldn't you,' was my response. But I wasn't letting on, I got away with it this time and I may be lucky next term. No passing out parade for me.

End of term was upon us. Although not parading in the Quad on the Saturday morning I still had to dress in my work uniform and make sure our washrooms, toilets and cleaning rooms were spic-and-span, before being able to finish packing my gear for going on leave.

Once more I'd spend my first week of leave at grans before taking the train up to Norfolk.

Les had asked me to accompany him to Silvermans to get a set of 58 so after going to the Chiefs office to collect my travel warrant I hung around in the room waiting for them all to come back from parade.

Eventually the lads started making their way back from the armoury, chaos reigned with lads moving rooms, others heading to the Chiefs office for pay check and travel warrants, others getting changed and some deciding to go for a meal before leaving.

We said our goodbyes to Smudge who would be moving to Course 8 lines and wished him well; he was staying behind another couple of hours moving his kit down to his new room. Les and I grabbed our cases and eventually boarded the transport to Dover Priory and fought for a seat on the train to London; a train packed with Junior Leaders going on leave.

We arrived at Silvermans to find that Les wasn't the only JL looking for webbing and boots there were others in front of us. Les knew what he wanted and knew what he needed; he was quite capable of managing the purchase himself as well as finding his way back to the 'Tube'.

I left him to it and headed back to the underground and my train from Paddington.

The Northern Ireland situation was grave and getting worse.

Since joining the army and being posted to Dover the previous September we'd become used to hearing of the troubles and the escalating violence.

Prior to joining up most of us had taken little notice; I for one hardly read a newspaper even though I delivered them daily. But now we had papers in our TV rooms, in the NAAFI and in the WRVS; we knew what was going on.

We'd been subject to numerous bomb scares, mostly during the night and laughingly took this in our stride believing that they were and would continue to be hoaxes.

However an IRA terrorist bombing took place in February of 1972 that brought home to us the fact that this was getting very serious. The Aldershot bombing was an attack by the Provisional Irish Republican Army (The Provo's) using a car bomb on 22nd February 1972 in Aldershot. The bomb targeted the headquarters of the British Army's 16th Parachute Brigade and was claimed as a revenge attack for the Bloody Sunday shootings by the Para's in the Londonderry, Bogside area of NI the month before in January.

In Aldershot seven civilian staff were killed and nineteen wounded. It was the IRA's largest attack in Britain to date and was a wakeup call to all that the war was now being waged on our own doorstep, not just across the Irish Sea.

We had been spoken to collectively by our OC following the Aldershot bombing and been warned that we needed to be constantly vigilant.

This warning sent alarm bells ringing in my head as I stood next to the wall at the end of platform two at Paddington station and watched a man walk away from a package he'd been stood next to a few yards from me.

What should I do? There were many other people around, but no one was taking any interest. The guy who I thought owned the package had vanished and not returned... I made up my mind; picking up my case I headed for a row of office doors running along the side of platform one. I opened one and went in only to be told to get out this is private, couldn't I read. Ignoring the comment I began to explain my reason for being there. A phone call was made and within thirty seconds my story was confirmed by a British Rail worker sticking his head round the door. From there it was a blur; whistles were blown, people were being moved and offices were being emptied. Obviously they had a plan.

I was taken to an office some distance away where I was left in the company of another BR employee. I could hear sirens. The police came (not the army) I was interviewed, asked all about myself my address taken and also the description of the man with the package. It was three hours before that part of the station was reopened. I was worried sick I'd get into trouble for what I'd done; it was a hoax.

However I had no need to worry, the senior Police Officer and the senior person from BR both praised me for my actions before I was sent on my way.

I tell this story to the present day – the day I emptied Paddington station.

Course 3 May 1972

We returned to Dover on 8th May.

A new term, Course 3; we were all very buoyed-up and happy; the last term of our first year.

We - the occupiers of room 96 had a new Room-jack a lad called Keith Harvey and a nicer lad we couldn't have wished for. Another Lance Jack (Pip Newman I think) replaced Mick Foster and life without Martin Hill as our Troop Junior Sergeant was a whole lot more relaxed.

We were now two rungs up the ladder and could do pretty much as we wished unless we were really out of order. No longer looked on as 'Sprogs', we'd come through the toughest two Courses and survived.

Room inspections would decrease dramatically, we could remodel our kit such as sewing creases in our denims, slashing the peak of our No2 dress hat, wear our berets in a two way stretch and even our hair was worn slightly longer without comment from our Junior or Senior NCOs.

Within a day of returning I was escorted down to the offices by our new Junior Sergeant Abe Bateman and deposited outside the SSMs office.

What the fuck was this all about? I was shaking in my boots.

Abe knocked at the door, stuck his head inside and said, 'Junior Sapper Burt Sir.'

'Thank you Sergeant Bateman, leave him with me.'

The SSM called me in while Abe disappeared.

I marched smartly to the desk and halted - Shitting myself.

'Junior Sapper Burt Sir,' I reported.

'Ah... Burt... I have in front of me two letters, one from the Chief Superintendent of Paddington Green police station in London; the other from a senior official with British Rail based at Paddington Railway station. It seems you caused a bit of a ruckus while heading home on leave. Are these facts true?

'I don't know what the letters say Sir,' I replied.

'Well Burt they are regarding your escapade at Paddington Station, I'm sure you know to what I'm referring and they both paint you in glowing colours... observant, quick witted and sensible, a credit to your Squadron and your Corps. That's a hell of a commendation after emptying one of the busiest main line stations in London. Well done; the OC wishes to talk to you. I'll leave you outside his door. When he calls you in, March in, close the door behind you, halt in front of his desk and salute. He'll tell you to stand at easy – not easy – you know the difference by now don't you?'

'Yes Sir.' I replied.

'Follow me.'

I halted outside the OCs door (Officer Commanding the Squadron or Company as opposed to Commanding Officer who would command a Regiment).

The SSM knocked and stuck his head around the door, 'Burt's outside Sir,' I heard him say.

The door closed and I was left waiting. Only a minute went by before Major Milsom called … 'come in Burt.'

I opened the door, went in, closed it and marched smartly, halted and saluted in front of the OCs desk.

'Stand at ease Burt…' *A pause while he continued to look at a letter in his hand…*

'Well Burt, it seems your leave got off to a bit of a hectic start. I think you can be very proud of yourself for the way you acted three weeks ago; these letters by the way never came directly to the Squadron they came via RHQ and the Adjutant, so no doubt I'll be spoken to about this by the CO in the mess, so I'd really like you to give me the facts in full.'

I did so…

When I finished my story he said.

'In this case it was a false alarm, but it could so easily have been the real thing, these are proving difficult times Burt, we lost another soldier shot in Belfast only last week.

At this point I said 'Yes Sir I read about it while I was at home.'

'You did? Good, you lads need to keep abreast of these issues; they'll quite likely affect you on leaving here and moving into adult service. Anyway, I'd like to say well done on behalf of the Squadron Permanent Staff group and I think Lt Rogers would like a word with you also. Carry-on.' (Which meant I was dismissed).

I came to attention, saluted, about-turned and marched out. The next time I was in this office it wouldn't be for praise, but for a bollocking and a fine.

I turned left and knocked at the Troop Officers open office door; Lt Rogers was inside.

'You wished to see me Sir?' I said…

Ah, yes Burt…

And so I went through the whole story again.

My fame was short lived and I soon put the whole episode behind me. It was back to the training routine and a slimmed down education curriculum. This was the term where we would be expected to complete our trade modules.

The three Infantry weapons had been learnt over our first two Courses; they now needed to be honed or perfected on the Ranges at Lydd and Hythe.

Most of our drill movements had been learnt, but again practice was the order of the day. Hours of drill were still written into our itinerary.

This term, our third term, was to be our final basic term, a term spent pulling all our skills together; as well as drill and weapons we would spend hours on field tactics and patrols; along with of course – fitness, fitness, fitness.

We would grumble every time we were dragged out to run the lanes and roads around Whitfield and Temple Ewell but we now took it literally in our stride.

We would also this term put our toe in the water regarding some basic improvised Engineering tasks.

For some of us the latter part of Course 3 would be the first step on the promotional ladder with the first step following an assessment Cadre to the rank of Lance Corporal, some would go higher, one lad from our intake Las Stewart eventually making Junior Regimental Sergeant Major, others, your truly among them would find themselves promoted and then within the space of 24 hours demoted again... I'll enlarge on that further on.

We were a couple of weeks into the term when I was called to the office and told I would be going home for a week to work in my local recruitment office. It was called the 'Satisfied Sapper' scheme and given to those who'd shown themselves to be worthy; in my case it was due to my alerting Paddington station to a possible bomb threat. Another lad who was picked to do this was Lee Wood from Maidstone. Initially I was pretty chuffed about this but then we were told we were expected to carry out this duty in full No2 dress, less best-boots. We would leave for home on the Friday and report back nine days later on the Sunday working Monday to Friday in the local army information office. A float would be given by the Chief Clerk, all expenses would be paid; of course this was subject to production of receipts.

I telephoned home and told my mum and dad the news and said I'd be home on Friday quite late.

At the end of works on Friday I packed my case and collected my travel warrant plus float from the Chief. The duty driver had been booked to take me and other lads from 'B' and 'C' Squadrons to the station. Lee's dad was driving over from Maidstone to collect him; the lucky bugger would go home in style.

By the time I got to Liverpool Street it was gone eight-o-clock and here I made a mistake of not reading the departures board, I caught the train standing waiting on the platform - it was the slow train. No train travelling from London to Norwich was quick in the seventies or eighties. Three and a half hours for the quick train, add an hour for the slower train that stopped at almost every station along the way. I got into Norwich at midnight to find no connecting train to Yarmouth; I lugged my case a mile to the bus terminus at the top of the city, just in time to get the last bus with all the night-club drunks back to Gt Yarmouth. The bus went through about twenty villages along the coast road before dumping me on a junction in the back of beyond; I was still a mile from home. It was gone 2am when I banged on the door and woke my family.

The following day mum and dad drove into Yarmouth and I asked to go with them, I needed to visit the bus station at the end of Wellington Road and enquire the bus times through Ormesby to Yarmouth and on to Lowestoft. I needed to be at the careers office for 0900.

I was horrified to read on the timetables that I'd need to leave home 0645!

The first bus I needed to catch to get me through my connections and to the office on time stopped two hundred yards up the road from our house at 0650; it took forty five minutes to get to Yarmouth, then a bus change and wait before another hour long trip to Lowestoft.

I dismounted the bus in Lowestoft at the 'Sparrows Nest' on the junction of North Parade and had to hike a mile down through the houses to the office on the junction of St Peters Street and Yeovil Road.

Getting home was a reverse procedure except that the bus never went through Ormesby; I had to get off the bus at the Caister and Scratby junction and walk almost three miles home. The walking itself didn't bother me it was what I was wearing; having to do this hike in my No2 dress uniform. By the time I'd left the careers office made the connection and walked those last three miles home it was passed eight thirty in the evening. What I thought would be a relaxing week turned out to be bloody hard work, as I said to my mates on return to Dover. I'd have rather stayed at Old Park with them. However it did look good on my report.

Mid-term exercise came round which this half term was held in the notorious Brecon Beacons National Park in Wales; notorious because it's a god-forsaken place which is never warm and always wet.

This camp certain individuals within Course 3 who had shown leadership potential would be chosen to manage section patrols and other tasks; temporarily we would hold the rank of Junior Lance Corporal and we would be assessed for permanent promotion later in the Course. I was chosen as one of these candidates.

The tasks we were to lead were chosen randomly and the Junior Lance Corporal arm-bands were passed on daily.

Although we were still only in Course 3 we were being given the grounding in basic improvisation. Improvisation is a word right up there at the top of the Sappers dictionary - Initiative, finding ways to get round problems, working with the basics, making things happen; and the phrase of today 'thinking outside of the box' these are all part of the job of being a 'Sapper'. Our instructors were looking constantly for those who showed those qualities.

No training area is great when you're living in a scrape in the ground – Dartmoor, Otterburn, they're all pretty bleak, but Brecon has to take the prize; even on a good day it's probably the most miserable training area in all UK.

We were to arrive and depart to and from Sennybridge Camp. A couple of nights would be spent in the huts, the rest of the time we'd be in scrape holes covered by ponchos and eating ration packs, on the hills of Brecon; without doubt in the pouring rain; utter bloody misery.

When we left from Sennybridge 48 hours after our arrival we were carrying a mountain of stuff and I was eternally thankful for my 58 webbing, this was the first time I'd used the large pack which easily took all my gear and was comfortable to carry clipped over the top of the yoke (cover photo). Loaded to the gunwales the trucks dropped us on the side of a mist shrouded minor road in the middle of nowhere.

In sections we formed up and tabbed for what seemed like miles to our lay-up area. Here we were to stay, digging in and going out both night and day for live-firing and patrol practice.

We were dug-in on the side of a hill overlooking a valley and stream, either side of the stream for yards was boggy marsh with humps of tussock grass.

Leaving at night on patrol we had to wade through this ice cold water both on the outward and return journey, it wasn't uncommon for some poor sod to end up face down having tripped over a hump of grass in the darkness. Our feet, boots, and the bottom of our trousers would just have dried out during the hours of exercise when they were drenched again on the return crossing.

Clipping our poncho's together (the new design poncho I'd bought in Silvermans had now replaced the old ground-sheet we were first issued with), we buddied up in our scrapes with a fairly large waterproof cover over our heads. We dragged stones and clods of peat, which were in abundance to build up a protective wall to the sides of our meagre accommodation. In our improvised shelter we slept and attempted to cook our 24 hour compo rations on our mini Hexamine stoves.

How many nights we spent on this hillside under the poncho-bashers I fail to remember but it felt like a lifetime. Our clothes were soaked, our sleeping bags were soaked and our instructors told us to quit moaning, what the fuck did we expect on a hillside in Wales.

One night when it was coming down like stair-rods we came under attack from what we thought was a Course 7 fighting patrol. They got as far as the stream before they were spotted and challenged by our sentries. No reply was given to the 'Halt who goes there!' Instead of answering our attackers stormed across the gulley flinging thunder-flashes left, right and centre and letting rip for all they were worth. Whistles were blown, Stand-To was shouted but it was to late – by the time we'd got out of our sodden sleeping bags they were upon us, we'd have all been killed in our beds, it was bloody frightening these guys cammed-up to fuck with blacken faces, bushes and branches hanging off them like walking shrubberies. They stormed across our position ripping down our bashers and kicking down our meagre stone and peat protection. We were totally screwed. Within minutes it was all over and they were gone leaving carnage behind them; we never fired a shot. It took us the rest of the night to sort ourselves out and regain some sort of order, rebuilding our bashers in the wind and pouring rain.

It turned out not to be any of our squadron at all; at least no troop owned up to it. When we spoke about it afterwards we decided they were too good to be our lot, they were probably a couple of sections of adult troops, territorials, (now known as reservists) or lads from Hereford who classed the Brecon's as their own back yard. They'd recce'd our position at some point and thought it would be fun to run amok among the Juniors. Until that point we all thought we were doing rather well...

However from this point on we were far more vigilant and a couple of nights later when Course 7 tried to take us by surprise they had a shock; we were prepared and reacted far quicker, hitting them hard before they had started to cross the stream and bog. They brought fire down on us from the other side of the gully but retreated without pressing home an attack. The attacking force Permanent Staff umpires giving us the victory. We'd learnt our lesson the first time.

The one outstanding memory I have of this camp was LMG live firing. The range extended for a good mile over the rugged hilly terrain with targets appearing from ground level, over vastly different distances. The variation in distance didn't allow time to change the sight range of the weapon; it was a case of point at the target and walk the rounds into it.

During my stint on the weapon a fully grown sheep, of which there are hundreds loosely grazing on the Brecon ranges came wandering round the side of a derelict house. This sheep was almost a kilometre away at the LMGs maximum killing range. Spriggsy my shooting mentor for the last year was down beside me in a shot...

'See that sheep Steve?' he said.

'Yeah I see it Corp.' I replied.

'Zap the thing' he said

'Are you serious,' I asked?

'Yes I am, do you good to shoot at something other than a piece of plywood; aim on the target and note where the rounds are landing, walk the rounds onto it, go on get stuck in.'

And that's what I done – the impact knocked the sheep clean of its feet, although it was a thousand yards away you could see bits of mutton flying off in all directions.

I don't think that poor old sheep felt much, here one second, gone the next; when we'd made safe we walked up to view the remains and the damage a five round burst of 7.62 to flesh and bone can cause. It was sobering and nothing like depicted in the movies, a couple of lads took on a greenish tinge.

We were all on the point of hypothermia and trench foot by the time we returned to what I can only say at the time seemed like five star accommodation at Sennybridge camp.

Exercise deployment over, we all had to return to Dover.

This time, unlike our trip to Stanford the previous November we had the responsibility of a personnel weapon, so we were obliged to return to Old Park, dump our kit, clean and hand in our SLR to the armoury before heading off on our short weekend leave.

Pete Bedigan from Newcastle came home with me for the weekend. He said it just wasn't worth going all the way to the north east for so short a time.

We both went up to Norwich on a jam-packed commuter rush hour train Leaving Liverpool Street around 1730. We managed to get a seat in one of the old fashioned compartments. These compartments sat six with the arm rests down and eight with them up, it was quite a squeeze at this time of day so the arm-rests were all up and we were tightly jammed in. Pete went off to get us a couple of bottles of beer; he would pass for eighteen, I certainly would not.

Purchase made Pete fought his way back through the rush hour, full to bursting carriage corridors. When he eventually got seated he handed me my far from cold lager while he took out his 'Jack knife' and flipped the top off his Brown ale bottle. It went absolutely everywhere! The shaking it had received on its travels through the train meant the beer shot out of the bottle neck like water out of a fire hose. The four people sitting opposite Pete got covered in sticky Brown ale. He was very embarrassed and apologetic but there wasn't much we could do about it. Of course we kept straight faced until the compartment emptied in Ipswich, and then we fell about laughing.

We returned on the Sunday afternoon for the final half of our third term. Now we we'd be taking our education exams for our trades and waiting to see who would be considered for their first promotion.

Prior to going on leave after Easter I had given Myleene my address and had kept my fingers crossed for a letter waiting for me on return. There wasn't one. I rang her number, the phone rang and went dead, that disconnected sound, so I concluded that the house must now be unoccupied; oh well she'll either write or not. She didn't; however Sunday the ninth of April would not turn out be the last time I would see Myleene. But I moved on and met another girl at the NAAFI dance; Gail Southerly who lived in Whitfield village; yes, Gail Southerly, how could I forget a name like that. She lived in a bungalow a few hundred yards up the Sandwich Road. I knocked around with her up to the end of the term but for some reason it ended, I never saw her again following post Course 3 leave. I remember her gran lived with the family and she had this really old book that told you how to read palms and tea-leafs and such like, the book must have been a hundred years old, nearly as old as her gran.

Trade exams finished I found I had failed two of the seven basic modules and had to re-sit them. This was not even taking into account numbers 10 and 14 the extra two I required to progress in my planned trade as a plant operator.

Things were not looking good; however I did eventually complete the required minimum. I was just not interested in anything academic at all even to the detriment of my own chosen future trade.

At the same time, our exams concluded, we were taken for trade interviews. These were carried out over in the trade training wing office by the education Officer Major Millsop, the trade training Officer, Captain Story and our Troop Officer, in my case Lt Rogers.

Bear in mind at this point I was still not an adult soldier I was only just sixteen years old as were the majority of my peers; the responsibility of our welfare and care had passed from our parents to that of the army. You would have thought that any major decisions that needed to be taken regarding our future at this point - decisions that were contrary to those that had been agreed on our signing-up - that our parents would have been consulted. But they weren't, not a bit of it.

The long and the short of it was, I was marched into an office, with, I might add, no prior warning; to face three Officers across a desk and make my own life changing decision on my future Royal Engineer trade training and my parents weren't even notified let alone consulted.

I was told that I was a good Junior Sapper; that I was doing well in all my training except my academic subjects. That I would not achieve the required modules needed for a plant operator in this third term and the only way I could do this was to agree to a further half course of full time education, Course 4E.

Now, as far as my parents were concerned, when I left home I left home to be a heavy plant operator. They'd never discussed a follow up plan or trade.

'Mr and Mrs Burt your son has proved he has the ability to be trained as a heavy plant operator', said the recruitment Sergeant and consequently that's what they believed I'd eventually become. Neither my parents nor I for that matter expected I'd be put in a position where I needed to make a choice, and I certainly was not the right person to be making that decision.

If the army had written to my parents and explained the situation I know exactly what my mum and dad would have said - 'half a term of full time education in 4E.'

There would have been no argument over it because that was the understanding between us when they agreed to let me leave home for a Junior Regiment of the army.

Thing is, they weren't consulted and I was left to make the decision myself with a certain amount of persuasion from a trade Officer who knew in what area of trade requirements the Engineers were lacking at the time.

'So Burt, you don't fancy continuing with your education at this time? You'd rather not go back to the classroom? Well we recommend for the interim you consider becoming a Combat Signaller. You can always carry on your further education when you reach your adult unit and obtain the extra modules you require and apply again to be a plant operator. You will also be put through your B3 driver training prior to leaving for your adult unit. How does that sound?' B3 was the military equivalent to a civilian class 3 heavy goods vehicle licence (HGV), except there was a great deal of maintenance and recovery theory that went with it. Of course my interviewing panel knew this was a sweetener; every kid wants to learn to drive and the bigger the vehicle the better.

The army wanted every soldier to be able to drive as well.

Now they weren't lying when they made this statement about continuing with my education when I arrived in Osnabruck; just over a year later I found Roberts barracks - the barracks of 23 & 25 Engineer Regiments had a very comprehensive education wing where numerous Courses were conducted and modules could be obtained, both in the day-time (if your Troop Officer agreed) and the evening. But the chances of me a young squaddie on the loose taking any progressive interest in furthering my education at that time of my life was pretty slim and it never happened.

Although at that particular moment in time standing in front of these Officers this route seemed like a good delaying tactic.

'Yes sir, if you don't object that would be my choice of career path at this time, I do not wish to carry on in 4E.'

Job done, I came to attention, saluted and marched out. My parents knew nothing about this until I let it slip while in England on a B2 Signals Course in summer 1975. Dad went ballistic!

Age was on my side; I was still very young and could have easily at this point done another four terms at Dover instead of three... in fact Steve Cottle did just that, passing out in the December of 73, whereas I passed out in the August. It was very peculiar how the powers worked it out, but make no mistake it was done to the army's advantage. They needed Combat Signallers in BAOR; they'd talked me into becoming one; so get Burt through training as soon as possible and into a front line unit (which of course BAOR was during the 'Cold War').

I left for my unit in Germany early November 1973. I was still five months shy of my eighteenth birthday. I served five months in my adult unit before I actually signed on as an adult soldier! I wasn't even old enough to go in the Squadron or NAAFI bar! (Although of course I did). Looking back on it now it hardly seems credible, but that's what happened and not just to me.

During the second half of term both Les and I had been put forward by both our Junior Course NCOs and by our Permanent Staff NCOs as recruits with the potential for advancement through the junior rank structure.

Every term new promotions had to take place to fill the gaps of those moving up to and into Course 8 and passing-out for 3 training Regiment at Southwood Camp in Farnbourgh.

I was very fired up in Course 3. Things were going well for me in every department other than education and that minor hick-up as I saw it had now been put to bed. I was delighted to think I could become a Junior Lance Corporal after passing the few tests we had to carry out to prove ourselves worthy. These were military based tests such as drill commands, marching a squad and leadership ability in field craft and patrols. I felt very confident on being able to fly through.

I also remember having to do a ten minute presentation in front of a group, a task that didn't faze me, I wasn't a kid who'd get tongue-tied. My talk was on the Humber one ton armoured 'Pig' as it was known. Designed as a soft skin vehicle in the early fifties it was converted to a wheeled armoured personnel carrier as a temporary stop gap until the six wheeled Saracen came into service. When the troubles in Northern Ireland kicked-off it was rapidly upgraded with armour and nearly 500 where deployed to the province.

It was a pig in every sense of the word. It not only looked like a pig, but it drove and handled like a pig as well, the characteristics of this ungainly mongrel I would experience first-hand in March 1974 when I was sent to Bordon in Hampshire to train as a driver on one of these things. It was top heavy and if you got two wheels on anything higher than a pavement the bloody thing would tip over. To top it off with a windscreen the size of a hanky you could barely see where you were going... But that was some way off and for the present all I had to do was research the vehicle and do a then-till-now presentation. This sounds easier than it actually was – bear in mind there was no internet in 1971; my only sources of information were from books or asking questions among our Permanent Staff group. However after some serious investigation I managed to collect enough information for a ten minute talk and it all went pretty smoothly.

As a group of prospective JNCOs we were put through our paces for a week before being informed of our promotion or non-promotion whichever was the case.

Les was definite promotion material, he'd been a

The Humber 1 ton or 'The Pig'.

cadet before coming to Old Park and he'd breezed through our first two terms with no problem, his downfall was his inability to know when to shut up; his mouth tended to get him into trouble. Put that aside he was proving to be a very good Junior Sapper.

So we were two of a number of lads given the good news, we'd passed and we would enter our next Course as Junior Lance Corporals.

Forty five years on I don't recall the names of all those promoted, but I do remember apart from Les and I two other lads and the reason for this is – for the four of us promotion would be very short lived.

We were not old enough to drink alcohol, although we all had and as far as I'm aware most of us enjoyed it.

The pubs in Whitfield and Dover were strictly out of bounds and most landlords wouldn't serve the obvious fresh faced and young looking Freds, so a trip into town for a beer was not worth the effort.

Shops and supermarkets didn't, in 1972 sell alcohol; again you had to buy from a designated 'Off-licence'. This wouldn't change in the UK until the early eighties.

However rumour had it that there was one pub in the town that would serve anyone no questions asked, this was apparently the 'First and Last' on East Cliff Road, a back street just off the Eastern Docks.

Les and I should never have listen to the two Dave's they'd already done 14 days in the guard room for being caught in the married quarters with a 'Pads' wife (married personnel were referred to as 'Pads' by single's) and that was in our first term!

Residents of the BER both Dave B and Dave B like us had completed the JNCOs cadre and been told of our upcoming promotion. (I can only say they must have been desperate in 'A' Squadron at the time). I have excluded their surnames to avoid any future law-suite or contract being put out on me.

Dave and Dave decided they would celebrate their change of status by frequenting the 'First and Last' for a jar or two... would we like to come along? For me a second major decision within a couple of weeks and again I make the wrong one.

'Yeah, sure love to,' we foolishly said.

So that evening, clad in our best we left for what we thought would be a 'cool' mature evening drinking a couple of pints of Watney's Red Barrel, eating a few bags of crisps and throwing a few arrows at the dart board.

It all went to plan for the first twenty minutes, the lass behind the bar had not batted an eyelid when we requested four pints of bitter and we retired to the back room where we couldn't be seen from the street – not that there was much we could have done to avoid capture as the back-room bar only led to two outside toilets, a 'his and hers' and a small yard – the pub backed right up against the While Cliffs with no rear exit.

Was this a chance inspection by one of Dover's boys in blue or had he been tipped off? After he'd taken our names and Squadrons we asked him but he wouldn't say and we never found out. I don't think he was tipped-off, I think we were just very unlucky, it was a random check, it was plainly obvious we were squaddies and young ones at that so the request - 'let's see your ID cards lads' was the question he was bound to ask and our IDs showed our date of birth. We couldn't lie and there was no point saying we were in 'B' or 'C' Squadron it would have taken no time at all for the Provost Sergeant to find out just which Squadron we belonged to.

We were sent on our way and our capture was phoned through to Old Park.

We walked more or less in silence back to the barracks all four of us knew we would be deeply in the shit; we never said anything to the duty NCO it would be on the SSMs desk soon enough and the whole bloody Squadron would know and we'd be on a charge as sure is eggs are eggs; sure enough that's what happened.

We walked upstairs Dave and Dave headed off to their room, Les and I to 96 where we sheepishly explained our evening to our roommates.

Keith and our three buddies' thought it was hilarious.

'That'll be the shortest promotion in history,' was the prediction given by our Room-jack and he wasn't wrong.

The 'First and Last' pub, up against the cliff. The pub where we were 'Nicked'!

The following morning we were called out of the ranks and marched into the SSM. He gave us a bollocking, an especially harsh one as he knew we'd all just finished Cadre the previous day.

'You four bloody morons, you know what this means don't you? No stripe for you four - promoted yesterday and demoted today, what the fuck were you thinking? You Dixon, you Burt... I expected better of you, as for you two, he was now glowering at Dave & Dave I told you after your last escapade I didn't want to see the pair of you in this office again. Who's idea was this?' He said staring from one to the other of us.

There was silence from the four of us.

'Not saying eh? Fine, I'll tell that to the OC I'm sure he'll be impressed with your loyally to each other... Right, outside my office at 1330 for OCs orders (we were on a charge or OCs orders as it was called).

191

At 1330 we were again outside the SSMs office we were relieved of our berets (we would not salute) and we were taken to stand outside the OCs door one behind the other.

This is how it worked – We stood smartly at ease.

The SSM would roar - Accused Accuseddddd SHUN! We would then come smartly to attention, the SSM would open the OCs door and we would be marched in at double quick time to the right side of the OCs desk, wheel to the left and halt. We would then be commanded Right TURN! And remain smartly at attention in front of our Officer Commanding. We would only speak when spoken to, the charge would be read, our defence would be listened to and the OC would make his judgement.

We would then be right turned and again marched out in double time. Double time instead of being Left – Right - Left - Right – Left, is more like eft-eit-eft-eit-eft-eit (very fast, get it?)

The SSM called us up and in we very briskly marched and halted and turned.

The OC looked up.

'The charge against you lads is that you were caught yesterday red-handed in a local pub by the Dover Constabulary. The Officer phoned your names through to the guard-room who informed the Sergeant Major who is far from happy. I'm also informed that you told the constable that you didn't make a habit of drinking but you were celebrating a promotion… is this correct?'

'Answer the OC Burt.' This came from the SSM who was stood behind us.

'Yes sir, that is correct,' I said.

'Well of all the ridicules things to do and on top of that get caught… I'm very sad about this but I have no option but to oppose your promotion and fine you ten pounds each. I would have been stricter but I realise that denying you promotion I'm also denying you of the increased pay that went with your stripe. Burt, you especially surprise me, you've had a very good term and we were expecting further good things from you. Hopefully all four of you will redeem yourself very quickly and lesson learnt we can review your promotion prospects in your following Courses. March them out Sergeant Major.'

'Accused SHUN! Rightttttt TURN! In double time Quick MARCH! Eft-eit-eft-eit-eft… and out we went.

'Burt, Dixon, return to your training; B and B come into my office.' Ordered the SSM.

Because of their previous conviction the two Dave's received seven nights behind the guard in No2 dress and banned from town for the rest of term.

Apart from temporary promotion during training exercise's neither one of us gained permanent promotion during the rest of our time at Dover.

End of term was drawing near and we were all keen to know what the following term held for us, we could go in a number of directions Courses 4, 5, 6 or Combat Engineering in Course 7.

We finished work one evening to find the list of our next Courses pinned to our Landing notice board.

I would be going to Course 7 along with Ray. Les, Doddy and Steve would be doing 4L. I found this a bit odd, I could understand Ray doing seven, he was the oldest of the five of us but I was the youngest in our room and probably our troop, I'd be entering a Course where the majority of lads were almost a year older than me. Still mine was not to reason why as they say.

Returning in Course 7 after our summer break in September; I would be on the lower floor – the old Course 8 lines.

Changes had been made to the way the final Course was structured. Course 8 would be moving to accommodation in 'C' Squadron block above the education wing, they would no longer wear the red, green or blue Squadron cravat, but would be considered a separate troop with no Squadron commitments. They would concentrate solely on Combat Engineering level B2. The only Junior NCO to retain rank would be the Junior Regimental Sergeant Major. Course 8 would be expected to manage themselves with no input from JNCOs and only minimal input from Permanent Staff trainers.

'A' Squadron would also change with a new OC; a Major Durey the gung-ho and forward thinking Darien Gap adventurer.

This coming Pass-out would see the departure of some good friends, admittedly they were lads who'd dished us out some shit in our first term, slightly less in Course 2 but had accepted us as equals in Course 3. Mick Foster and Smudge were two of them.

In two weeks I'd be travelling with Smudge down to Bath Spa for the last time.

I would be returning in Course 7; basic would be finished, we'd now be getting our hands on the real Royal Engineers equipment including mines and explosive.

We had a troop jolly in Margate, ninety plus of us let loose in a small seaside town. We had a great time spending most of the evening in the funfair; Les won a bet with Spriggsy by bringing back a pair of girl's knickers. His roommates knew this but others found out later that he'd bought them from some slapper he'd met during the evening; he offered her half of what he'd bet Spriggsy; paid a pound and won two; typical Les.

A week later I reported sick with an Achilles problem.

'You'll have to watch that ankle Burt; you've got an obvious weakness there.'

'Yes Sir,' I said.

I'd got away with it again, for the second time my supposed injury had not been linked to the forthcoming Pass-out parade.

We broke up on Saturday 12th August for an extended four week break returning Monday to start work on Tuesday 12th September.

Tony Cooke, Smudge, Taddy, Gerry and me all travelled together from Paddington. It was summer and we were all in good spirts. Tony got off in Swindon; Gerry said he'd come over to Winsley for the day while I was down at grans and I gave him my aunties telephone number before he got off the train in Chippenham. Taddy's mum and dad were waiting for him on the Bath platform, he had only a five minute drive up to Twerton a suburb of Bath very close to the city centre. He introduced me to his folks who I'd end up seeing quite a lot of over the next year and a bit. Taddy would also be joining me in Course 7. Smudge was waiting in the station for his connection to Westbury and we said our goodbyes on the platform; he'd been a great mentor and friend, I'd miss him. I wished him well on the next stage of his Sapper journey – his final six weeks B2 Combat Engineering at Southwood, completing subjects that couldn't be taught at Dover due to their not being the correct facilities.

He told us on the train that ex-Freds and Chepstow apprentices arriving at 3 Royal Engineer Training Regiment got crapped on from a great height.

We were all very young and yet we were very highly trained; basically when it came to training we'd 'got the 'T' shirt' and because of this the instructors took us down a peg or two by putting us through hell.

This was not a rumour but a solid fact passed down from one group to another. But as Smudge said, 'fuck em we can take it.'

He kept his promise giving me his Pea-greens, which he told me weren't allowed to be worn at Southwood.

Once again I was back in my favourite place – Winsley.

Jeff and Sticky were both working but Bern and Kev were at home. Angie also had a job she was working at the mushroom quarry in Bradford. I'd had the occasional letter from her over the last year but what had started out as regular correspondence had dwindled somewhat. I'd not been the most loyal boyfriend... but boyfriend may not be the right word to use. We hadn't been boyfriend, girlfriend for a few years, but when all was said and done she was still the girl top of my list and I desperately wanted to spend some time in her company. I made a point of knocking on the Holt's door whenever I thought Angie may be in; more often than not she wasn't. I was no longer on the scene; some other lucky bugger had won the heart of the girl I'd loved throughout my school years.

But I was nothing if not resilient and wouldn't give up that easy. I would continue to regularly write my exploits from Dover and hope I'd impress with my stories of daring-do... meanwhile in the interim I hopped on the bus to Melksham to meet with my old flame Clare. She still gave up her time to meet with me and with Clare there was always the chance of a leg-over, it was summer and quite warm in the long grass beside the canal.

Evenings in the village we'd sit outside the Stars as we had for years, or walk down to the Viaduct Hotel at the bottom of Brassknocker Hill in Limpley Stoke where Jeff had a job of standing up Skittles for the Skittle teams, it paid fifty pence and all the coke you could drink. Moggie Cliffe (Maurice) who'd taken over our council house when we left Winsley was the bouncer on the door (shows what type of establishment it was) he'd got him the job. I remember one evening walking down Winsley Hill and we could hear the music from the Hotel blasting out across the valley; number three in the UK charts Silver Machine by Hawkwind; what a great record. Another hang out in the evening was the social club or working men's club in Westwood. We'd walk through the old village past Lavington's and the cricket field down the footpath to Avoncliff in the valley then up the really steep hill on the other side of the canal to Westwood village. No one bothered about our age and we could listen to a band, sink three or four pints before staggering back to Winsley around 11pm.

Eventually mum would be on the phone to my aunt Dorothy, demanding I come home, so I'd pack my bags and head reluctantly to Norfolk.

Two weeks in Norfolk was enough, although this visit home was mid-summer and at least I could get my bike out and ride to the beach at Scratby or Caister, a short three miles away.

It had been a year since I'd left home and a year since the family had moved to East Anglia, I got the feeling that my dad was resigned to being in Norfolk but not necessarily happy. I settled down to being a soldier far better than my parents had settled to being chicken farmers.

It was Monday 11th September my mums birthday; we had a family birthday breakfast; I gave her a card and present and once again boarded the train to Dover.

Course 7 September 1972

Our September 1971 Intake had been lucky enough to remain in the same lines for a year, but now we had to move to new rooms and new lines.

We carried out this mad room swap following passing-out parade on the Saturday morning prior to going on our summer break.

Courses 4, 5 and 6 lines were on the second floor, far side of the block looking out over RHQ and the stables.

My new room in Course 7 lines - the ex-Course 8 lines was on the ground floor looking out onto the quad the first on the right through the fire doors.

I'd skipped the Pass-out parade four weeks previously and that morning while my mates had been pounding the square in their best kit with rifle I'd spent in a leisurely couple of hours moving all my kit plus mattress and bedding to my bed space of choice three floors below.

Following my move I relieved the Chief Clerk of a nice pay cheque and travel warrant then relaxed and waited for everyone else to return from parade, get changed and manically rush round doing the same thing.

Lads came to 7 not only from 3, but from 4, 5 and 6 as well. There was to be a total of thirty five of us of which over half were from my own intake. Ray and Taddy had joined me, also Jago and Jackson the two scroungers; thankfully they weren't in the same room as me.

As well as 'A' Squadron the other two Squadrons had Courses of equal number, so over a hundred lads at any one time were learning how to build and blow sky-high anything from a tree stump to a bridge. Oh what fun!

We paraded in the quad on the first morning to be addressed by our new Officer Commanding. He stood on the office step; we were formed-up smartly in three ranks in our troops.

Our SSM stood by his side as did the other commissioned Officers.

'Men,' our SSM roared. 'I will call you up and fall you out, you will gather in an informal group in front of the steps.'

'PARADE! PAAARADE SHUN!' This was one single crash as we brought our left boots to the floor in unity.

'PARADE, FALLLLL OUT! Again as a single body we swivelled to the right, brought our left foot to the floor and marched three paces before splitting and gathering in front of the steps.

'Good morning lads, and welcome back,' the OC greeted us.

'Morning Sir.' Came our muffled, first morning back, less than enthusiastic reply.

Right lads, I'm Major Durey and as I'm sure you knew before the summer break I've taken over command of the Squadron from Major Milsom. I'm also pretty sure you've been informed of where I have been and what I have been doing over the last six months. (Nods and muffled yeses).

For those of you who haven't heard, I made my way with a group Sappers and other assorted personnel along the Trans America highway from Alaska to Cape Horn. Two hundred and fifty miles of that journey was through the swamp and forest of the Darien Gap in Panama, that section of the journey took us three months on its own. To say we must have been crazy is somewhat an understatement, once we'd started on that section of the trip there was no going back. I will, over the coming months offer to show film footage of our journey and give talks to any of you that are interested.

However to the present... I've now found myself with a slightly quieter life that I expect to be different but no less interesting and no less enjoyable. I've been told I've inherited the best Squadron in the Regiment and I have no doubt that you men will prove to me that this is the case. I have ideas to modernise the Squadron to introduce some home comforts to your rooms and slightly relax the rules. In return I expect you to continue to strive to be the best Squadron in the Regiment. I don't like second best in anything. As we move forward into a new era I wish you all well and hope that over the course of time I'll get to know each and every one of you. Carry on Sergeant Major.'

With this comment and before the SSM could call us up he turned and with the other Officers made his way back into the office area.

'LISTEN IN!' Roared our SSM.

'Reform in your troops and continue with whatever duties you have; fall out.'

As a group we made our way back to our troop positions and formed up in three ranks.

Our Permanent Staff Sergeant for this term would be Sgt Farmer; he would also be one of our main Combat Engineer instructors. Other Combat Engineer instructors would stand in for different subjects of which in total there were four main ones, Demolitions, Field Defences, which encompassed a multitude of minor subjects within, such as barbed wire entanglements, holdfasts, trench-works and sangers; Bridging which in Course 7 consisted of the Bailey Bridge along with improvised bridging and finally anti-personnel and anti-vehicle Mine Warfare.

As well as this huge step into full time practical Combat Engineering subjects we had to train for the assault course competition, the patrols competition and this term Course 7 would take part in the all services British Legion March & Shoot competition an annual event held in the Autumn. It was going to be a full on term.

Sgt Farmer called us to attention, left turn and marched us over to the West Square Combat Engineer training wing. He stood us easy and explained what would happen during the term.

We would tackle our theory or classroom work as a troop; there were three classrooms in the wing used and laid out for different subjects. We would alternate through these rooms with the lads from 'B' and 'C' squadrons. When doing practical tasks such as section trench digging on Dover cliffs or building improvised holdfasts we would be divided into sections of roughly 5-8 lads depending on the task.

We fell out to the classroom for our introduction to our Sapper trade - Combat Engineering.

The first item we were presented with was the R.E.P.B. The Royal Engineers Pocket Book, a small thick book measuring roughly six by four inches. We would each be issued with a copy for our time on the Course and we were strongly recommended to buy one. The sales pitch left me wondering if our instructors were on commission.

Joking aside this little book contained everything you needed to know in the way of calculations, weights, minefield configurations amounts of explosive required to do away with numerous man-made and natural structures, plus heaps of other stuff; it was indeed the Combat Engineers Bible. The pages were held by sprung loaded clips, new sections could be added and amendments changed. Not dissimilar to the eighties fileofax for those who remember the forerunner of the Ipad...

I didn't buy one at the time choosing to sign for mine and hand it back when I left Dover; but twenty five years into the future while Clerk-of-Works overseeing the building of a marina in Co Fermanagh Northern Ireland (a Peace & Reconciliation Project) I got hold of one again on Ebay and found it incredibly useful while planning and installing the groundworks, jetty and pontoon system; this copy I still own.

There is no doubt that we all suddenly felt a great buzz being in Course 7, especially those of us that had come directly from Course 3; you may even call it smug and big-headed. Our instructors were well aware of this and very soon put us in our place. Sloppy drill was quickly picked up on and nipped in the bud.

During our first three Courses we were made to swing our arms chest high when we marched and all leg drill movements such as the turning movements and 'Halt' required the knee to be at a right angle to the hip. We considered this a bit over the top and had witnessed a far more relaxed approach to drill movements such as swinging the arms across the body to waist height and dragging the foot through the 'Halt' by Course 8.

Within the first day of our new term we'd try to emulate this style only to be given an ear bashing and thirty minutes hard marching drill by our instructors just to remind us that we hadn't quite got there yet. Although they very soon let the bullshit slip and as long as we didn't over-do-it would turn a blind eye.

Every morning of the Monday to Friday week we were up at sparrows-fart in our boots, denims and 'T' shirts, road bashing around Whitfield and Temple Ewell; this in preparation for both the assault course and march and shoot competitions. Green Lane in Temple Ewell was the killer; down the back hill to Buckland then over the main road, the river and the railway we would bash our way up Lower Road to Kearsney railway station; this was the easy bit we'd then get onto Green Lane a narrow road that in 1972 ran all the way up to Whitfield and when I say up I mean up. The back hill from Buckland to the Barracks was steep enough but Green Lane was in another dimension – a killer! As the weeks went by we cursed this hill; if we had a bad morning our PTIs would make us run up and down twice, swearing and shouting at us,; they would make us ran up it backwards or carry an equal sized colleague on our back or over our shoulders.

We progressed from 'T' shirt order to skeleton-order (ammo pouches only) and then battle order, full belt kit with ammo and weapon. I don't think I've been so fit in my life and I would never be at that point of physical fitness ever again.

On the actual day of the competition we entered two teams of eight men and covered the seven miles in forty minutes.

We didn't win or even get placed. I was not one of the sixteen guys picked but my good friend Alan Tadd took part and on completion his foot was so raw on the bottom that blood freely dripped from his boot.

For the assault course competition we carried no weapon but instead carried a lump of telegraph pole. This was an Inter-Squadron event in which I did take part and that term, we, 'A' Squadron won the day.

Along with shooting, running was my forte, I was really swift and had the stamina to go the distance however I was lazy and not inclined to put myself forward for anything that caused me to break into a sweat. I could quickly assess a situation and slip out of the line of sight. It was a failing of mine which probably didn't go unnoticed among my instructors.

We had one lad in our Course 7, Pete Eastwood - he'd joined a term before me in April 71. He was fitness mad, a Junior Sergeant and would be posted to the same Regiment as me in Osnabruck Germany. He would become a Regimental PTI in 23 Engineer Regiment. When you were fitness training under PTI Eastwood you bloody well knew it. I'd love to know where he ended up and what he ended up doing on leaving the army. Many PTIs became PE instructors at schools – I pity any school kid that had Pete as an instructor; killer Eastwood we called him in 16.

We soon settled back into the routine of Squadron life and our new OC was true to his word. Each room had television; the old flat iron that had to be shared between two or three rooms was replaced with a steam iron, one in each room. Other little changes took place, I can't remember what they were now he was a good bloke and when he held one of his Darien Gap talks I went along, it was very interesting.

We were only a week into the term when Les who now doing 4L came down to tell me he was off to Towyn (Tywyn) in North West Wales to the outward bound school, I was pretty envious, I was stuck with a term of Combat Engineering while my mate was swanning off for a great time in an outward bound centre in Wales - Snowdonia National Park. Still… almost certainly due to my age I'd be doing 4L the following term along with my B3 Signals Course, I hoped I'd also get the chance of an outward bound centre visit.

However as it happened my good pal Les was not going to enjoy his 4L as expected; within a few days of his leaving for Towyn word filtered back that he was in hospital and would remain there for some time. He'd fallen from the Death-slide and broken a number of bones. I can't remember now how many breakages he had, but the rumour mill was rife with stories of his back, neck, hips, legs… in fact if you listened to the talk around the lines it was a wonder he'd ever walk again let alone be a soldier. The Death-slide at the time was aptly named… a tower among the tree tops with a wire rope leading to ground level, now we call it a Zip-wire, and you're clipped on and wearing a harness. In 1972 you had no harness, just held tightly to a length of rope with a few knots in it. The day Les jumped at the rope it was raining, the rope was wet and his hands were muddy; he couldn't hold on and plummeted to the ground.

I... or should I say 'A' Squadron never saw Les again until the very end of term, almost four months after his accident; he came down for the last couple of days to move his gear with the rest of us. He told us he'd spent quite a while being rebuilt and then gone to convalescence. But he was as good as new and returned in January 1973 for his Course 7;

At this point in the term life was pretty hectic but the new challenge, the Combat Engineering was interesting.

We learnt our subjects in the classroom and then put them into practice.

Mine warfare and Field Defences practical we would carry out on the clifftops between the Dover Eastern Docks and St Margret's Bay; in fact pretty much where the present day Coastguard Station stands; the road out to the present Coastguard Station is the same road we took in the 4 tonners laden with the tools of our trade.

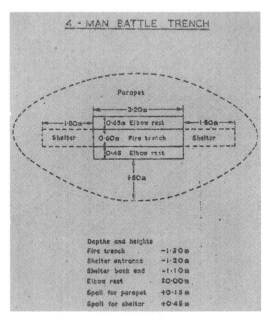

Up here on top of the cliffs we would erect coils of wire entanglements and dig different types of trenches single person defensive scrapes, one man trenches for longer term occupation with a ground sheet and earth covering; in sections we'd dig large mortar pits and headquarter trenches with timber reveting and roofing covered by three or four foot of earth.

It was lovely up there on the cliff top we were at the end of September, entering Autumn 1972 was a real Indian summer; we were very lucky, out on the top of the white cliffs in shitty weather was not the place to be; but we worked shirts off in the late summer sunshine with views all the way across the channel to France. At break times and lunch we would sit eating the rations from Hay-boxes, drinking tea and smoking and at 1600 hours pile onto the trucks back to Old Park.

However it was back breaking work and as fit as we were we would be exhausted by the end of the day, all our efforts had to be filled-in or dismantled, gear had to be loaded on the trucks and on our return to the Combat Engineer Wing the equipment had to be meticulously cleaned till it gleamed and then packed away in the exact place and condition as we'd signed it out. Only then could we form up and march the 150 yards back to the Quad and the cookhouse for our evening meal.

At six in the morning we'd tumble out of bed – form-up and once again hit the roads around Whitfield or the cross country track; training for our forthcoming competitions. Our bodies during Course 7 took a hammering daily that they never seemed to recover from. Our shoulders were raw and tender from carrying the pole; feet were blistered; even the area around the hips was sore where we were constantly running with loaded webbing. On top of that every muscle ached from the daily Combat Engineering tasks we were preforming. We were knackered.

Course 7 was relentless and I think it began to wear us all down. Petty squabbles and arguments were becoming frequent. Some nights following a hard day out on the cliff tops laying a minefield we'd be back doing night time mine retrieval, regardless of the weather; crawling on our bellies in the darkness marking safe lanes and searching for the mines with prodders and electronic detectors. Tea, truck, stores, wash and bed we'd be up again at six for our road bash in the morning.

As well as the night time Combat Engineer training we had to prepare for the section patrols competition, this was also carried out under the cover of darkness. We'd finish work, go back to our rooms and get our works-dress ready for the next day then into combats, and webbing, with cam-cream or burnt cork smeared over our faces we'd be over to the armoury for our SLR, magazines and if we were lucky a blank adaptor. Lucky because there were never enough adaptors to go round.

Blank adaptors fitted to the end of the barrel and held in place by the bayonet lug allowed the weapon's working parts to move as they would with a live round; the gas content in a blank round filled only with sawdust is not great enough to push the working parts back to expel the spent case and pick up a new round from the magazine. The adaptor effectively prevents or blocks the few gases of a blank round from being expelled out of the mussel using it to re-cock the weapon. If you don't have an adaptor fitted each round fired requires the cocking lever to be manually pulled back, the weapon to be manually rearmed.

The thing is, without an adaptor the filling inside the blank is discharged from the muzzle in exactly the same way as a bullet, although within a few yards of the end of the barrel the wood-dust residue is quickly dispersed. Technically it should do a person no harm - unless of course the barrel is close to another person when the trigger is pulled and this is exactly what happened to me.

We were on a patrol in the dead of night when we were overheard by a listening patrol consisting of lads in Course 3. They opened fire on us, we hit the ground and our patrol commander decided to overrun their position. We were on our feet and charging, screaming and firing toward the dug-in position. In the heat of the fire fight Smudge Smith a huge guy from North London who I'd end up travelling to Osnabruck with the following year was running behind me; he pulled his trigger and discharged a blank round inches from the left side of my lower back. Of course I didn't have a clue what had happened, we were surrounded by noise, it felt like a dozen wasp stings all at once; I screamed and fell rolling on the floor with my hand over my back. However this was adrenalin pumping moment with rounds

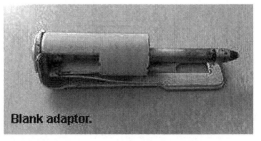
Blank adaptor.

being loosed off, lads shouting, thunder-flashes flying through the air and exploding and parachute flares floating down from overhead.

Not the time to be wimping, I was only on the floor for a millisecond before I was back on by feet and charging again through the position. My back stung like hell and I had no idea what had happened. We overran the position and regrouped moving off to lay-up and take stock.

Once we had accounted for our numbers our patrol leader asked if we were all ok. I said I'd had a problem with my back and didn't know what it was; in the light of a masked torch he looked at my jacket. 'Fucking hell Steve,' he said, 'you've got a hundred bloody holes in your jacket, what the fuck done that? Let's have a look at your back.'

But I said I'd rather not - it would wait till we were back at the main RV but fucking hell it was sore. We moved off and eventually the exercise for the evening was over. I took my combat jacket off and there in the back of the jacket just above the point my belt would lie were a multitude of little holes. When I felt my shirt it was damp with blood and the skin on my back beneath the shirt was rough with small blisters and indentations. In the beam of the trucks headlights everyone had a good look at my war wound. It was the size of a cricket ball in circumference; it was red, angry and very sore. Of course our Permanent Staff knew exactly what had happened and the only culprits could have been one of those not sporting a blank adaptor. Of the four lads without adaptors it could only have been the not so quick on his feet Smudge who was behind me when we launched the attack. He effectively (had it been a live round) killed me – one of his own side and a comrade in arms. Our Permanent Staff were not amused and used me as an example of lack of care and weapon safety in a hot situation showing my wound to all those present.

A mug of tea, a bun - whacked out we'd clamber aboard the trucks for the trip home, we'd get comfortable, the chatter would cease; someone would light a fag and in the glow of the lighter you'd see blokes asleep, their heads on their webbing lying on the floor of the truck with arms wrapped round their rifle, or their head on the shoulder of the guy next to them. For some strange reason at that time of night surrounded by your mates, sharing a ciggie, dirty, sometimes wringing wet and tired there was a great sense of comradery and achievement; we felt like Soldiers.

The following morning I paraded with the sick lame and lazy and went off to the quacks to have my back looked at. The doc cleaned up the wound and gave me antiseptic cream and that was the end of it. I had to change my combat jacket and shirt which created a hoo-ha, the QM saying I'd damaged the kit and had to pay for it. I resolutely stood my ground on that one and won the day. But it just goes to show how easily you can be wounded or killed by friendly fire when all hell is breaking loose around you.

As I wrote at the end of the last chapter, Course 7 would be a Course of highs and lows. I had two portions of bad news this term. This first came during the first half of the term which really hit me for a six, I had a letter arrive from Angie, the first one in ages and of course I was overjoyed.

While in Winsley during the summer break I'd not seen her and had received only a couple of answers to my letters the previous term. So this was the first correspondence of any type for quite some time. In happy anticipation what my letter may hold I sat on my bed and ripped open the envelope, in which I hoped I would find at least a bit of affection being shown from her to her old flame.

But no, quite the contrary. It was an honest and frank letter telling me some news of a new boyfriend and asking me not to write to her or look her up anymore – in old fashioned terminology 'A Dear John'. I was gutted – ok perhaps I'd not been that faithful - but then we weren't exactly boyfriend girlfriend any longer in the remain loyal sense, but for me through all those years of growing up in Winsley, the year in North Bradley and my year in the army I had it in my head and really believed that one day Angie and I would seriously get back together. Now came the crushing realisation that this was not going to happen.

This letter, as daft as it sounds now had a real effect on my moral. Remember I was only a sixteen year old teenager; although in my everyday working life I was participating in, and working at, very adult type jobs, I suppose a piece of me was still very childlike and Angie's rejection was not something I could cast-off or move instantly on from. Even adults are affected by relationships closures and for me as a youngster this hit me hard.

This 'getting the boot' from my girl, along with the intensity of the workload put me in a real downer. It was the only time during my army career that I wanted to quit, give it up and go home.

I carried on – I had to, had no choice, I had gone past the point of being able to quit even if there'd ever been one. As I said before if you wanted to get out you had to be literally kicked out and then it would be on your final record – dishonourable discharge and no one wanted that – unless of course you were mega desperate.

I was quiet and withdrawn; my roommates all who were older than me and had not been in my Intake Course had no sympathy and took the piss something cruel. I was run down, uncommunicative and my standards were dropping to the point I was called in front of my Troopy and questioned. He listened without too much sympathy and told me to buck up.

I did - I had to - in the end putting my love life on the top shelf and getting on with the whirlwind itinerary of Course 7. However I decided that I would take my half term leave in Winsley; the desperation of a teenage broken heart...

The week prior to half term once again we left for our field training exercise; a second trip to the Stanford training area in Norfolk. This trip instead of learning field craft as we'd done a year earlier in Course 1 we'd be concentrating on improvised engineering exercises - Improvised lifting

Raft command! Stanford Oct 1972

equipment such as building a Gin & Shears, improvised bridging and rafting, as well as close-quarter combat range and other shooting practise. It was a great week and we took turns as acting section commander.

My leadership task was building a raft and transporting a trailer across a lake. We carried this out with coils of rope, and by rope I mean real natural rope, hemp and sisal, not polypropylene or nylon; scaffold 'deals' and 45 gallon oil drums.

We had to build a raft capable of taking the loaded military trailer. It was great fun and I was one of the first to be put in charge of the task. The photo shows Mog Fawsett front right and the rest of my section doing the work while I stand at the stern dishing out the orders.

I also won ten pounds on the close quarter battle range with the highest score of the day. The range consisted of a path through a forest; along the way twenty targets appeared from ditches, from behind trees, from trenches in the ground and windows of ruined buildings... you get the idea I'm sure. We had to move with stealth along the course snap shooting two rounds at each target when it appeared, sometimes two at a time.

While doing this we had to be aware of the rounds in our magazine, count the shots and change the mag when it was empty. We all threw fifty pence in the pot, I won the tenner, the runner up got a fiver and third place got three quid. I dropped two rounds out of forty and Spriggsy was amazed when I put two rounds into the middle of a target that swung out of a tree as I was crossing a track. I literally fired from the hip. Pure luck I'm sure, but well impressive.

We were back in the old Nissan huts with the pot-bellied coal stove sat in the middle of the room with a tin chimney out through the roof.
Brian Bridson and I were on guard duty one night, it was freezing and we went into a hut to get warm. The fire was almost out and Brian had the bright idea of throwing a jam-jar full of petrol into the stove to bring it to life. It was a wonder the stove didn't explode. Brian removed the cast iron plate on the top and ludicrously, very slowly tipped in the petrol. This was the craziest way to do it... well, anyway you tip petrol into a lighted stove is going to be stupid but this took the biscuit. Of course the petrol ignited back to the jar. Brian was effectively holding a Molotov cocktail which in panic he dropped into the stove, glass and all.

There was an almighty explosion and the flame shot out the top of the stove as high as the ceiling above. All the sleeping bodies in the room came instantly awake while we rushed for the fire buckets (note fire buckets not fire extinguishers). All hell broke loose but fortunately by the time Permanent Staff arrived the fire was out and we lied through our back teeth that something had gone pop in the stove as we were patrolling past and that we'd dashed in and saved the day. Hero's both of us... we were bloody lucky not to get fourteen days in the 'Nick'.

Unlike the year before when mum and dad had picked me from Brandon station I chose to return to Old Park and head west for the weekend. We embarked from Brandon on the Thursday, and those of us going home for the weekend were free to leave Old Park on the Friday morning. Again I'd requested my train warrant to Bath Spa. The usual crowd of us travelled together round the Circle line and onto Paddington; Tony, Taddy, Gerry and myself, the topic of conversation this trip was - one - would I be able to keep my girlfriend and two – tattoos. Loads of lads had arrived at Dover with tattoo's Les and Pete Bedigan having more than anyone else put together. The Tattooist in Dover wouldn't tattoo Junior Leaders, whether there was an age restriction on when a person could or could not be tattooed I don't know, if this was the case then why did so many lads of only fifteen and sixteen years old arrive at Dover sporting a kaleidoscope of artwork. Anyway whatever the reason the lads who wanted a tattoo or a further tattoo went elsewhere, Deal, Chatham or Folkestone. Gerry was planning on getting a Geisha Girl on his upper arm. He would get this done in Bath. He did... and on return after the weekend it was much admired. Me? Not a cat-in-hells chance. I liked my skin just the way it was; also I didn't fancy the pain.

I had a nice weekend with gran; I never saw Angie but got the true story from Jeff. I didn't feel at all like returning to the army following that weekend, I was gutted. Bern said I should desert, I could hide out in their garden shed. Although the facilities on offer were five star I declined and returned to Dover for the second half of the term.

I knew I had to get myself back on track, there was just too much going on for me not to have my head in the right place, also the training we were going through didn't allow for anything less than hundred percent concentration. These next few weeks would see us on a two week practical Bailey Bridging course in Chatham and live demolition work at Yantlet on the Isle of Grain on the North Kent coast. Lack of concentration in either of these two subjects can cost you your life.

Again we were really lucky with the weather, we spent two or three days practicing live Dems at Yantlet and the weather was gorgeous. We'd load up the trucks with PE4 explosive, detonation cord and fuses; plus other assorted stuff to make improvised shaped charges, nail bombs and booby-traps.

One of the improvised charges we made was a bee-hive charge from a champagne bottle.

We tied a petrol soaked length of string tightly around the middle of the bottle lit the string and allowed it to burn out. Plunge the bottle into cold water and tap it on a solid surface 'voila' the bottle parts neatly in the middle where the string has been tied. Then tape three or four six inch nails to the bottom of the bottle to act as legs that hold the base of the bottle roughly four inches above the item in which you want to blow the hole. Pack the bottle base with explosive, pop in a fuse or det-cord and retreat a safe distance. BANG!! The inverted conical glass sphere in the bottle base is blown downward and through whatever your improvised charge happens to be stood on. I believe we used a lump of thick steel plate – powerful and impressive stuff.

The Bangalore torpedo was also demonstrated to us. This is a mine safe-lane or wire obstacle clearing charge; five foot sections of 3" pipe full of explosive are screwed together to make a charge up to fifty feet in length; this is pushed into the minefield or under a barbed wire defence and initiated. Your torpedo goes off and the safe lane is cleared. We built a section of wire defences and set-off a couple of joined lengths. This was the only time during my army service I used or saw this piece of kit in action, a simple idea that does a bloody good job of safely clearing whatever obstacle lies in your path.

A friend of mine and fellow member of the present Junior Leaders Regiment old comrades association, I'll just call him Stewart, told me of his memories of visiting Yantlet while in 'C' Squadron Course 7.

He was so excited about doing demolitions he decided his parents had to see what he was doing. He left the range with fuse cord, detonator and a lump of PE on his head under his beret. I suppose he was planning on blowing a hole in his parent's garden, maybe they wanted a pond in the back garden or his dad needed the shed dismantling in quick time? Whatever - Stew was on the bus when he was caught with the gear... he was very lucky; whoever the instructor was that day he was certainly a decent guy. Stewart got off with a bollocking. It could have been a hell of a lot worse. Stewart went on to do well in adult service climbing the promotion ladder (I believe) to the rank of SSM.

The British Legion March and Shoot came and our team along with 'B' and 'C' Squadron teams left for Pirbright; the military camp that was hosting the competition. I can no longer remember where our team or the other Squadron teams were placed; I can remember that for all the sweat and agony the lads went through, we didn't come in the top three.

Our next mission was a week's practical Bailey Bridge building at Chatham. In works dress with kit bags and suitcases we boarded trucks for the half hour drive up the A2 to the Medway towns.

Chatham is the home of the Royal Engineers, it's also home to the School of Military Engineering and many of the RE training courses take place either in Chatham, Chattenden or Upnor. Plant operations, bomb disposal, Bailey and Medium Girder Bridging (MGB) as well as Watermanship, these were and are just a few of the courses taught in and around the Medway towns. This would be my first trip to Chatham but during my army career I would visit many times.

We were housed in Kitchener barracks overlooking what was then the Chatham Naval base. The barrack rooms not dissimilar to our rooms at Dover. From here we were trucked daily across to Chattenden where we struggled and sweated with the massive Meccano-set that was the Bailey Bridge. This assault bridge was really the king of self-assembly. Used extensively through every theatre of the second world war they are still used today and still to be found seventy years on from the end of the war spanning ravines and rivers on the back roads of continental Europe.

Huge panels held together with pins the bridge is almost limitless in configuration and the weight which it can hold. From a single panel high and wide to a triple, triple there are even photos of the Bailey being trialled as a suspension bridge.

At single level the bridge can be built without the use of a crane, the side panels, transoms and stringers all being man portable, dare I say with a bloody struggle as the parts description and weights in the following paragraph will show.

The building process is not complex, the landing transom or bank seat is carried over with 2 base plates on the leading nose section; when it reaches the other side a team run over the bridge, position the pads and the beam/rollers and as the bridge grows so it is slowly pushed across in situ; this is because the landing pads and bank-seat need to be

Bailey Bridge, still in use in France.

in place as a firm base for the leading nose of the bridge.

The bridge is built on a roller carriage and as the tail of the bridge grows so it's pushed psychically forward while more sections are added. Once positioned on the other side of the obstruction the bridge is jacked down, the leading nose section removed, the wooden planked roadway laid and away you go.

The Bailey uses a multitude of components; the two heaviest being the Panel; the basic bridge member constructed of welded steel. Each panel top and bottom chord has interlocking male and female lugs into which the panel pins are inserted. The panel weighs 570 pounds or 259kg. The Cross Girder or Transom is 18 foot long, 10 inches high and 4 ½ inches wide and is clamped to the panels using transom clamps. Transoms had five sets of lugs on the top surface to locate the roadway stringers. There are holes drilled through the transom to allow the transom to be carried using lifting bars, these weigh in at 445 pounds or 202kg.

As well as these large sections there are many others... In total, there are 28 standard and over 100 specialist parts.

A completed bridge has two main girders, left and right. These are made of multiple panels, pinned together.

They are arranged in one, two or three trusses and one, two or three storeys high. This is where terms like 'double-double' or 'double-single' comes from.

The first describes the number of trusses and the second, the number of storeys. A 'double-double' Bailey bridge therefore has two trusses (panels) wide and two storeys high.

To provide extra stability and reduce twisting, sway bracing are connected in a diagonal configuration under the bridge deck to the corner of each panel.

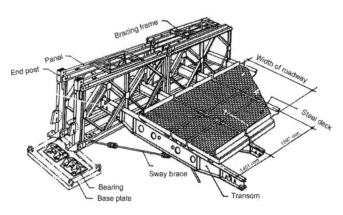

Stringers sit on the transom beams as a base for the timber decking or chesse's and the ribands are bolted to the outer stringers to form a kerb.

Specially strengthened ribands are used to create a ramp at the ends of the main bridge section.

Footwalks can be attached to the overhanging transoms using footwalk bearers, this separates foot and vehicular traffic.

Variations on panels, transoms and storeys can be used depending on the span and load carrying requirement.

If you ever see a 'triple-triple' it's one hell of a bridge!

Sorry... I got carried away there – hope you're still awake.

I will admit right now that we were very excited to get stuck-into the Bailey Bridge building, but very soon realised just what hard work it was to build one. We were boys – not mature men and how none of us done ourselves permanent back injury lifting panels weighing in at two hundred and fifty kilo's is a bloody miracle. No one seemed to ask that question, like walking round with detonators and plastic explosive in our hands it was our job and par for the course – we got on with it.

During the day while we were bridging over in Chattenden a tea and sandwich van would come round selling soft drinks, pasties and chocolate. I've got to put this in because I'm sure anyone of you reading this having been through this experience will remember just how the poor guy who owned the van got robbed blind. I'm sure it was not just our Course 7 but those before and those after. Both sides of the van opened up to display his tucker, but of course he couldn't serve both sides of the van at once, consequently lads would walk off with pockets full of his stock without paying. This seemed to go on day after day. He must have realised at the end of the day that his stock sales didn't match his takings but the way he went about it never changed. We all had our share of free pasties and soft drinks during our time over the river.

Another surprising incident occurred in the last couple of days at Chatham.

I was heading into town with Bri Bridson one evening when who should I see coming toward me on the arm of a sailor; none other than the delightful Myleene. It had only been a matter of 6 months since she'd moved from Dover. I'd heard nothing from her; she wasn't the letter writing type of girl. But here she was coming toward me. I stopped as she came along the road and of course Bri asked 'what's up.'

Brian had come to Course 7 from 4L and 5T, he wasn't from my Intake Course and was unware of my fling with Dover's answer to the young Diana Dors.

'My ex,' I said.

His eye's almost popped out of his head. 'Your ex... blimey you lucky sod, what's she doing here with him?'

I quickly gave him the low down as Myleene and the matelot approached. As she got within a few yards of us I saw recognition dawn on her face.

'Hello soldier boy,' she greeted me in her familiar fashion. 'Fancy seeing you here.'

Without hesitation and with no regard to the sailor she gave me a smacker of a kiss.

Seeing her again and looking so good sent both my heart and 'Y' fronts pulsing. She had the mischievous look in her eye and started talking completely ignoring her companion.

I asked after her parents and family, her aunt – the reason for her move to Chatham; and also what she was up to. She avoided the question about herself but said she'd left school and was working. *(I wouldn't mind betting I know what she was up to!)*

After a few minutes of chat with the sailor in the background shuffling his feet she said 'here's my number, give me a ring.'

Diving in her bag she brought out her pen and once again just like all those months ago grabbed my arm and wrote her telephone number on it.

'Phone me,' she said blatantly with no regard for the matelot who was not looking to happy. She turned with him and began to walk away.

We were fifty yards apart when she once again like so many times in the past turned and gave me her parting shout.

'Take care soldier boy and remember what I told you last time; don't wash it off!'

With a wave she was gone.

I rung the number the next day but it wasn't her's. I'm sure it was her little prank to make the guy she was with jealous or to give herself a buzz. Like I said – that's just the type of girl she was.

I never did see her again.

We returned to Dover for the last few weeks of term, Saturday Regimental Parades and the assault course competition.

The day came when our teams lined up in front of what you could call the adult version of an adventure playground.

Two teams from each of the Squadrons Course 7s.

We were dressed in our red PT vests with denim work trousers; 'B' & 'C' Squadron were in their Blue and Green.

With our ten foot length of telegraph pole between us, each section of eight waited to pull their running order position from the beret.

The race started by hitting the assault course with the pole, after negotiating the course we ran across the West Square and onto the circular roadway for one circuit before finishing back at the assault course. The competition was judged on timing; the team completing in the shortest time was the winner.

Every term the competition varied slightly in its composition.

I don't remember where exactly my team were placed in the running order. What I do remember was being acutely aware that this would - after weeks of practice, be the last time we'd have to go through this agony.

Supporters were there in their droves having been given time out from daily subjects or classes.

We were off! Four lads either side of the pole the, first obstacle was the six foot wall. Over went the pole followed by team members. The scramble net, the under wire crawl, the inclined wall and jump and the elevated zig-zag walk-way; negotiating some of these obstacles meant only two guys could keep hold of the pole - pre-agreement during practice had determined who these would be. Then came the agony of the twelve foot wall; two guys were launched upward first, then the log was passed up, pulled over the top and dropped on the far side before the rest of the team came over. The lightest and lankiest lad came last because there was no one left on the ground to give him a leg up. The two strongest remained on top of the wall while the guy below ran and jumped grabbing their wrists - then - wrist holding wrist, this last person would be physically pulled upward till he could grab the top of the wall and pull himself with the aid of the other two hauling on the seat of his pants, over the top. All three would then drop the twelve foot to the ground below. It was more like thirteen foot because a big hollow had been formed over the course of time in the earth and mud at the foot of the wall.

By now the rest of the team had moved on for the last couple of obstacles - the watery mud jump, tyres, sandpit and a quick exit from the course across the West Square. At this point muscles were screaming, but this was also the point where seconds lost on the assault course could be made up.

Keeping rhythm by shouting at each other we gave it our all; round the half mile circuit, back across the square to the finish line.

That year - that term - an 'A' squadron team won; the team I was a part of. In fact we came first with a 'B' Squadron team coming second. The rivalry always seemed stronger between 'A' & 'B', probably because we were mutually joined by our accommodation block and the cook house; we lived and worked in closer proximity with each other rather than with 'C' Squadron.

'C' Squadron on the other hand felt themselves a cut above due to the fact that they were over the other side of the barracks.

Regardless of team, Squadron or event we all had this driving ambition to win; it was all good clean fun and as terms went by all three Squadrons had their winners in one competition or another.

As with all the competitions there was an Inter-Squadron trophy for the assault course, this joined other cups in the Squadron silver-wear cupboard, including a team cup I'd helped win in the Inter-Regimental Course 3 shooting competition.

The last week of term came, we took our B3 Combat Engineering exams and I went sick... of course the assault course competition had played havoc with my Achilles tendon and that last week of term I just couldn't march.

Shucks, there goes Passing-out parade again.

Exam results published, we'd all passed. The other notice gave us information for the following term. I was to take 4L for the first six weeks this would be totally committed to canoeing. Along with white water canoeing and surf canoeing we would train for, and compete in, the hundred and twenty five mile Devizes to Westminster canoe race. The second half of term would be Signals B3 in 5T.

My new room for the following term was over the other side of the block on the first floor looking out over the grassed area to RHQ, the stables, and the English Channel in the distance. It was a really nice room.

Les was back, repaired after his multi-bone breakage, he returned to move his gear to the lower floor Course 7 lines I'd just left; we'd both meet up again in 8 – April 73.

He and I moved our gear; we seemed like the only two people in the very quiet block; after we'd done we sat in the cookhouse and drunk a mug of tea while I filled him in on what to expect in his coming Course 7.

We left later on the Saturday for a well-earned break. For me it had been a gruelling term which at times I'd found very difficult and been very miserable, especially at the point when I'd been given the brush-off by Angie.

However I'd also had some high points – I'd passed my B3 Combat Engineering, done well in leadership skills and was still winning prizes with my shooting, I had also been a part of the team who completed the assault course competition in the quickest time.

Heading home once more with my West Country mates I boarded the train leaving Paddington.

I stayed with Gran a week before heading to Norfolk on Friday the 22nd December.

Another portion of bad news greeted my arrival home; Rosko our German Shepherd had been knocked down on the main road outside our house and had been killed. Mum and Dad not wanting to burden me with the bad news had waited till I got home to tell me. I was very sad; he had been a lovely dog. A little waif of a puppy when dad had rescued him from a scrap metal yard where he was malnourished, starving, and suffering badly from Rickets. We nursed him to good health and he was good tempered and obedient pet; it was a sad loss to our family.

On the up side a Christmas card from Monika posed the question could she visit us in Norfolk at Easter. My parents could see no reason why not and that good news perked me up no end.

Christmas and New Year came and went and in no time I was heading South for my fifth term at Dover; six weeks in 4L doing nothing but canoeing followed by six weeks Signals; with the woes of the previous term behind me I couldn't wait – I'd done the first three basic terms, I'd completed the first of my Combat Engineering courses. I now felt as if I was a soldier... a Royal Engineer with knowledge of my Corp and Military trade.

Course 7 Sept – Dec 1972

Top row 2nd left Gerry, 4th left me for some reason the only one in a pullover. In the middle with two stripes big Smudge Smith, 4th from right Ray.

Front kneeling 2nd from the left Bri Bridson holding a lifting bar, 5th and 6th from left kneeling Pete Eastwood our fitness fanatic and Taddy.

Course 4L & 5T January 1973

As hard as I'd found the previous term this present term was a doddle, real fun, relaxed and easy going.

Apart from Course 8 who were a separate troop anyway, we were now senior in the Squadron and I'm sure all of the lads who'd done 'Intake' with me felt the same way. The only lads who may have done a Course longer than us were those who'd been back-squaded due to failing their B3 Combat Engineering or had completed an extra term of education.

Our seniority felt good and we were treated well by our Permanent Staff.

Most of the first six weeks of this Course we wore civi-clothes and more or less done our own thing.

We were introduced to canoeing in early January... in fact as soon as we kicked off the term.

Shivering in our bathing trucks while sleet lashed down on us we had to pass the army canoe swimming test. This we done off the pebble beach inside the Dover break-water. It was fucking freezing! We had to swim out 100 yards from the beach – swim under a canoe, turn, go back under the canoe and make the beach. I can't for the life of me remember if we had wet-suits or not but I can't imagine for one minute that we didn't, there is no-way we'd have survived the cold without one.

Everyday we'd be off to a different canoeing location; sitting in the back of our Bedford RL, followed by a Land Rover towing a trailer loaded with canoes.

On stormy, windy days we would surf canoe off the beach in Deal or Dover, riding the tips of the rollers as they crashed in on the beach. The gravel pits in Sandwich where we were taught to roll and right the canoe and days away in Devon on the river Dart and South Wales canoeing the river Wye at Symonds Yat, Ross-on-Wye.

We didn't parade in the mornings and were rarely there for room inspections, choosing to make our way to the canoe club early. Mind you, room inspections had taken a turn for the better since Major Durey's arrival. The daily drudgery of bed packs and stand-by-your-beds had been reduced to only twice a week providing beds were neatly made and rooms were kept clean and tidy. Permanent Staff NCOs would inspect the lines daily on their own and providing they were happy with what they found life was sweet. Of course if they weren't happy the punishment of extra room inspections and loss of privileges would soon be reinstated.

From single canoes we rapidly progressed into the sleeker racing doubles. These we would be using for the hundred and twenty five mile race along the Kennet and Avon Canal from Devizes to Westminster Bridge. We had two types of double canoe, K2s and C2s - Kayak or Canoe; the Cs tend to be a bit more stable than the Ks but in numbers we had half and half of each. Most of us wanted a C2, you had a better chance of staying in the bloody thing, but our instructors only allocated the Cs to those who proved totally inept at keeping a 'K' upright.

My partner in a canoe was Dave Hopwood the boxer from Doncaster. As good as we were in white-water and surf canoes we were fucking useless in the doubles. However others must have been worse because he and I were lumbered with a 'K'. Getting in the thing was a bloody nightmare – the amount of times we capsized before even moving from the river bank I lost count of, and as the days went past we seemed to get no better. A bit like a bicycle, if you stopped you toppled over. Our instructors at times got completely exasperated with us; we were none too happy either I might add.

The DW was a big thing – they called it the world's toughest canoe race. All government service teams and independent clubs wanted to win. The majority of these teams were volunteers who wanted to take part – they weren't Junior soldiers who'd been ordered too; I don't believe many of us had that driving ambition to win; I know for a fact I didn't and neither did Hoppy. We were quite content to make leisurely paddle of it and stay dry.

I feel I've got to fill the reader in on the details of the race, so here follows the history...

Unlike many of the world's great races, the Devizes to Westminster Canoe Race (or DW as it's often called) does not follow an immediately obvious or logical course. It is not a complete descent of some mighty river, nor is it an epic journey from one great city to another. Devizes is a market town set in the English farming county of Wiltshire. Running through the town is the 200 year old Kennet and Avon Canal, a navigation that once linked the sea port of Bristol to the town of Reading, and onwards via the River Thames to London. Westminster in contrast to Devizes is the seat of British Government; it contains the present day nation's law-making and administrative nerve centre. Why then do these two vastly different places represent the focal points of the world's toughest canoe race?

The answer is, of course, peculiarly British.

It starts with a group of men in "The Greyhound" pub in the village of Pewsey, just outside Devizes. It was 1920 and a national rail and bus strike was looming. Alternative means of transport were discussed in the bar, and the outcome, as with all good bar-room talk, was a wager: whether or not it was possible to get down the River Avon from Pewsey to the sea at Christchurch in under three days, a distance of some 70 miles. Four intrepid souls took up the challenge in a 20-foot sculling skiff and duly won the bet with 10 hours to spare.

In 1947 one of the original Avon descent participants, Roy Cooke, was planning to try to reach London via the derelict Kennet and Avon Canal and the River Thames in less than 100 hours (27 years to come up with that idea - they're quick workers in Pewsey! SB).

He was unable to see this through; the project was taken up by the Devizes Scouts, with the encouragement of locals who put up a sum of money for Scout funds if they could succeed in taking a boat from Devizes to Westminster in under 100 hours, all food and camping kit to be carried in the boats.

A year later, Easter 1948, Peter Brown, Brian Walters, Laurie Jones and Brian Smith, all aged just 17, set out on the first DW run. Great interest was generated nationally, with progress reports and photographs appearing in the national press, and the local cinema in Devizes interrupting programmes to give reports of their progress. At the finish a large crowd turned out at Westminster Bridge to see them successfully complete the challenge in a time of 89 hours and 50 minutes. Later that year several crews tried to make the run, but were defeated by thick weed on the canal. So it was established then that Easter was the best time to run DW. (Weed killed off, following the winter chill).

The following year, 1949, despite no formal race having been organised, nearly 20 boats set out from Devizes to attempt the run. Most failed. Two crews from Richmond Canoe Club brought the time down to 49 hours 32 minutes.

The interest shown in the event prompted Frank Luzmore, a member of the Richmond crews, to run an annual contest.

1951 saw an outstanding performance by the SAS crew of Dansie and Dry bringing the time down to just over 24 hours. A phenomenal achievement given the primitive boats and the requirement to be self-sufficient. Despite success from Richmond in 1952, crews from the Royal

Marines, SAS, and the Paras were to dominate the race for the next 20 years.

DW has always attracted strong characters and over this time competitors included Paddy Ashdown for the Royal Marines, and Chay Blyth and John Ridgeway who both competed in 1961 for the Paras.

One reason for two decades of domination by Forces crews was the similarity between active service and the demands of DW. Each was like a military exercise, demanding training, preparation, teamwork and logistical planning. The Royal Marines were, in effect, professional canoeists. The special boat section of the Marines had been formed at Poole Harbour during the Second World War, and their exploits in canoes were made famous in the film "Cockleshell Heroes". To this day the British Canoe Union annually awards the Hasler Trophy, named after the leader of the "Cockleshell Heroes", Blondie Hasler, to the most successful canoe club in marathon racing.

As all entrants stretched the rules to the limit, and the rule book grew in size to close loopholes, the decision was taken in 1971 to allow crews to receive support along the course. Gone were the spurious food items and equipment that met the requirement for "all food and camping to be carried in the boats". And gone too were the clandestine rendezvous at hidden points along the course that made a mockery of the idea of being self-sufficient.

1971 was a defining year in the race, with civilian clubs and military crews in a genuine battle for supremacy. Richmond Canoe Club, in many ways the pioneers of the race proper, took up the challenge. They entered a strong team of four boats, all with paddlers who had all represented Great Britain at international level. One member, Peter Lawler, had even been to four Olympic Games and had previously set the Junior DW record that had stood for nearly 10 years. Lawler with his partner Chris Baker won, bringing an end to the services' stranglehold on the race. With their other crews coming in 3rd, 5th and 7th, Richmond also broke the team record, and more importantly, gained the first ever team victory by a civilian club.

JUNIOR RACE

The demand for a junior race was met in 1953 when compulsory overnight stops were introduced. Originally there were only two overnight stops, but this soon developed into the present-day format of three overnight stops at Newbury, Marlow and Ham, with a mass start to Westminster on the final day. The first race saw only two crews entered, both of which were from the Chippenham Sea Cadets and finished in a *time of 37 hours 18 minutes. By 1961, with the entry of **Junior Leader Army Regiments** and police cadet units, numbers grew steadily, reaching a peak in 1970 when 100 crews were entered. The establishment of a Schools Trophy in 1975, however, has produced a steady influx of public schools into the race, and entries are now rising again. Schools are now responsible for 90 percent of the junior entries.*

I'm not going to lie – I nicked this information and its quite old information. What it doesn't mention is that following the Second World War the K&A fell into serious disrepair. It was no longer used as a commercial waterway and maintenance of banks and locks never took place.

In the early sixties many sections were drained and others were left to drain naturally. When we, a mixed bag of reluctant participants took part in the Spring of 1973 there were numerous dry sections to be run with crew carrying the canoe. These were called portages and each time we reached the end of a wet section or a lock gate we would need to climb out of the canoe and back in! We practiced this many times desperately trying to avoid the dunking that seemed inevitable. We would (this is Hoppy and me) come into the bank as fast as we could, we would grab and hold on for dear life to any vegetation including stinging nettles and brambles – anything to prevent the boat from going over. Then one of us would climb out while the other kept the craft alongside. Whichever one of us was out the boat would keep it upright while the second crew member precariously clambered out; then repeat the performance getting back in. It was exhausting.

I did enjoy canoeing, I canoed often during my time in the army and when I left the service I bought two of my own which I used regularly during the summer on the rivers, Norfolk Broads and off the local beaches in Norfolk. But following the DW in 1973 I never again sat in a double canoe.

The canoe teams put forward by the Junior Leaders Regiment Royal Engineers in 1973 consisted of lads from all three Squadrons; in all there were around eighteen of us, six from each Squadron. Others from our respective Squadron 4L Courses were off doing other stuff, Outward bound in Towyn or Otterburn, sailing, skiing or some other activity.

No one in authority thought it might be a good idea to <u>ask</u> what lads might be interested in canoeing? I'm sure if names had been requested from the three Squadrons; eighteen enthusiastic potential canoers would have been found and they would have put in a Stirling effort. Instead, the JL delegation of 1973 were a bunch of reluctant misfits press-ganged into competing, so consequently some of us, of which Hoppy and I were two, lacked enthusiasm...

However canoeing did have its advantages. We canoers were excused mid-term camp. It goes to show how seriously the Regiment was taking our entry to the DW. Instead of shivering in a hole in the ground on the Otterburn training area we would be spending just over a week in the lovely counties of Wiltshire and Berkshire practicing along the route of the forthcoming Devizes Westminster canoe race. Ok we may get wet but we'd be wearing wetsuits which go a long way to keeping a body warm. At the end of the day we'd change into warm dry clothing and climb into a lovely dry sleeping bag; content in the knowledge that our assigned chef would be preparing eggs and spam fitters with hot tea for breakfast. Good luck in Otterburn lads!

Back to Dover we went and off for a long weekend at home. The good news that greeted my arrival was that Monika would be coming over from Munich and staying with us for the whole of my end of term break in April.

On return from our long weekend I started in 5T doing my Signals Course.

The canoe race didn't take place till Easter which this year was 20th to 23rd April, very late. Although some of our canoe team (such as myself) would be moving out of 4L we would still be expected to turn up at the club and continue training for the main event six or seven weeks ahead.

Alan and Steve. B3 Signals Course, April 1973

There weren't many of us on the Signals Course, twelve of us in total; a few like Taddy were doing two 5Ts. The first half of his term he had taken driving lessons and driving test in a Land Rover. I had been unable to do this as I was still under the age of seventeen. I would be learning to drive later in the year after finishing Combat

Engineering at Southwood Camp in Farnbourgh.

The topic of conversation had moved on from buying our own kit to the buying of cars, motorbikes or scooters for Course 8; a few of us were intending to splash out on a set of wheels.

Both Taddy and Hoppy who were now doing their Driving Course were hoping to buy cars. I wanted a scooter, a Lambretta 150 SX, this would fill the gap till I took my driving test, I was at least old enough for two wheeled transport.

We trained on two vehicle or base station sets, the C13 HF set used where VHF was not appropriate and the C42 - VHF transceiver, for mobile communication in the forward battle area.

We also trained on the man portable A40/A41 set which would be carried by the patrol radio operator. These sets were part of the Larkspur system replaced in the early eighties with Clansman.

We had to learn correct terminology, the phonetic alphabet and codes for individuals such as Sunray and Sunray Minor.

A Sunray could be of any rank it was a code for a leader or commander at any level; Sunray Minor is obviously his or her second in command. The code for a Royal Engineer representative was HOLDFAST which is pretty neat compared to the REME who were BLUEBELL, poor sods.

Then there were encryption codes... I remember there were two types of coding system but I can only remember the one – 'Slidex'.

Slidex had first been used in World War Two and continued to be used into the eighties. It was considered pretty water tight as a battlefield instant coding system. It consisted of two parts; a card with 12 columns and 17 rows producing 204 rectangles and two coordinate strips, one vertical strip on the left and one horizontal strip on the top. The card and the coordinate strips were placed in a metal frame.

If you wanted to send an encrypted message via Slidex you'd open your communication with 'Slidex message over'.

The listening station would acknowledge and you would return with the sheet number you wanted to use. The squares on the different sheets would hold different words to suit differing situations. Then you'd read out the coordinate strips from the side and top of the board.

The rectangles on the coordinate strips had a random letter, so that each word could be represented by a bigram.

Each rectangle on the Slidex card had a word or phrase on it plus a letter or number. The words or phrases were those most likely to be used by military units, for example DIVISION, ARTILLERY, ATTACK AT ONCE etc.

What happened if you wanted to send a word that was not on the Slidex rectangles? In order to allow for that eventuality the same rectangles had numbers or letters printed on them. This allowed the operator to spell words that were not included in the Slidex card, or include numbers.

In order to do so he had to use one of the SWITCH ON rectangles (there were several). After that he could use the letters or numbers in the rectangles and then end this part with one of the SWITCH OFF rectangles.

The coordinate strips changed daily. Usually it carried low and mid-level traffic (up to division) however it was sometimes used for higher level messages.

Its main advantage was that it was easy to use by fighting troops.

Set tuning, codes, phonetic alphabet and how terrain and weather effect signal transmissions were all the stuff we learnt on B3.

Later during the Course after we'd completed theory and radio set tuning training in the classroom; we were out in the lovely Kent countryside and sunshine practicing mobile communications from the back of a Land Rover, driven by those three or four lads who had completed and passed their driving test six weeks previously.

I'd just like to add before someone points out that I'm breaking the official secrets act with this very old information; everything I've written is freely available on the web...

The photo shows us on the last day of our Signals Course outside the Chequers Inn in Slaugham, Sussex where we went for an end of

Course 'Chicken in a Basket' pub lunch. (There's now a porch across the front where the pub sign is mounted).

A few of these faces on the photograph I remember.

I'm four from the left with Taddy on my right side. Joe Frazer our boxer is the

B3 Signals Course

big guy in the middle, Joe was the lad who held me up on my tiptoes by the scruff of the neck during our Intake Course when I accused him of nicking a pair of my socks. To Joe's left in the front is Pete Stevenson he was 'B' Squadron and had done 5T with Taddy. To his left is Geordie Goldsmith who would join me later in 16 Squadron. Behind him and on the end is Steve Hadlow, a good mate of Pete's, also 'B' Squadron, a hard-nut and completely fearless. He was always in some kind of trouble but army through and through. It was as if he had too much energy to burn off, I think he ended up in the slammer three times while at Dover for one thing or another. He was with me during the canoeing and we became good friends. Taddy Steve and I were the first guys to wear DMP (camouflage) combats. At that time combats were still Plain olive-drab; where we got hold of them heaven only knows, but even in the army image was important. What this black and white picture doesn't show is my Pea-green denims which I'm also wearing.

My seventeenth birthday came and went.

Our term was nearing an end; we would break-up for the Easter on Saturday 14th following Pass-out parade. But prior to leaving for home our kit had to be moved over to Course 8 lines above the education block. A few more days and the red cravat would disappear; although Squadron loyalty would remain all three Squadron Course 8 lads now became one single troop, all ninety one of us.

Preparation work had to be put in place for the following weekend; Easter weekend was the Devizes-Westminster race weekend. The competing teams would go home for a few days then return to Dover on Wednesday. The idea was to get everything prepared and loaded on the trucks before we broke up so we could jump on board on the Thursday morning and shoot off to Devizes. This allowed a few of us to bunk-off Pass-out Parade; no need to limp to the M.R.S this end of term.

Saturday morning we had one last inspection of our kit and canoes, we packaged and loaded our stores onto the trucks and with the last jobs completed returned to our rooms and started moving our personnel gear to the education block.

The rooms had our names pinned to the door allocated alphabetically regardless of our root Squadron. I'd landed on my feet with this bed space, it was a corner space with a window at the side of my bed looking out over the back hill and the wooded area where the Officers married quarters were built. My room mates were - Bri Bridson and Dave Buckley ex 'A' Squadron along with three from 'B', Mick Blyth, Taff Brown and Paddy Butler; plus one lad from 'C', Blacky Blackwell.

Roll on Course 8.

I'd spoken a couple of times on the phone with mum and dad; well mum really, dad didn't do telephones. I'd told them I wanted to find myself a scooter and how much money I wanted to spend. Dad was none to chuffed with my choice of transport wanting me to have a motorbike or just go straight for a car. However I wanted wheels now not having to wait till I'm seventeen and mum thought the scooter idea was safer and less likely to get me killed.

While home we were told to open a bank account, no longer would we join a pay parade, this would be the last leave we'd take home a Giro and next term after submitting bank details our salary would be paid monthly direct into our accounts; grown up stuff indeed.

This leave I would not be going to Winsley, I'd head straight home to Norfolk. Monika would be flying over on the Saturday of the Easter weekend; she would be at ours when I returned from the DW on the Monday. She would fly back to Germany on Saturday 5th May and I would return to Dover on Monday 7th with my new second-hand scooter. My final term would kick-off on Tuesday 8th May.

When I arrived home Saturday evening I found that dad had already bought the local paper and circled a few scooters for sale. Typical dad he couldn't wait to be out there helping me buy a bike. On Sunday morning I phoned two of the four adverts only to find they'd been sold however the other two scooters were still available and dad, Pete and I set out to view them. In the end I settled for a Lambretta LI 150 special in blue and gold. I paid sixty five pounds for it; as I'd not had a chance to cash my Giro cheque dad left a deposit for me; I done all the paperwork on the Monday and we went back Monday evening to collect it. I was well chuffed.

On the 18th, the Wednesday I boarded the train again for Dover, returning to take part in the DW.

Thursday morning - a final check of our gear, the collection of some fresh rations and by lunch time with all the paraphernalia needed to keep us out in the field for four days we set off for Devizes in some very unpleasant weather.

We erected our tents that evening in a cold easterly wind, set up the field kitchen, ate and turned in. In the morning the weather was no better we were in for a rough ride. After a good hot breakfast we donned our wet suits and prepared for our timed departure. Fortunately the change of rules a few years previously meant we no longer had to carry any food or gear with us; our canoes were empty and therefore lighter to Portage.

Hoppy and I done thirty five miles the first day ending up knackered in Newbury. I remember vividly the weather being shite and on looking up the forecast of the time found my memory to have served me well.

1973: (20th - 23rd April)
CYCLONIC/EAST OR NORTH EASTERLY - LOCAL SNOW IN SOUTH.
Warmest: 14degC (Glasgow/23rd):
Sunniest: 12.9h (Stornoway [Western Isles]/22nd).

An area of rain moved south across the UK during the night of the 20th Good Friday, 21st Saturday, and morning of the 22nd Sunday; the rain was heavy in some parts of southern England, with snow in places; showers followed, more frequent over East Anglia, the Midlands and northeast England, with thunderstorms. Rain which affected southeast England and the east Midlands during the night 21st Saturday 22nd Easter Day moved slowly west to the west Midlands, South Wales and southwest Midlands during the 22nd. While over northern areas, it was mostly dry.

On the Monday, England and Wales had widespread rain with hail and thunderstorms. Winds were often strong and gusty, from the north or northeast, with a considerable chill.

For London specifically, based on Kew, a total of 29mm of rainfall fell during daylight hours Sunday and Monday.

So that was the weather for Easter 1973. We couldn't have had it worse – lashing it down, with wind in our faces.

We were wet, tired, sore, and miserable. Both Hoppy and I had spilled out a number of times and by the time we got to Newbury we were almost suffering hypothermia. We ate a hearty meal in one of our 8 man tents of compo stew put together by our cook, a lad from the cookhouse who had drawn the short straw.

The following day, Saturday, we were off again another thirty five miles to Marlow.

The weather was freezing, sleeting and blowing easterly almost directly into our faces. We just about completed the day.

The third day we got as far as Shepperton lock checkpoint and we were retired by the marshals who considered us unfit to carry on. We had done 87.7 miles capsized to many time to remember and we were both carrying blisters on the palms of our hands from the paddles, along with scratches on our legs and shins from the edge of the canoe cockpit caused when climbing in and out at the portages. Our - Hoppy and my DW adventure ended there.

Hoppy and I weren't the only two that failed to complete; many other competing teams had dropped out before us and others gave up that last day. However a couple of our teams did make it to Westminster Bridge and good on them. The DW is a gruelling race on a good day, but that particular year the unseasonal weather made it particularly vicious.

By Tuesday night I was home again and pleased to see my friend from Germany, Monika.

Two years had gone by since we were last together, she'd become a very attractive lass and I was well and truly bowled over. She'd taken on the hippy look with an Afghan coat and brought her guitar with her. We had a lovely couple of weeks before I took her back to the airport to catch her plane. It would be another two and a half years before we'd meet again while I was on a winter training exercise with the US Army Special Forces based in Bad Tolz in Bavaria.

I'd made enquiries with British Rail as to whether I could take my scooter back to Dover by rail, an idea put to me by my parents. It turned out to be pretty inexpensive. The scooter would go in the guards van to

London, I'd unload it and ride it through the city to Charing-Cross and back on the train to Dover; simple.

And it was, completely hitch free.

With my bag held by bungie cord on the seat behind me I arrived in Old Park to find a few more of my mates had returned with either two wheels or four.

We all left our bikes in the corner of the drill shed on the West Square. Hoppy bought and drove back a Mark 2 Ford Cortina. Taddy bought an Austin 1100 but had left it at home. I was now itching to move onto bigger things, like a car.

Course 8 May 1973

Our final term would be taken up solely with Combat Engineering, no distractions as in Course 7. The B2 was a serious Course which on passing would put us leagues ahead of our contemporaries entering directly into adult service.

The junior rank structure had been left behind us, the only junior soldier to hold and to continue to use his junior rank was that of the JRSM (Junior Regimental Sergeant Major). This term the honour went to 'A' Squadrons JSSM (Junior Squadron Sergeant Major) of the previous term, Las Stewart.

Las had worked damn hard during his time at Old Park; joining in the same intake with me he had diligently worked his way up through the rank structure to become the first black JRSM in the Regiment for that matter he was probably the first black JSSM as well. Now in 2016 this would not really be considered anything special. But in 1970 if you weren't white you were very much in the military minority and the cards were stacked heavily against you. It was well deserved; he was a model Junior Soldier and no one who knew him, or joined with him would begrudge him his place as head Junior Soldier of the Regiment and his Course 8. I'm sure all who knew him would agree with me when I say all these years later, well done Las!

Our bank details were collected and those who had failed to open an account while at home were introduced to a representative from Lloyds Bank in Dover, sat down and made to open an account, as the Regimental paymaster told us 'no account, no pay'. I'd opened an account at mum and dads bank the National Westminster on the Market Place in Yarmouth.

Oddly I found I never used my scooter. Because so few of us had transport we still decided to walk out as a gang. If Mick Blyth or Dave Hopwood went out they'd go in their cars (Mick had a Mini Cooper) and four or five of us would go with them.

Something major finally went bang in Hoppy's Cortina engine and it was using more oil than petrol we ended up dumping the Cortina in the local scrapyard.

The lad in the bed next to me Blacky Blackwell from 'C' Squadron tied himself in with a lass from St Margaret's bay. Almost every night he'd catch the bus to see her. In the end he asked if he could borrow my bike, so I lent it to him for a price - ten fags a go or similar. Eventually he asked if he could buy it off me I said no at first but dad had spotted a small 998cc MG Midget in a local garage for £250.00 it was still there when I got home on mid-term leave it was a lovely little car and I really wanted it. I borrowed the money from the bank plus £100.00 for the insurance and bought it. Twenty five pounds a month repayments over two years. It was a heck of a lot of dosh!

When I returned to Dover after the mid-term break I told Blacky he could have the bike for the same money as I paid for it, he agreed and said he'd give me the money before the end of term. He never did and on the last day of term I went hunting for him for the money, the twat done a runner and I never saw him again until we got to Southwood. I threatened to do him over unless I got the dosh; he told me the bike had packed up and he couldn't use it anymore.

'Tough,' I said, 'it was working all term while you were off seeing your bloody women in St Margaret's now I want my money and I want it soon.' Anyway I never got it, he disappeared at some point during our time at Southwood, where he went or what happened to him I don't know. I remember the word at the time was he 'Deserted' (ran away for the non-military readers) to be with his girl, whatever the reason I'm still waiting for my £65.00 with interest. Not a small amount of money in 1973 I can tell you. I hope he ended up in Colchester Military Nick, it'd serve him right.

During Course 8 we could go home every weekend if we wished; leaving Old Park on a Friday evening at cease of works we had to be back for Monday morning parade.

Friday at 1700 you'd see a crowd of Course 8 lads in uniform on the Canterbury road out of Whitfield thumbing a lift for London.

Thumbing or hitchhiking was very common and there was never a problem getting a lift if you were in uniform. Over the next few years as the troubles in Northern Ireland got worse we were advised not to do it. But many, me included still did.

I decided one Friday to hitch to my Grans for the weekend and Paddy Butler my roommate said he'd come with me, it took us hours. We were dumped around midnight on the M4 roundabout junction 17 at Chippenham; the car that had brought us down from London going off to the right to Malmesbury. We walked almost all the way into Chippenham before getting a lift as far as the A4 - Bradford-on-Avon junction in Corsham. We decided to sleep in the bus shelter and finish the journey in the morning. A police car found us there and took us the rest of the way to grans. It was gone four in the morning when we woke her. She made us a plate of pickled beetroot and ham sandwiches and gave us a slug of brandy which she kept for medicinal purposes only.

Gran paid the train fare back to Dover for us on the Sunday. She was a real Gem.

Another lad in our room was Taff Brown, yes he was Welsh. He told us his brother had lost an eye in an accident at work, he had been fitted with a glass eye but lost it one night while out on the beer so his opo's at work made him a wooden one painted it red and varnished it. His party trick was to take it out in the pub and float it in his beer. Taff also told us they would hang it on the dart-board and throw darts at it. We didn't believe these stories so he asked his brother to bring it down to Pass-out and show it to us.

Lee and me doing Combat Engineering home work. Course 8

Sure enough he did.

He did have a new glass one of course.

We had one small lad with us who never had any money, can't remember his name or which Squadron he'd come from but to subsidise his income, or should I say put some extra money in his pocket he'd do a fish and chip run to the chipper on the London road down the back hill on the way into town. We'd all chip-in (excuse the pun) a few pence for him to get himself a meal or keep the money for something else. It was worth it, it was a hell of a trek and he had to almost run back to make sure the food wouldn't be cold. The local kids found out he was doing this and mugged him for the food. He'd come back almost in tears worried that his clients, us, might get the idea he'd kept the dosh for himself. This happened a couple of times, the local kids thought he was easy pickings until a crowd of us followed him down one night and when the locals jumped him we jumped them and beat the shit out them. He wasn't troubled after that.

Course 8 was hard work but fun, we were a troop from all three Squadrons that worked together well and I don't remember any particular lad being unfriendly or the type to throw their weight around, a problem with a couple of lads during my Course 7.

All Course 8 had access to the Junior NCOs club, The 'Chev8 Club' adjacent to the NAAFI shop; we could go and relax in what was a kind of private club; it had a soft drinks bar and we could buy toasted sandwiches and other simple food.

The weeks passed by as we moved toward August and our passing out parade. I now had a car waiting for me at home a lovely little MG with a Gold-Seal reconditioned engine that had only done 36,000 miles. I couldn't wait to pass my test and drive it.

MGB Chatham
Course 8

No mid-Course camp this term; as Course 8 we were off for a second three week stint in Chatham. Once again we headed up the A2 to occupy our temporary accommodation in Kitchener Barracks.

Ninety of us divided into three troops we alternated between Watermanship on the river Medway at Upnor; practical building of the Medium Girder Bridge (MGB) and Plant Roads & Airfields (PRA). All three subjects were very interesting... well at least PRA and Watermanship were; MGB was again a case of slotting together this giant, bloody heavy metal Meccano set.

Unlike the Bailey Bridge being constructed of panels the MGB is constructed of rectangular box sections. The bridge parts are not quite so heavy but as the photo shows, the lifting of these box sections is carried out by four men instead of the six required to lift a Bailey panel.

The role of the bridge is more of a quick assault bridge rather than a bridge that stays in place for an unspecified length of time. It's quicker

234

to assemble, less complex in construction, but doesn't have the almost unlimited weight capacity and other characteristics of the Bailey.

Our PRA training consisted of three rapidly laid modular surfaces. PSP (Pierced Steel Planking) sections of ten foot by two foot clipped together. This stuff you see just about everywhere with its round perforated holes. It was rapid and easy to use. Class 60 roadway that is laid in individual planks and the Summerfield Track this model laid as a road or large mat area.

We also practiced using the Class 30 roadway, a vehicle launched rapid road system that is deployed from a reel over the cab of a truck. This roadway is used primarily as a temporary surface leading to and from a bridge crossing point or beach-head. The photo above shows my section preparing the Class 30 reel; I need to have a chat with the photographer, he chopped my head off.

Another PRA task that our three troops rotated through was the construction of a new car park at the Royal Engineer Bomb Disposal Wing at Chattenden. This was a fun project which we carried out with very little input from our instructors. We cleared the site levelled off and done the whole job including the final pouring and levelling of the black-top (Tarmac).

At Upnor we were taught boat handling skills and the minor mechanics of the two stroke outboard engine, we all got a chance to pilot the alloy assault/work boat doing handling on the river as well as docking skills. We all found this very enjoyable and completely different to any other skill we'd learnt.

Training completed, job done we returned once again to Dover.

We were now down to the last few weeks of term, this meant full dress rehearsal for Saturdays Regimental parade. Our kit was gleaming; we were old timers now, we'd tuned in to army life, we knew how to prepare our kit and what was expected of us. Yes we had a couple of inspections with our No2s laid out but no trauma's.

B2 exams came round these were in three parts. I passed 1 and 3 but failed 2. It wasn't uncommon, a few lads would fail one of the three modules but they could be retaken at Southwood during our six weeks Combat Engineering finalisation.

During our last couple of days certain items of kit were returned to the QM stores – our 37 pattern webbing for those who'd lived with it throughout their time at Dover, (I'd handed mine back at the end of Course 2); our REPB pocket books, the great coat that was only ever worn in the middle of the night when we had a bomb scare, BDs and plain olive combats. The new style DMP (camouflage) combats were already being issued to Intake courses, we'd get reissued our new look DMP at Southwood.

Friday night 10th August and families started arriving. My mum, dad and brother came down with the caravan, any family with a caravan or a mobile home could park it on the West Square; washroom and toilet facilities were made available in the Combat Engineer wing.

We were doing our last bit of preparation while our families came into the block and walked around the rooms. I gave mum and dad a case and kit bag of gear to take back to the car; I kept the minimum in my locker overnight to pack up the following morning.

My 58 webbing had already found a new home.
Best kit prepared some lads went off to have a meal with their folks. Blacky promised me he'd have my payment for me the next day. I was a fool to trust him.

Pass-out parade. Las leading Course 8 on the march-past.

We awoke to glorious sunshine and in civi's Dave Buckley and I went early for breakfast. When doing a serious parade stint like the one we had ahead of us we needed food in our belly's, if not it was a sure-fired way to faint on parade.

Families were invited to breakfast and I'd shown my parents where to go, however I would not join them, I was eating early and going straight from the cookhouse to the armoury for my weapon. My parents and brother wouldn't see me again until I marched onto the East Square at 1000hrs.

111 collected plus bayonet I returned to my room to get on with chores and get changed.

The lines had to be left spotless. Mattresses, pillows and blankets would be left on the springs for the next group of lads moving in and they'd be hard on our heels as we moved out.

There was a real feel-good factor in the lines, a great deal of banter and laughter coming from all the rooms. We changed into our immaculate No2s and very carefully made our way out to the front of the block. Thank God the weather was good there was no back-up plan for rain. We walked like tin soldiers hardly daring to bend a leg or arm and very cautious not to bang our boots into anything or anybody. We formed up in open order and our troop Permanent Staff inspected us. Two years' worth of bullshit had resulted in us being at this point; as immaculately turned out as it was possible to be.

A small tug here or there to straighten a collar or a tie; but no negative comments. We were all immaculately turned out.

Now it was the turn of our JRSM to drill us onto the square and through the Parade; only the second passing out parade I'd done in my six terms.

'Trooop Trooop SHUN!' Commanded Las.

CRASH! 91 boots hit the deck as one.

'SHOULDER ARMS!'

Family groups walking toward and onto the viewing platforms on the square stopped in awe to watch.

'The troop will move to the left in threes! LEEEFT TURN!'

CRASH! Again a perfect execution of the movement.

This really was stirring stuff especially with our audience of families.

Las was in fine voice.

'BY THE RIGHT – QUICK MARCH!'

We were off toward the guard room and trade wing where we would halt and wait while the rest of the Regiment moved onto the parade square.

Here we stood easy until once again Las called us up and on we marched halting in front of the saluting dais and out front of the whole Regiment.

Then one by one each JSSM brought their troops to attention and open order.

Las then gave the same command to Course 8.

We awaited the arrival of our Officer group.

Our inspecting Officer that term end was the Chief Royal Engineer; Lt Gen Sir Terrence Meekin KCB OBE, and as he came up the steps onto the square with the CO, Adjutant and all the other Officers from the Squadrons Las gave the order to the Regiment...

First the Shoulder Arms. Then the Present...

'JUNIOR LEADERS REGIMENT! JUNIOR LEADERS REGIMENT! PRESENTTT ARMS!'

Mum and me after parade. Pass-out Aug 73.

Three movements; our SLR was held in front of us in the present and remained there until the Officer group had taken their places. Then the command to shoulder and order arms was given again.

In open order we stood to attention as inspecting Officers from Squadron and Troop walked through the lines.

We, Course 8 were inspected by the CRE. He walked through the ranks with the CO, Adjutant and Las looking us up and down and at times stopping to talk to one of us.

While this took place the Regimental Band played; for around twenty minutes they marched up and down in front of the visiting families all who were sitting on raised staging behind the Officers.

Inspection over the Officers returned to the Dias and the Regiment went through the march past and march-off routine; Course 8 leading the Regiment.

We marched straight to the armoury where for the final time I handed in my SLR number 111, it had served me well during my two years at Dover.

After handing in our weapon and bayonet we reformed for a Course 8 photo on the West Square returning afterwards to an area that had been designated for families and photographs, this was on the green outside the junior ranks club opposite 'A' Squadron. There was also a small finger buffet.

We all milled about talking and posing for pictures our Permanent Staff with us. After half an hour Dave Buckley, (whose family were unable to come down for the Pass-out), and I said goodbye and shook hands with our instructors, marched smartly back to the block and got changed into the few remaining civi's we'd kept in our lockers.

We had one final train warrant to collect. In a couple of weeks we'd all be headed to 3RETR (Royal Engineer Training Regiment) on Southwood Camp Farnbourgh. Here for six weeks we would finish our Combat Engineer training. Some, me included would then spend a couple more weeks learning to drive a four ton Bedford RL truck; others would go straight off to their new posting in adult service.

Now in civi's with No2s on a hanger and the remainder of my odds and ends in a case I said goodbye to my mates, had a final hunt round for the sneak who still owed me for the scooter and failing to find him but content in the knowledge that he'd turn up at Southwood I returned to my parents car and the trip home.

My time at Dover completed.

3 Training Regiment Royal Engineers

We had been warned by those who'd been before – we would be shat-on from a great height when we arrived at Southwood. Cocky ex-Fred's would be taken down a peg or two.

We didn't take much notice, we had the 'T-shirt what could they do that hadn't already been done. We were in for a shock.

We only had a short time at home; although some of us were only half way through our seventeenth year and not one of us was yet eighteen we were now classed as adult soldiers, no longer juniors with school type terms and holidays.

We had been given strict instructions as to our arrival at Southwood. We would arrive at Farnborough station between 1300 and 1400 hours only. We were to wear full No2s less best boots. This meant peaked cap not beret. Our kit would be carried in military case or kitbag only, not multi-coloured cases or holdalls.

We would be collected only at the station. We were not allowed to bring our own cars at this point in time and any ex-Fred arriving by car with family should be dropped outside the train station not at Southwood. The logic behind this was that we would all arrive together and all go through the same induction all at the same time. Some lads from Scotland and the North had to leave the day before to ensure they would get the designated train.

The train for Farnborough left from Waterloo.

91 of us arrived on the same train. To arrive within the time slot given there was only the one train from Waterloo. We had been told that those who missed it would really suffer.

A couple of military green coaches were there to pick us up, a truck for cases and kitbags along with a bunch of hard-nosed instructors who wasted no time in screaming at us to get our gear on the truck and our bodies on the bus. Blimey!

Both the buses and the truck stopped just inside the gates of 3 Training Regiment and we were shouted out to collect our gear which was unceremoniously thrown to the ground; we fought through the pile to find our own bags and rapidly formed up in three ranks.

I Whispered to Taddy, 'surely were not expected to march with this lot, are we?'

'Looks like it,' he replied.

'STOP FUCKIN TALKING IN THE RANKS!' Was bawled at us.

Bloody hell...

It was August, the weather was boiling, we'd travelled from our homes in full No2s including the killer collar and collar stud. I was sweeting buckets.

We formed three ranks and the NCOs gave us a quick look over screaming blue murder at those who'd loosened their tie and collar stud.

'NAME!! You untidy fucker?!'

The guilty gave their names only to find out they would be on the next nights guard duty and fire picket. What a start.

You will now march to your 'Spider' Block.' We were loudly told. (Spider huts - six long rooms with the ablutions, toilets, and cleaning rooms across the middle as you can see on the photo of One and Three training Regiment).

I couldn't believe it, how the hell were we expected to march with all this gear – but we did. As a rabble, being shouted at every step of the way, we kind of marched – if you can call it that - up the side of the square till we got to a block of huts and halted.

We were told in no uncertain terms that we were a mess, a bunch of shite. 'Is this the standard of turn-out from Dover? We'll sharpen you lot up fuckin pronto!'

They started this sharpening up process by forming us up in three ranks in open order. Then the NCOs walked slowly through the ranks looking at each lads cap - looking for the slashed peak.

There were only a small minority of us who hadn't slashed the peak of our No2 dress hat while at Dover; it improved the look and made you look less like a bus conductor. After Course 3 it was another expected modification. We would cut the stitching either side of the peak just below the strap buttons and push the edges of the peak upward into the side packing, this would make the peak sharper in angle, the more vertical you could make the peak the better.

The 3RETR instructors were out to get us – defacing military equipment.

Everyone with a slashed peak was told to remove it and place it on the floor in front of them.

When we'd all been checked and with only a few still wearing a hat we were given the order... 'One step forward MARCH! - MARK TIME!'

1 & 3 Training Regiment
Royal Engineers. Between the road
and the railway line.
1 RETR is the area in the forgound.
3 RETR with 56 Driver Training Sqn
are the buildings in the top half of the photo.

Marking time in a nutshell is marching on the spot. We were marching on, and in the process crushing, our hats.

We, the majority had to buy a new one; our names were taken and added to the forthcoming guard rosters.

Following this we were told to lift our trouser legs. Of course we were all wearing civilian socks in a multitude of colours, it was summer, it was hot, who wants to wear thick issue socks in August? We were given three minutes to change into our army socks.

You can't begin to imagine the melee - cases, kitbags and contents strewn everywhere while we desperately rummaged for our issue footwear and our instructor screamed at us to get a move on.

Clothes and other kit lying all over the place, but we were all back in three ranks, looking I might add, pretty ragged.

We were then told we were to run round and round the outside of the 'Spider'. One at a time we'd be picked to fall out and march into the block and into an office room. Halt - salute give name rank and number.

If - and I mean if, we done this satisfactorily we'd be given a room number and bed space. If not we'd be back outside running. I passed on the third attempt, hot and sweaty I dragged my gear into this massive room crammed with sixteen beds; our whole Course 8 had to fit into the one Spider, six rooms. Fucking hell, we'd been spoilt at Dover.

Eventually we were all in - in more ways than one.

Our training NCO, who had a cupboard like room at the door end of the dormitory, informed us there would be a room and locker inspection at 1900.

I'm not going to go into too much detail only to say we were at it nearly all night.

They used white gloves on the locker tops and roof beams! They looked for dust on top of the water in the fire buckets and then tipped them over. They used every trick in the book. We thought we'd seen it all at Dover; boy were we wrong.

Lockers that were not presented to satisfaction were chucked unceremoniously out of the window, civi's an all!

This went on for days or should I say evenings because during the day we were still training on Water Supply modules of our B2.

A couple of nights where inspections went into the early hours of the morning, lads would sleep on the floor so their bed packs weren't disturbed for the early morning inspection! That's how bad it was.

We hated our instructors and would willingly have killed them, our lives during these six weeks were hell and for those who'd held high rank as Junior Soldiers, such as Las, JSSMs and Junior Sergeants, their lives were made even more of a misery. Our instructors had never been Juniors; they'd joined as adults in 1 RETR and had a really jealous streak against the superior (as we saw ourselves) Fred's.

We had no weapon issue during our time at Southwood; when on guard duty we carried a pick axe handle in place of a rifle so we could beat an intruder to death instead of shooting him or her.

One of our training NCOs owned a Lotus Europa sports car and one night both his headlights got smashed. Rough justice I say. I wouldn't know who the culprit or culprits were though.

Needless to say the whole guard of that night got a weekend duty as punishment for not spotting or apprehending the vandal.

If... we managed to avoid doing anything wrong during the week and avoided weekend guard or fire picket we could go home. In fact we could go home every night of the week if we wished and as long as there were no room inspections or locker inspections and we were back in time for parade the following morning.

Taddy had his Austin 1100 at Southwood and he decided he would go home to Bath on a Wednesday evening, have a meal with his folks and drive back the 75 miles for midnight or just after. I would go with him; bung him fifty pence for petrol, (it was 25p a gallon at that time, gallon that is NOT litre!) he'd drop me at my grans where I'd have a meal then I'd go and play darts down the pub with my mates; he'd pick me up at the pub – 'The Plough' at Bradford Leigh and back to Southwood we would go.

One Wednesday evening we were heading home on what was then a very quiet M4 motorway when the engine blew up just to the east of Swindon. We walked to the emergency phone, made a call and eventually after a long wait the AA turned up. The engineer pronounced the car dead. This didn't require a great deal of working out – a piston rod is not supposed to stick out the side of the crank case.

'I'll have to get you a tow truck,' said the AA man, 'they'll tow you into our depot in Swindon.'

We got to Swindon around 2200 and decided to continue on to Bath and borrow Mr Tadd's car to get us back to Farnborough, Alan was sure this would be ok.

So we made our way to the station. At the station we were told trains had been suspended from Paddington due to a bomb scare; an event which was now becoming common place.

We eventually got on a train at 0130 and arrived at Alan's at 0230 after almost missing the stop at Bath because we'd fallen asleep. We jumped off the train as it was pulling out of the station; we missed the end of the platform and like two escapee's in a war movie, rolled head over heels down the embankment leaving the door swinging open behind us.

We walked from the Station up to Twerton and eventually when we arrived woke Alan's parents who fed us. Feeling tired but slightly more human we started back to Farnborough in his dad's car at 0330, getting back to our room at 0500. We lay on our beds for half an hour before we were up and on parade. Knackered!

Alan's dad retrieved the car from Swindon, had it repaired and told him that he could swap cars the following weekend.

So nine days later we started out again. He'd drop me at grans and pick me up on Sunday afternoon to return. This time instead of going motorway we'd go the A4.

All was well till we got to the top of the hill just outside Marlborough on the edge of Savernake Forest when again something went bang in the engine. (I made a mental note not to buy a Morris or Austin 1100). Two engine seizer's within ten days... not bad going eh?

We coasted down the hill and into the car park of the 'Roebuck' pub where we drank a few pints and waited for Mr Tadd to come out and tow us to Bath. I couldn't expect Alan's dad with a car in tow to drop me to Winsley so I went as far as Alan's house and caught the bus back to grans. On Sunday evening Alan turned up at grans in his own now repaired car and off we went.

We still laugh about this now.

Les, who was to join me in 56 Driver Training Squadron following the completion of our B2, and I decided we'd go home one weekend and collect my car. Could I drive? Of course I could drive I'd been driving since I was 11 years old; I just didn't have a license.

We'd tell my mum and dad that Les had his test and then I could drive back to Farnborough with 'L' plates. No worries.

And this is exactly what we done. I'm guessing my mum and dad knew what we were up to, had they asked to see Les's license we'd have been stuffed, but they didn't, seeing us off with a cheery wave and a 'take care', on Sunday evening. We shared the driving entering North London on the A1 from Baldock and then heading out to the West on the North Circular road. We joined the A4 to Slough, from there south to Camberly and Farnborough. We didn't have a care in the world as we zipped along in the Midget.

My first car April 1973

I now had my car with me, parked with others in the corner of the parade ground.

After six weeks of hell we all took our final B2 exams, which I passed.

This was the end of an era; here our Course 8 and many lads I'd joined with in September 1971 would part company, a few of us would be moving on to 56 Driver Training Squadron but the majority would be leaving for their adult Squadrons and Regiments.

Our new postings were published on the notice board; there was an air of excitement as we crowded the board to see where we were going. We had been asked our first and second preferences, but in reality we went where we were sent.

There was no parade, party, or piss-up. We were finished, we said goodbye and wished each other well. Some of us would meet again when we reached our adult units; others would meet again later in their service. Some of us wouldn't meet again until the formation of the Junior Leaders Association in 1999. Others, many years into the future would get a surprise message turn up on social media; this has happened to me a couple of times.

For me along with a bunch of mates including big Smudge who'd shot me in the back, Dave 'Hoppy' Hopwood, Les and Alan we were going to move to another Spider which was a part of 56 Driver Training Squadron. We would be taking our B3 heavy goods vehicle class 3 Driver Training Course and test.

Happy days.

56 Driver Training Squadron

And they were happy days - all the shite, guard duty's and fire pickets that had been piled on us during the last six weeks evaporated. Life suddenly became very good. Every morning a truck would take us over to Cookham to the driver training centre; bring us back for lunch and again in the evening. We were housed in a Spider with guys from all Squadrons of the Sappers, some a great deal older than us who were doing B2, A2 and A1 driver Courses; also mobile crane training. They came from RE units almost worldwide and we listened with interest to the stories they told.

One by one we passed our HGV test, packed our bags and moved on. Hoppy and Alan were the first couple to leave. They had taken their Land Rover license at Dover so it was a quick couple of weeks for the upgrade to a four ton truck. Alan left for 43 Field Support Squadron in Osnabruck and Hoppy to Hamelin both in Germany.

I found the driving Course easy and took to driving a truck with no problem at all, a week or so after my two good friends left I took my test and I passed first time.

The following day I was given my posting orders; I was to report on 27th November to 16 Field Squadron RE, also in Osnabruck Germany. I had two weeks leave before flying to Gutersloh from Luton. Smudge would also be going to 43 Field Support within the same 23 Engineer Regiment - the same Squadron Alan had joined; he'd be flying with me.

I loaded my kit into my little MG Midget said goodbye and good luck to the few mates remaining and headed west for a final visit to my friends and gran in Winsley.

In two weeks I'd be flying off to Germany to join my Field Squadron; another Cold War Soldier on the 'Iron Curtain' front line.

Epilogue

At Dover we had large and very capable complement of Permanent Staff trainers - Officers, Corporals, Sergeants, and Staff Sergeants.

Yes, we got bawled at - my tale of Jones on the drill square is not made up; incidents like this occurred and occurred quite regularly during the first two terms from Permanent Staff and Junior NCOs alike.

But the truth is, and I'm sure most would agree with me, our trainers done a great job in setting us on the road to a career in the Royal Engineers. For me Johnny Spriggs will always stand out; he was a great mentor and if he reads this I hope among all the hundreds of recruits he saw through Old Park he may remember me.

My two years at Dover was a long time ago and even with help from friends who were there with me at the time, remembering all the names is impossible; those that I, or I should say we, did remember are mentioned by name, some I've changed and others I've had to fill-in. There will no doubt be some elements of the book that others may not agree with; it stands to reason that we view things differently and the lapsed time is considerable, no two person's memories can be exactly the same after forty five years, however having consulted with friends who were with me at the time I believe I've gone the extra mile to ensure accuracy.

I would like to remind readers that this memoir is from a Junior Sapper in 'A 'Squadron...

I write about 'A' Squadron being the best, our NCOs and Officers telling us we were the best; but the same speech was given in each Squadron. All three Squadrons believed they were the best and it was drummed into us daily; best is what we were constantly pushed to achieve as individuals, as a Troop and as a Squadron.

At times the training and the induction during our first two terms was brutal, and I mean that sincerely. But together we hung-in there.

I made outstanding friends who became more like brothers.

For my first three terms I shared a room with a great bunch of lads and I mean the best; Steve, Les, Ray, Paul and Gary who left us.

Also Alan, Gerry, Dave Hopwood to name just a few, and our Room-jack Smudge - a great lad; I never saw him again after Dover but I hope life treated him well.

Other lads from my Intake I went on to serve with later in BAOR and a couple I'm still in touch with now through the Junior Leaders Association or through social media.

I look back now from the age of sixty to my time as a Junior Soldier (Sapper) at Old Park Barracks Dover with a sense of pride and achievement.

Was it the right decision or the wrong one? Without any hesitation I can say it was the right one. It suited me and it suited my personality. I was going nowhere at school and the outlook was grim...

When I compare my school reports with my reports as a Junior Leader there is no comparison. My lowest grade during my time at Dover was a 'C plus'. At school they'd been at the other end of the alphabet. Sure I still struggled academically at Dover; but in other subjects, military and trade I excelled.

In Course 7 I had a bit of a hick-up but it didn't last and my report from that term was equally as good as the other five; my final report from my final term was very good indeed. I'd never been able to say that in my young life before.

Would I change anything? Would I - knowing post event what it was like have changed my chosen path?

The answer is emphatically no.

Course 8 August 1973. Steve Burt, back row, 4th from the right.

Las Stewart, Alan Tadd and Steve Burt - JLRRE Dover reunion 2000